LINGUISTICS AND
THE ENGLISH LANGUAGE

D1362230

LINGUISTICS AND THE ENGLISH LANGUAGE

A Transformational Approach

Bruce L. Liles
University of Missouri, St. Louis

 GOODYEAR PUBLISHING COMPANY, INC.
Pacific Palisades, California

Copyright © 1972 by

GOODYEAR PUBLISHING COMPANY, INC.
Pacific Palisades, California

All rights reserved. No part of this book may be reproduced in any
form or by any means without permission in writing from the publisher.

Current printing (last digit): 10 9 8 7 6 5 4 3 2 1

Y-5295-4

Library of Congress Catalog Card Number: 71-187700

ISBN: 0-87620-529-5

Printed in the United States of America

Contents

Preface

As with many other areas of learning, our knowledge of human language has increased rapidly during the last few decades. This book is designed to introduce the reader with no background in linguistics to part of this information. No attempt is made to direct the content toward any one kind of reader. It is doubtful that the person who is reading the book to learn something about language or to prepare for teaching needs a different introduction from the student who is preparing for more advanced linguistics courses.

The topics presented have been selected to show that language is systematic and that much of the system can not be seen from a superficial inspection. To avoid giving the impression that the English language is unchanging and uniform, I have included chapters on language change, regional and social dialects, and the current standard dialect of American English. A generative-transformational framework has been selected for the chapters on syntax, morphology, and phonology; and language change and contemporary variation are discussed within this framework.

Just as an introductory physics text does not include everything known about nuclear physics or the quantum theory, this book does not give an exhaustive treatment of linguistics. It does present basic information on a number of aspects of the English language and provides bibliographies for further reading. It also attempts to lead the reader into making investigations on his own. At the end of each chapter in this book there is a brief listing of works which discuss chapter topics in greater detail or which give views different from those found in the chapter. The works have been selected because their content and presentation are within the grasp of the beginning student. References to works found in the general bibliography at the end of this book are made by author and date only.

There are several ways in which this book differs from most other introductory works in linguistics. Because there is much controversy over how rules should be stated, there are no formal presentations of base or transformational rules. Formal statements of rules have limited value to the person being introduced to linguistics, and they can be better approached at a more advanced level. Also, syntax is presented first and phonology last, rather than the earlier convention of phonology, then morphology, then syntax. This arrangement has been selected because the theory of phonology employed in this book relies on syntactic information for many of its applications.

At a time in which almost all aspects of language study are being actively debated, it is often hard to decide which approach to follow in an introductory book. Not only is there disagreement among different schools of linguists; there is also much diversity among scholars in any one of the schools, such as the transformationalists. A uniform approach has been selected for the book, not because the others are necessarily faulty, but because a certain degree of consistency is useful for a person beginning any field of learning. After a person attains a basic understanding of one approach, he can study the others more easily.

I would like to thank all of those who have helped me in the preparation of this book and to give special thanks to the anonymous reviewers.

LINGUISTICS AND
THE ENGLISH LANGUAGE

CHAPTER ONE

The Meaning and Scope of Linguistics

Although the word *linguistic* was in use at least as early as 1837 and *linguistics* as early as 1855, neither term was used with any great frequency until the 1930s, when the structuralist movement first became popular in the United States. During the 1930s and 1940s, *linguistics* was a term widely used by scholars who studied the structure of contemporary languages. Since the prevailing goal during those years was to employ scientific precision and objectivity in the study of language, scholars were fairly well agreed that linguistics was "the scientific study of language." So long as the word was used almost exclusively by specialists among whom there were no major theoretical differences, the meaning remained fairly constant.

By the mid 1950s the word was no longer the exclusive property of specialists, and during the 1960s the term came to the attention of the general public through the controversy over *Webster's Third New International Dictionary* (1961) and through the introduction of new subject matter into the English programs of most elementary and secondary schools in the United States. When words pass from the technical vocabulary of specialists to the everyday vocabulary of the general public, well-defined, precise meanings give way to less exact and even new meanings which vary from speaker to speaker. We have seen this process apply to *inferiority complex, extrovert, seminar, martyr, tragedy,* and a great many more words which no longer have just their original technical meanings. *Linguistics* is no exception as a word that is used in various ways. Because of this lack of consistency in meaning, it is essential that any book on the subject, especially one which is called *Linguistics and the English Language,* begin with a definition of the term.

Most linguists are still concerned with precision and objectivity in language study, but basic differences in theory are so pronounced among linguists today that there is no general agreement as to how to attain these goals. To some linguists it seems pretentious and inaccurate to speak of their discipline as a *science.* Probably the only definition that a great many linguists would accept today is that **linguistics is the study of language.** This definition includes the study of the structures of individual languages such as English, German, or Navajo as well as the study of language in general. It also includes all approaches with which the person studies language: traditional, structural, transformational, tagmemic, stratificational, and others. Let us look at some of the questions that have been asked about language in the past and see how people have approached them.

Questions About Language

The etymologies of words have long intrigued people in most parts of the world. Frequently in the Old and New Testaments, origins are given for the names of places and people. We read in the sixteenth chapter of Genesis that the angel of the Lord says to Hagar, "Behold, you are with child, and shall bear a son; you shall call his name Ishmael ["God hears"], because the Lord has given heed to your affliction." Later we read that the city to which Lot flees is called Zoar, "Little," because of its size (Genesis 19:22). The Greeks also were interested in origins of words. In Plato's *Cratylus* many etymologies are suggested, most of them highly fanciful and inaccurate. For example, the name of *Pluto,* the god of the underworld, is linked with the Greek word *ploutos,* "wealth," since wealth comes from the earth. In this work Socrates feels free to remove, add, or rearrange letters to obtain the desired result. The speaker of English can gain some idea of the extreme measures used if he tries to justify the name *radio* because it is something we *hear.* By dropping the *h* and *e* of *hear* and rearranging what is left from *ar* to *ra,* we have the beginning letters of *radio.* Most etymologies like this, though interesting, are linguistically worthless. Speculations about etymology did not stop with Plato, for we find such later accounts as those by Quintilian (first century A.D.) and Isidore of Seville (seventh century A.D.), in which the Latin *bellus,* "beautiful," is given as the origin of *bellum,* "war," because war is not beautiful. Similarly, *lux,* "light," is given as the origin of *lucus,* "a grove of trees," because light is not found there. Nor is such speculation dead today. Recently an American tourist was overheard explaining to her husband that the Danish peninsula of Jutland was obviously so named because it **juts** out into the sea. It apparently did not occur to her that Danish might not have the English word *jut.* A better guess would have been "land of the Jutes."

There have also been more systematic studies of word origins. Generally speaking, local historical societies are in agreement with the facts when they say that the names of their towns originated from topographical features (*Flat, Redwater, Longview, El Paso*), the names of older cities (*Carthage, London, Rome*), or a prominent person (*Washington, Lincoln, Columbus*). Starting with the eighteenth century, we find English dictionaries giving etymological information, often inaccurate at first but later generally reliable. In addition to dictionaries, there are a number of other books which record systematic studies of word origins. The interest in etymology is still alive.

Many investigations of language have dealt with questions other than etymology. One question which was asked periodically for centuries concerned the relationships of the languages of the world. In Genesis we find the account of how all men spoke the same language until God made divisions at the Tower of Babel. For many centuries there was a widespread belief that all people originally spoke one language and that it was still in existence, perhaps Greek or Hebrew. All other languages had changed except this one. The Greek historian Herodotus (fifth century B.C.) tells of an earlier Egyptian ruler named Psammitichus, who conducted an experiment to determine what this original language was. Reasoning that infants who never heard any language would be uncorrupted and speak the natural language of mankind, he had two babies isolated at birth from all human contact except for a single shepherd who saw that they were fed. When they were two years old, the shepherd returned to Psammitichus with the news that the children had greeted him with "becos," not once but on several occasions. Since *becos* was the Phoenician word for bread, it was concluded that Phoenician was the original language. More than two thousand years later, James IV of Scotland tried the same experiment, but his children were reported to speak Hebrew.

Today we know that children have to be exposed to a language before they can learn it; those who through rare circumstances have not heard people speaking have not developed any spoken language. Also, we know that all languages which are alive are steadily changing, so that if all languages are derived from a common source, it is not a language which is still being spoken in its unchanged state. There are enough written records to show that such modern languages as French, Spanish, Italian, Portuguese, and Rumanian developed from Latin and that most of the languages of Europe, including Latin, are ultimately descended from Indo-European, a language spoken around 2000 B.C. and earlier, whose speakers did not have a writing system and who, therefore, left no written records. We can group many of the languages of the world into individual families such as Indo-European, but with our present state of knowledge we are unable to show any relationships among these families which could definitely indicate a common source for all. These ideas about language relationships, of course, are relatively new. Two hundred years ago people were still looking for the original language of mankind among those that were then spoken, and many people still thought that Latin was a corrupt form of Greek.

We will say that asking questions of this nature is taking a philosophical approach to language study, as opposed to making etymological investigations or descriptions of such matters as sentence structure. Another philosophical question about language which has been asked periodically is found in Plato's *Cratylus,* the work we mentioned earlier in which *Pluto* is derived from *ploutos,* "wealth." Plato's chief interest was not in word origins but rather in the nature of words, and he was using the etymologies as evidence for his argument.

Cratylus and Hermogenes, after arguing over whether names are natural or conventional, bring Socrates into the argument. Hermogenes argues that names are conventional, that one name could have been given to a person as well as another. Similarly, common nouns such as *sun* and *moon* (Plato, of course, uses the Greek *halios* and *selēnē*) are not inherently "true" but rather names accepted by convention and agreement among the speakers of the language. We could add to Hermogenes' argument and say that if by chance the words *sun* and *moon* had been interchanged sometime in the past that we would today speak of the body that rises during the day as the *moon* and of the one at night as the *sun*. If all speakers of the language agreed on this convention, these names would be as true as the ones we now use. Cratylus and Socrates, on the other hand, take the opposite position, arguing that names of people and things are natural, not conventional. The etymologies are used as evidence. This argument is the earliest record we have of whether names are natural or conventional.

Today the prevailing opinion is that they are conventional, that parents could name their daughter *Betty* as well as *Susan*; the name they happen to select will be her real name, and there is no single one that is by nature "correct" for the child. Or from another viewpoint, we can say that a young male human is called a *boy* in English only because of circumstances of the past and because of general agreement among speakers of English to continue using this particular combination of sounds. *Boy* is no more "natural" than *puer, garçon, muchacho, Junge,* or *mal'chik*; or, for that matter, than the potential English word *taz.* Yet no doubt, there are many nonlinguists who feel the same as young Stephen Dedalus in Joyce's *A Portrait of the Artist as a Young Man*: Although God understands Frenchmen when they refer to Him as *Dieu,* that is not His real name; His real name is *God.*

Another question has been raised as to the relative merits of various languages. To the Greeks there was no problem: The only real language in the world was Greek. A suggested origin for *barbaros,* the term applied to non-Greeks which later became the English word *barbarian,* is *bar bar,* a derisive imitation made by Greeks of the sounds produced by people who they felt could not talk. In recent times some speakers of French and English have held similar xenophobic attitudes, refusing to learn any other language and showing extreme impatience with anyone who speaks their language with a foreign accent. This attitude is made particularly clear in Flannery O'Connor's "The Displaced Person" as Mrs. McIntyre and Mrs. Shortley are preparing accommodations for a Polish refugee family who are coming to live and work on Mrs. McIntyre's farm. They have learned that the members of the refugee family speak only Polish, and Mrs. Shortley wonders whether people who "can't talk" will even know what colors are. Such naive reactions are not restricted to fictional characters or to people in rural areas. One of the contributions various Europeans claimed to be making to their colonies was that of introducing a civilized language to replace the native "dialects."

The opposite situation also occurs, in which people of a country feel that some other language has more prestige than their own. During the nineteenth century, German was spoken among the upper classes in the regions that are now Hungary and Czechoslovakia; the ability to speak French was a sign of cultivation in Russia and Sweden. In Europe until the sixteenth century, almost all serious writing was done in Latin. With the rise of nationalism and the spread of literacy to a much larger segment of the populations of Western Europe, the vernacular languages such as English, French, and Italian began to replace Latin as the language of scholarship. The controversy continued for a long time over whether a language such as English was as suitable as Latin for philosophical and scientific study.

The same kind of situation exists today when people ask whether the languages of emerging nations are adequate for the demands of the twentieth century or whether the people in these countries should learn some "better" language such as Russian, French, or English. During the nineteenth century there was a widespread belief that the languages of the world were in various stages of evolutionary development and that some languages were still very primitive whereas others were in a high state of refinement. Today few linguists believe in this theory. The languages of the most primitive people in the world today have been shown to be as systematic and grammatically complex as those of more civilized peoples. The vocabulary of each language is adjusted to meet the cultural needs of its speakers. English had to add many new words during the early modern period to handle ideas previously discussed only in Latin; during the twentieth century it has had to add many more to adjust to technological advances. In the same way all languages are potentially adequate for handling any ideas. In most cases new words must be added to the vocabulary to accommodate ideas that are new, but this is an easy process.

One of the most productive periods of philosophical investigation of language began during the second half of the seventeenth century. A representative work of the movement was published in France in 1660, a book by Lancelot and Arnauld with a long title which is usually shortened to *Grammaire générale et raisonnée*. Noam Chomsky in *Cartesian Linguistics* (New York: Harper & Row, 1966) has shown that many of the ideas which linguists are investigating today were introduced during this period: linguistic creativity, deep and surface structures, and linguistic universals. These topics will be explained in later chapters of this book.

Another question about language was raised during the eighteenth century when many Englishmen realized that they had no sources for deciding questionable points of usage. In the Age of Reason it went against the grain not to have a clear-cut code of standards. During the course of this century, therefore, there appeared a number of English grammars by such men as Robert Lowth, Joseph Priestley, John Wallis, and George Campbell. The purpose of these works was to provide a norm for English to be used by native speakers. Just as it was unthinkable to people of this age that two roads could be equally desirable for reaching a given destination, they found alternate forms of speech such as *backward* and *backwards* unpalatable. One had to be right and the other wrong.

Although there was no disagreement over the desirability of a system of standards, there was no uniform opinion regarding how to decide on the standards. Some people felt that language should be regulated by reason. A linguistic judge would use his own opinions to make decisions about what constituted good usage. Even if the prescribed form was not in use, the judge was to institute it. In fact, one feature in most eighteenth-century grammars was a listing of errors which everyone, including the best writers, committed. Rules which are based solely on the tastes of a judge are necessarily subjective, and there was much disagreement among the would-be legislators of the language as to the content of their rules. For example, it is almost impossible to find two books from the period which agree in all details about the use of *shall* and *will*. Another opinion was that standards should be based upon the actual usage of educated people. If a particular form is in widespread use among the educated, that is enough to make it correct. According to this view, there can be no errors which everyone makes. Most of the grammarians who held this opinion were inconsistent in their application of it, mixing their own attitudes with their observations. These two opinions are still found today, especially in attitudes toward practices of dictionary editors. During the last decade linguists have discovered that language is far more complex than anyone had ever suspected. Because of this complexity and our lack of information about more than a small fraction of it, many scholars have abandoned all hopes of making mechanical translations from one language to another, at least for the near future. Since the present state of knowledge about language is this limited, it is hard to see how one person or group of people, even with impeccable taste, can have the wisdom needed to legislate usage.

The Development of Traditional Grammars

Instead of investigating etymologies or philosophical questions about language, a person may decide to describe linguistic structure. Grammatical study as we think of it today began during the fourth century B.C. with Plato's most famous student, Aristotle. Following suggestions made earlier by Plato, Aristotle said that each sentence or proposition was composed of classes of words called *onomata* and *rhēmata*. It is tempting to refer to an onoma as a noun and to a rhēma as a verb, but in each category Aristotle included more words than are normally included under our present classifications of noun and verb. The principal difference which Aristotle drew between these classes was that rhēmata designate time, whereas onomata do not. He also said that the onoma is that about which something is predicated and that the rhēma is that which predicates. He also added a third class, *syndesmoi*—words which have little meaning in themselves but which show relationships between onomata and rhēmata.

After the death of Aristotle, the study of grammar was continued by the Stoics and by the scholars of Alexandria. During the first century B.C., Dionysius Thrax, an Alexandrian, wrote a grammar of fewer than 400 lines in length. In spite of its brevity, this was the first real grammar of Greek. In it we find the culmination of grammatical study up to its time. Thrax gave a brief account of the alphabet, but his main interest was in the parts of speech and their properties. Aristotle had given three classes, and the Stoics and Alexandrians had gradually expanded the number. Thrax listed eight: noun, verb, participle, article, pronoun, preposition, adverb, and conjunction. (All terms are given in their Modern English forms, as derived from Latin. The Latin terms were translated from Greek.) As properties of the noun he discussed gender (masculine, feminine, neuter), number (singular, dual, plural), and case (nominative, genitive, dative, vocative, and accusative). He listed such properties of the verb as mood (indicative, imperative, optative, subjunctive, infinitive), voice (active, middle, passive), person, number, and tense. Although there is much about the Greek language which Dionysius Thrax did not describe, his little work provided the model from which grammars of Latin, English, and other European languages were written for the next eighteen centuries.

Along with most other aspects of Greek learning, the Romans borrowed their grammatical tradition and later transmitted it to the countries of Western Europe. Many Greek scholars had studied grammar for the purpose of learning about man and his institutions; grammar was part of the larger subject of philosophy. The Romans studied it for other reasons. First of all, part of their educational training involved a study of Greek, the language used for many scholarly writings. Furthermore, a knowledge of Greek was considered a cultural accomplishment, just as French was later in the Prussian court of Frederick the Great. Wealthy Roman families had Greek tutors to teach their sons Greek grammar. The Romans, then, studied grammar as an aid in learning a foreign language, Greek. Another reason for studying grammar concerned rhetoric. The ability to sway people through public speaking was considered a highly desirable attribute in Roman times. One way of developing this skill was to study the speeches of great orators, and for such a study a system of talking about and analyzing language was needed. Hence, Latin grammar was studied as an aid in the mastery of rhetoric.

Of all the Latin grammarians, two are especially important for the influence they exerted on future studies: Donatus (fourth century A.D.) and Priscian (sixth century A.D.). During the Middle Ages the most widely used elementary textbook of Latin was by Donatus, but the longer grammar by Priscian was more influential in providing a model for future grammars. The works of both grammarians were distinguished from those of earlier writers because of their organization and presentation of information rather than by the contribution of much that was new. They continued the practice of classifying words as to parts of speech and parsing each one according to its properties. Donatus in his *Ars Minor* discussed quality, comparison, gender, number, form, and case of the noun. For the verb he discussed quality, conjugation, gender, number, inflections, tense, and person. The definitions offered by Donatus and by Priscian were derived extensively from earlier grammarians, especially Dionysius Thrax.

During the Middle Ages there was little advancement in grammatical studies. Since Latin was the language of scholarship in Western Europe, the study of this language was as much a part of the curriculum as are reading and writing today; and part of learning Latin was mastering its grammar. During this time there were a few isolated occurrences of original linguistic study, such as the twelfth-century description of Old Norse known as the *First Grammatical Treatise*. The techniques used in this volume to analyze the Old Norse sound system are closer to those of the twentieth century than to the Middle Ages. Works such as this were generally known only in limited areas and had no lasting influence on linguistic study in the centuries that followed.

The sixteenth century witnessed a rise in prestige for the vernacular languages of Europe, although the movement had begun earlier. Eventually English, French, Italian, and the other vernaculars replaced Latin as the language of scholarship, but this process was not completed until the nineteenth century. The study of Latin grammar continued to have sufficient prominence in the curriculum that elementary schools were called *grammar* schools. Grammars of English began appearing during the sixteenth century, and they continued the tradition of parsing parts of speech according to the categories established for Latin.

Starting with Roman times, the interest in the study of grammar as an aid to reaching other goals (such as mastering a foreign language or learning to speak one's own language eloquently) witnessed an unbroken tradition. Until the eighteenth century in England, the chief reason for studying grammar was as an aid to learning Latin. The sixteenth-century interest in an ornate prose style for English could easily have led to widespread study of English grammar for rhetorical purposes, but there is no evidence that it did. Such prose writers as Lyly and Sidney apparently used Latin rhetorics as their guides, rather than new rhetorics of English.

During the eighteenth century, the interest in providing standards prompted the writing of a number of grammars of English. For the most part, they followed the outlines laid down earlier by Priscian and by Dionysius Thrax. Throughout the eighteenth and nineteenth centuries, there was little research performed on English grammar. Many school texts still in use during the third quarter of the twentieth century continue to follow the traditional format and definitions.

Since these school grammars are the continuation of a tradition going back to the times of the ancient Greeks and since they have been the object of attack during the last three decades, we should examine the content that is typical of them. The first section defines the sentence as a group of words expressing a complete thought and introduces the subject and the predicate, both simple and complete. The second section, usually the longest in the book, defines the eight parts of speech and discusses the properties of each. The third section classifies phrases, clauses, and sentences. The fourth section discusses punctuation and such matters of usage as pronoun case forms, dangling modifiers, and subject-verb agreement.

There is a great deal of consistency among the school grammars as to their definitions of the parts of speech. The following are found in most of them, occasionally with slight modifications of one or two words:

A *noun* is the name of a person, place, or thing.
A *pronoun* is a word used to take the place of a noun.
A *verb* is a word which expresses action, being, or state of being.
An *adjective* is a word used to modify a noun or a pronoun.
An *adverb* is a word used to modify a verb, an adjective, or another adverb.
A *preposition* is a word which shows relationship between its object and some other word in the sentence.
A *conjunction* is a word which connects words or groups of words.
An *interjection* is a word which expresses strong feeling or emotion.

Most of these definitions are very close to those given earlier by Thrax, Donatus, and Priscian.

Some words do not fit easily into these categories.

1.1   Your *answering* the question so rapidly was rude.

Answering is the name of a thing (a noun) and is a word which expresses action (a verb). It has the *-ing* ending of a verb, and like a verb it has the object *question* and an adverbial modifier, *rapidly*. At the same time it is like a noun in that it is modified by *your* and is the subject of *was*. Words like *answering,* which have properties of nouns and of verbs, are called **gerunds** in traditional grammars.

1.2   The woman *holding* the umbrella is his cousin.

Holding is a word which expresses action (a verb) and which modifies a noun (an adjective). It is like a verb in having the *-ing* suffix and in taking the object *umbrella*; it is like an adjective in that it modifies the noun *woman.* Words like *holding,* which have properties of adjectives and verbs, are called **participles.**

1.3   The *poor* are happy.

Poor is a word which is normally an adjective, but here it appears to be a noun since it is the subject of *are.* Although many traditional grammars do not provide discussions for words such as this, one rather frequent solution is to say that there is an understood word such as *people* which *poor* modifies and which is the real subject of *are.*

1.4   *Mike's* shirt is torn.
1.5   *His* shirt is torn.

Although most traditional grammars classify *Mike's* as a possessive noun, there is no consistency in their classification of *his* in 1.5. It can be classified as a pronoun, an adjective, or a pronominal adjective, depending upon the text. The conclusion to be drawn from most school texts is that English grammar is a finite subject which has been described completely. There are a few thorny problems, such as those illustrated by sentences 1.1–1.5; but even these have unique solutions, and when confronted with them, the best course to take is to find an authority who can give the correct answer.

During the last years of the nineteenth century and the early years of the twentieth, such European mavericks as Henry Sweet, H. Poutsma, E. Kruisinga, and Otto Jespersen made significant contributions to the study of English while working basically within the traditional framework. They realized that there were still many aspects of English grammar which had not been investigated, and they produced creative works which linguists today find informative. Unfortunately, scholarly research was largely ignored by the writers of school texts, many of whom looked upon the study of language solely as a means of avoiding errors in writing and speaking.

Recent Approaches to Linguistics

During the second quarter of the twentieth century, there emerged a new school of linguists, known as **structuralists** or **post-Bloomfieldian linguists** (from Leonard Bloomfield, whose book *Language,* published in 1933, is often cited as the real beginning of the movement). It was the structuralists who first gave wide currency to the terms *linguistics* and *linguist.* No doubt they used these terms in referring to their discipline and to themselves to dissociate themselves from all other students of language and to designate themselves as scientists.

There were a number of reasons which caused the structuralists to become disenchanted with traditional grammar and to try to develop a more satisfactory approach. One of the greatest problems they found with the traditional approach was that it was inadequate for describing many languages. It was impossible, for example, to analyze the American Indian languages according to the eight parts of speech. The structures of these languages were incompatible with traditional classifications.

Furthermore, they noticed that the definitions did not follow any logical pattern. Some, such as those for the noun and the verb, were based on meaning; others, such as for the adjective and the adverb, were based on function. This is equivalent to classifying people into blonds, tall people, and young adults. Naturally, there will be much overlapping in such a system, since logic would demand a single basis for classification: hair coloring, height, or age. Similarly, they felt that some single basis for classification should be devised for the parts of speech.

Since the structuralists looked upon the meanings of words and sentences as something intangible that they could not measure with scientific precision, they tried in their analyses to use elements of structure that were not based on meaning. Various schemes were worked out during the 1950s, all of them having much in common.[†] One scheme that evolved made two separate groupings, according to form and function. According to form, a word could be a noun, a verb, an adjective, an adverb, or an uninflected word. A word which may be pluralized (*dog, dogs*) or be made a possessive (*girl, girl's*) is a noun; one that may change tense (*drop, dropped*) or take such endings as *-en, -s,* or *-ing* (*eaten, eats, eating*) is a verb; one that shows comparison (*fast, faster, fastest*) is an adjective or an adverb. Certain other suffixes and prefixes also can be used to distinguish classes of words:

Nouns:	ship*ment*, conform*ity*, happ*iness*
Verbs:	summar*ize*, wid*en*, solid*ify*
Adjectives:	love*ly*, industr*ial*, courage*ous*
Adverbs:	rapid*ly*, back*ward*, length*wise*

[†]The following works are representative: Charles Carpenter Fries, *The Structure of English* (New York: Harcourt Brace Jovanovich, 1952); H. A. Gleason, Jr., *An Introduction to Descriptive Linguistics* (New York: Holt, Rinehart and Winston, 1955, 1961); Charles F. Hockett, *A Course in Modern Linguistics* (New York: Macmillan Co., 1958); Archibald A. Hill, *Introduction to Linguistic Structures* (New York: Harcourt Brace Jovanovich, 1958); W. Nelson Francis, *The Structure of American English* (New York: Ronald Press Co., 1958); James Sledd, *A Short Introduction to English Grammar* (Chicago: Scott, Foresman and Co., 1959); David A. Conlin, *Grammar for Written English* (Boston: Houghton Mifflin Co., 1961); and Norman C. Stageberg, *An Introductory English Grammar* (New York: Holt, Rinehart and Winston, 1965, 1971).

All other words are classified as uninflected words. This includes the traditional prepositions, interjections, and conjunctions; and it also includes some words traditionally classified as other parts of speech: *the, a, tennis, here, there,* to name a few. Any word which does not permit one of the characteristic suffixes or prefixes is an uninflected word.

The second means of classification is according to function in the sentence. A word is a *nominal* if it functions as a subject or an object, as a *verbal* if it predicates, as an *adjectival* if it modifies a noun, and as an *adverbial* if it modifies a verb, adjective, or adverb. This dual system of classification permits different analyses for the troublesome words in 1.1–1.5 than those provided by the traditionalists. The sentences are repeated here for convenience:

1.1   Your *answering* the question so rapidly was rude.
1.2   The woman *holding* the umbrella is his cousin.
1.3   The *poor* are happy.
1.4   *Mike's* shirt is torn.
1.5   *His* shirt is torn.

According to this system, *answering* (1.1) is a verb by form, a nominal by function; *holding* (1.2) is a verb by form, an adjectival by function; *poor* (1.3) is an adjective by form, a nominal by function; *Mike's* (1.4) and *his* (1.5) are noun and pronoun, respectively, by form, adjectivals by function. In most instances nouns are nominals and verbs are verbals:

1.6   Her newest accomplishments enlightened us.

Newest is an adjective (*-est*) and an adjectival (modifying *accomplishments* or coming between *her* and a nominal). *Accomplishments* is a noun (*-ment, -s*) and a nominal (subject). *Enlightened* is a verb (*en-, -en, -ed*) and a verbal.

For other elements of structure, they identified *The little dog was barking loudly* as a sentence not because it "expresses a complete thought" but because of the rise in pitch accompanied by heavy stress on the first syllable of *loudly* and because of the drop in pitch and pause at the end. They said that *the little dog* forms a unit as opposed to *was barking loudly* not because the words were related in meaning but because of stress, pitch, and juncture.

They felt that they should not use sentences that they had invented for analysis since these would be selected subjectively. They felt, rather, that it was more objective to analyze sentences that other people had spoken, preferably sentences from normal conversations that were recorded without the speakers' knowledge.

Since the late 1950s, structural grammar has been challenged by **transformational grammar**. The transformationalists agree that the study of language should be objective, and they are very much concerned with providing valid evidence for their analyses; but their attitudes toward what constitutes valid evidence differ from those held by the structuralists. Many transformationalists believe that meaning is an integral part of linguistic description and that it is impossible to analyze a sentence apart from its meaning. They feel that limiting oneself to a body of sentences, such as those recorded from telephone conversations, imposes restrictions that are too severe for producing an adequate grammar. Such a group of sentences will necessarily contain many poorly formed structures if the speaker becomes distracted and changes his sentence in midcourse or if he is interrupted by another speaker and does not finish his statement. Unless the investigator uses his knowledge of the language and meaning, there is no way for him to isolate mistakes from well-formed sentences. Also, certain important structures such as passives or questions could easily be missing from any given collection of sentences. The transformationalists are as interested in specifying which sentences are possible, though not yet observed, as they are in describing the sentences in any particular collection.

Many transformationalists do not reject traditional grammar, but feel that there is much that is good about it. In fact, it is obvious that many of them are well versed in the writings of Otto Jespersen. Generally, transformational grammar is more explicit in its explanations than traditional grammar. The traditionalists would have recognized the sentence *Aunt Penelope detests smoking cigars* as ambiguous. They would have said that for one meaning the object of *detests* is the gerund phrase *smoking cigars* with *cigars* as the object of *smoking*. For the other meaning, *cigars* is the object of *detests,* with *smoking* a participle modifying *cigars*. Transformationalists do not disagree with this interpretation, but they do show more explicitly how these two analyses are possible. Paired with each meaning for a sentence there is an abstract structure which unambiguously specifies the meaning. For the meaning "Aunt Penelope detests cigars that are smoking," there is the abstract structure *Aunt Penelope detests cigars (Cigars are smoking)*. For the other meaning, that Aunt Penelope does not like to smoke cigars, there is the abstract structure *Aunt Penelope detests (Aunt Penelope smokes cigars)*. By a sequence of operations that we call **transformations** these structures are both converted into *Aunt Penelope detests smoking cigars.* Similarly, 1.1–1.5 are represented on different levels, such as (*You answered the question so rapidly) was rude* for 1.1. The abstract structure clearly shows the relationships stated by traditional grammar. These relationships are also those which the native speaker understands. Transformationalists feel that their grammar should account for as much of this knowledge as is possible.

Within the last 25 years the most widely used approaches to language study in the United States have been the structural and the transformational. As evidenced in most scholarly journals and in published books, the transformational approach has vastly outdistanced the structural approach during the last ten years. Within the United States there have also been other kinds of linguistic investigation, such as the tagmemic and the stratificational, but very few articles have been published which report research following these approaches.

One should not assume that interest in linguistics has been limited to the United States. Research in the field has been active and substantial in Europe, in Canada, in Japan, in Australia, in South Africa—in fact, in most educational centers of the world. Nor should it be assumed that American linguists are necessarily the leaders in the field. Their counterparts in England, Scotland, Czechoslovakia, and elsewhere are at least as distinguished and as productive as they. It is useful for a person beginning his study of a subject to limit himself to one school of thought and after he has passed the introductory stage to investigate other approaches. It is for this reason that this text limits itself to the transformational approach.

Descriptive Linguistics

Regardless of the approach a person takes, he must describe the language with which he is working. For descriptive purposes one can study the sounds of a language, its **phonology**; he can study meaning, **semantics**; or he can study how different elements of the sentence relate to one another, **syntax**.

In studying **phonology**, a person may be concerned with how sounds are produced by the human speech apparatus. He can study the movements of the tongue, jaw, lips, and vocal cords as they produce various sounds, and he may use machines to make precise measurements of the actions of these parts. Or he may study the perception of sounds by a listener, or the exact modifications of sound waves in speech production. Usually American linguists speak of the branch of phonology that studies how speech is produced, transmitted, and received as **phonetics** and of that part that deals with the modifications of sound waves as **acoustic phonetics**. Phonetics is only one aspect of phonology. A person may study which sounds a particular language uses. For example, English does not use the sounds spelled *ö* and *ü* in the German words *Möbel* and *früh* or the sound spelled *ch* in *ich*; German does not use the sounds spelled *th* and *w* in English *thin, then,* and *west.* Also, all languages do not permit the same arrangements of sounds. English permits *ts* to occur at the end of a word, as in *wits,* but not at the beginning (for some speakers *tsetse* is an exception); both German and Russian permit this combination of sounds at the beginning of a word. Or the student of phonology may be interested in patterns in the language, such as the regular shifting of stress with the addition of certain suffixes and the accompanying change in pronunciation of the vowels: *admíre, admirátion; télegraph, telégraphy.* The addition of suffixes may cause other phonological alterations, such as the change from *t* to the *sh* sound in *actívate, activation* and *relate,* *relation*. Many students of phonology are interested in learning how sound patterns are related to other aspects of language.

The person who studies **syntax** is interested in learning how the various parts of a sentence relate to one another. Most approaches to language study have recognized that words are restricted as to the functions they may perform, as illustrated by the following sentences:

1.7	(The) *apples* are good.	1.8	We discussed (the) *apples.*
1.9	*People* are good.	1.10	We discussed *people.*
1.11	*Cars* are good.	1.12	We discussed *cars.*
1.13	**Of* are good.	1.14	*We discussed *of.*
1.15	**Pretty* are good.	1.16	*We discussed *pretty.*
1.17	**Quickly* are good.	1.18	*We discussed *quickly.*

The asterisk indicates that the sentence is not well formed. *Apples, people,* and *cars* are words which may function in a way that excludes *of, pretty,* and *quickly.* Traditionalists spoke of classifying words as to their **parts of speech,** structuralists as to their **form classes.** As we have seen in the preceding pages, linguists have disagreed about how to describe these classes. Then what about the study of the functions themselves? The italicized words in the following sentence illustrate five different functions:

1.19   *Fred* opened the *door* for *Bill* with the *janitor's key.*

Fred is the agent who performs the action. The door is the object which is acted upon. Bill is the one for whom the act is performed. The key is the instrument used to perform the act. The janitor is the one to whom the key belongs. There has been no widespread agreement on how these functions should be explained. One method is introduced in Chapter Two of this book.

Some linguists feel that their syntactic descriptions should go beyond explaining the obvious relationships among parts of a sentence. They feel that they should account for the knowledge possessed by a fluent speaker of the language, or at least as much of this knowledge as is possible. Here are some of the observations that a fluent speaker of English can make:

Two sentences may have the same meaning although they differ in form.

1.20   The idea which Bill proposed astonished me.

1.21   I was astonished by the idea proposed by Bill.

A sentence may be ambiguous, with two or more meanings.

1.22   He read the magazine you gave him last week.

A sentence may clearly indicate ideas which are not overtly expressed by words; all native speakers of the language agree on which ideas are implied.

 1.23   They can't play the trumpet, but I can. (*Play the trumpet* is understood after *can*.)

Two sentences may be alike in structure; the only difference between them is in the choice of words.

 1.24   *Charles* is eager to please.
 1.25   *John* is eager to please.

Other pairs of sentences may look as though choice of words is the only way they differ.

 1.26   Charles is *eager* to please.
 1.27   Charles is *easy* to please.

This similarity in structure is only apparent, however. In sentence 1.26, Charles pleases someone else; in 1.27, someone else pleases Charles. The difference between the two sentences is more extensive than just the choice of words.

As these examples show, the native speaker knows a great deal about English sentences, much of which is not explained by a superficial analysis. One problem confronting students of syntax is how this knowledge is to be included in their descriptions of language.

The third major area of descriptive linguistics is **semantics**, the study of meaning and the ways in which meaning is associated with other aspects of the grammar. People have investigated the meanings of individual words since the time of the ancient Greeks, who argued whether the meanings of words were natural or conventional. Dictionary editors since the eighteenth century have been concerned with determining and recording the definitions of individual words. Linguists have known for some time that the meanings of words change with time; in fact, most of the words which have been in the English language for several centuries no longer have their original meanings. *To counterfeit* originally meant "to pretend, assume, imitate" anything, such as happiness; now it usually means to imitate or copy money. A *deer* was at one time any animal; now it is a specific kind of animal. Also, words may change in meaning through metaphoric association, such as *head,* a part of the body, can be applied to cabbage because of the shape, to the first person in a line because of position, or to the director of an organization because of function. Examples of metaphoric extension applied to colors can be seen in the sentence "Blackberries are red when they are green."

The study of definitions of words and shifts in meaning is still alive, but we usually think of other areas of investigation when we speak today of the study of semantics. During the 1930s and early 1940s, Alfred Korzybski, I. A. Richards, C. K. Ogden, Stuart Chase, Hugh Walpole, S. I. Hayakawa, and others made contributions to a field known as *general semantics,* which was more closely related to philosophy than to linguistics. During the 1930s, 1940s, and 1950s, the structuralists tried to avoid the use of lexical meaning in their analyses. They did this not because they thought the study of meaning was unimportant, but because they felt that it was too intangible to be handled scientifically and because its use led to circular reasoning. There was very little research performed on semantics by the structuralists. Within the last few years, linguists have been investigating ways of incorporating meaning into their grammars. One group of transformationalists have argued for *generative semantics,* in which meaning determines much of the syntactic and phonetic shape of a sentence. There is still much to be learned about how meaning should be represented and where it should fit into a grammar.

Historical Linguistics

For the greater part of the nineteenth century, most students of language were interested almost exclusively in studying earlier forms of the languages of Europe and parts of Asia and in determining how they are related to one another. Scholars had long known that Latin and Greek were in some way related because of many words that are similar in form and meaning:

	Latin	Greek
"ten"	*decem*	*deka*
"I eat"	*edo*	*edo*
"mouse"	*mus*	*mus*
"he is"	*est*	*esti*
"I carry"	*fero*	*phero*
"thin"	*tenuis*	*tanaos*

There are also other similarities such as the declensional endings, as illustrated by the noun meaning "foot":

	Latin	Greek
Nominative	pes	pos
Genitive	pedis	podos
Dative	pedi	podi
Accusative	pedem	poda

The usual explanation for these similarities was that Latin was a corrupt form of Greek.

In 1786 before the Asiatic Society, an English judge in Calcutta, Sir William Jones, made an address which later proved to be highly influential in promoting linguistic scholarship in Europe. His interest in languages and in the earlier culture of the Hindus led him to study Sanskrit, the oldest recorded language of India. In his address of 1786, he noted that there were correspondences among the vocabularies and inflections of Sanskrit, Greek, and Latin which could not be the result of accident and that these languages must have developed from a common source which may no longer be in existence. This idea was novel, because at least since the time of the Egyptian Psammitichus men had been looking for the original language of mankind among those still spoken.

During the course of the nineteenth century, a name was given to this earlier language which Sanskrit, Greek, and Latin held in common: **Indo-European**, from its geographical limits of India in the east and Europe in the west. Other names such as **Indo-Germanic** and **Aryan** were also in use at various times, but in the English speaking countries *Indo-European* is the one most often used. It was discovered that not only the classical languages but also most of the other languages of Europe were ultimately descended from Indo-European, which broke into distinct language groups around 2000 B.C. Since the Indo-Europeans did not have a writing system, they left no written records. By comparing words and forms from the oldest extant languages which are derived from Indo-European, linguists have been able to reconstruct the probable sound system, inflections, and vocabulary of the original language. For example, the Indo-European forms below can be reconstructed from the corresponding words in the later languages:

	Indo-European	Sanskrit	Greek	Latin	Gothic
two	*dwo	dva	duo	duo	twai
three	*treies	trayas	treis	tres	þrija
eight	*okto	asta	oktō	octo	ahtau
nine	*neun	nava	ennea	novem	niun
father	*pəter	pitar	pater	pater	fadar

The comparison of languages was also extended to those outside of the Indo-European group. Today linguists are interested in establishing relationships among the languages of the people of Africa, of Asia, of the Pacific Ocean, and of the American Indians.

Historical linguists are interested in a great many problems. For one thing, they describe earlier stages of various languages, such as Chaucer's pronunciation,

Shakespeare's syntax, or Milton's verb forms. The results of their studies have been used for many purposes, such as explaining previously obscure puns in Shakespeare or rhymes in Pope. By comparing successive stages in a language, they are able to recognize certain drifts or directions in which the changes in the language are moving. Some historical linguists are interested in explaining the meanings and etymologies of hard words. To study the earlier stages of a language, a linguist is largely dependent upon written records and is concerned with interpreting alphabets, handwriting, and spelling conventions. Some are concerned with **palaeography**, the study of manuscripts, which includes dating them and analyzing the handwriting. Some linguists have provided us with valuable studies of the history of writing systems such as our alphabet. In addition, there are many other questions that have long intrigued historical linguists: Why does change occur? Is the rate of change predictable? Why do some languages change more slowly than others?

Until the middle of the twentieth century, historical linguists were generally not concerned with the work of the descriptivists. Since then the folly of ignoring the scholarship of the twentieth century has been generally recognized, and developments in descriptive linguistics are now having a considerable influence on historical studies. Increased knowledge has shown a need for reevaluating earlier studies and has suggested a great many avenues for research in previously untouched areas. Neither descriptive nor historical linguistics should be pursued exclusive of the other since these branches of language study are able to make substantial mutual contributions.

Interdisciplinary Studies

When a linguist describes the language of a particular time or compares different stages of a language, he is undertaking a very important and useful study. But descriptive and historical studies by no means constitute all of linguistics. Language does not exist in a vacuum separate from man's other activities. Since the primary function of language is communication, it is naturally affected by the context. There is no major activity in which man engages that does not require the use of language. For many of these activities he even uses a special vocabulary: bowling, crossword puzzles, music, fishing, electrical engineering, and others. He shows that he is a member of certain groups by the language he uses. He expresses endearment or distance by his choice of words. His language reflects his social and regional background, his age, his sex, and his degree of creativity. To a lesser degree it may reflect his religion, his race, his prejudices, and his profession.

Sociolinguistics is the study of the relationships between language and society. This approach is relatively new, and the term *sociolinguistics* is so recent that it is not recorded in *Webster's Third New International Dictionary* (1961). The sociolinguist, like the descriptivist, believes that language is systematic, but his major interest is in linguistic differences and the ways these differences correspond with social systems. Most sociolinguists are convinced that there is a definite correlation between a person's language and his culture; they are not in agreement as to whether this influence is in just one direction (and if so which direction) or whether it is mutual.

Many variations in language can be limited geographically as well as socially, such as the pronunciation of *aunt, path, pen, closet* or the choice of words to refer to an object, such as *freeway, expressway, thruway, turnpike.* The person who specializes in this kind of variation is studying **dialect geography**. We often speak of the study of regional and social linguistic differences as **dialectology** and of the person who studies them as a **dialectologist**. Although many sociolinguists are interested in dialectology, all dialectologists are not necessarily sociolinguists. In fact, much of the research conducted in the past on regional dialects virtually ignored social influences.

Descriptivists usually ignore variations in language, choosing to base their research upon either the grammar of one person or upon that of an idealized speaker whose grammar is some kind of average of the grammars of many speakers of that language. Some dialectologists have questioned the validity of this approach which ignores variation. Many of them think that variation is systematic and should be accounted for in an adequate grammar.

One aspect of sociolinguistics is the study of languages that come in contact with each other, primarily through bilingual speakers. A linguist may study the influence of English on the Norwegian settlers in the United States or the influence of Norwegian upon English. Other obvious avenues for study are the influence of English upon Spanish, French, Czech, German, Yiddish, and other languages within the United States. For some people the form of English they use in school and at work is so different from the form they use at home that they are virtually speaking two different languages, although we call both of them English. Linguists are interested in studying these contact situations for descriptive and comparative purposes, and other specialists are able to use their information in trying to meet the social and educational problems that result from the situation.

Instead of studying language in its social context, a linguist may study it in relation to the mind and behavior of man. This study of language is known as **psycholinguistics**. Psychologists for some time have been interested in the language of people who have psychological problems or who have suffered brain damage. Before they can make the most effective use of deviant speech, they have to know what is normal; hence, they must use the results of the descriptivists. Also, much testing involves language ability, thereby providing another fruitful area for psycholinguistic research.

Transformationalists insist that their principal concern is with **linguistic competence**, the person's knowledge of his language, rather than with **linguistic performance**, the actual production of sentences. The effect on performance of such features as memory limitation, distractions, embarrassment, haste, and fear fall under the domain of psycholinguistics rather than descriptive linguistics.

An avenue of psycholinguistic investigation that is currently of great interest to other linguists is that of child language acquisition. Earlier studies limited themselves to vocabulary size and sentence length. We are now more interested in other aspects of the child's grammar: how he forms certain structures (questions, negatives, passives, etc.) at various ages and how these compare with adult structures; when he acquires syntactic and phonological elements such as auxiliary verbs and the various speech sounds; and in what order he acquires these elements. One of the most controversial subjects in language acquisition is whether the child is born with a linguistically blank slate and has to learn everything about language from his environment or whether he is born with a certain amount of knowledge so that language learning is a matter of selecting the relevant material from this knowledge. The fact that a small child can master such a highly complex system as language even under poor learning conditions certainly suggests the possibility of some kind of innate knowledge.

Still another area in which linguistics interacts with another discipline is education. This is the area which is often referred to as **applied linguistics**, although this term is used with much less precision than *sociolinguistics* or *psycholinguistics*. Theoretically the term should be applicable to such areas as cryptography and telephone communications systems, but it has rarely been found outside of education. There are three major places in the curriculum that questions concerning linguistics have been raised: in the teaching of foreign languages, in the teaching of reading and spelling, and in the teaching of the subject usually called English.

Because of various reasons, many native speakers of English are notoriously inept students of foreign languages. No amount of linguistic study can overcome the obstacles of poorly prepared teachers, poor teaching techniques, and student apathy. On the other hand, there are many teachers who do have a good command of the language they are teaching and who are able to cultivate student interest. For these teachers linguistic studies can be an aid. Comparative studies of the grammars of languages such as German and English, Spanish and English, and Italian and English provide exact information on how the two languages are similar and how they are different. Such information if used well can provide direction to the teacher and student in mastering difficult syntactic and phonological features. Also, linguistics can help to provide answers to various questions. How old should a person be when he begins to study a foreign language? Which languages are the most beneficial for a person to learn? Which dialect of a particular language should be taught? Should language teachers concentrate on the spoken language or on the written form? As rapidly as world conditions have been changing during the twentieth century, it is impossible to predict which languages a person will need to speak and read ten years from now, much less twenty or thirty. Missionaries, social workers, businessmen, and diplomats do not visit only major European countries. The person with a good linguistic background should be able to learn a new language with more speed than a person without such training.

In teaching basic skills such as reading and spelling, teachers have raised many questions. How should reading be taught? Should phonics be taught? How effective is it to teach the child to read by some alphabet such as the Initial Teaching Alphabet before teaching him to read words in conventional spelling? Would reading instruction be improved if only words with regular spellings were introduced first? Should the teacher emphasize the sentence rather than the word? If the child is not pronouncing the *h* sound in *where, which,* and other words spelled *wh,* should he be taught to pronounce it in his reading? How should the child be taught to pronounce *a* and *the*? Is the reading teacher introducing the student to new sentences, or is he teaching him the printed representations of structures he has already mastered in speech? If the language a student speaks is radically different from that found in most readers, would it be to his benefit to develop reading materials that are written in his own language? It has been shown that trying to teach spelling by the use of word lists which the student memorizes is a waste of time. How should spelling be taught? How should remedial reading and spelling be taught to students who have advanced to the fourth grade, high school, or their freshman year of college without attaining even a pretense of literacy?

The questions that are raised in teaching English classes are at least as numerous as those which arise when teaching foreign languages, reading, and spelling. What is the purpose of studying the English language? If the only purpose is to teach standard English, why should students who already speak this dialect be required to take the course? If a student who speaks the standard dialect of one region moves to another region, should he be taught the standard dialect of his new location? Will a knowledge of English grammar aid a student in his composition and in his understanding of literature? Which kind of grammar should be taught: traditional, structural, transformational, or some combination of these? Once one of these approaches is selected, which concepts should be presented at each grade level? Is the purpose of studying grammar to learn to analyze individual sentences or to learn how language operates and how to approach the study of language? Is there more to studying language than just studying grammar? Should grammar be taught? How should students who speak a nonstandard dialect be taught?

These questions could very easily be multiplied, and none of them have been answered definitively. The indifferent teacher will either pretend they do not exist or will attempt to answer them from intuition and bias. The conscientious teacher will see the need for familiarity with linguistics before attempting any answer.

It is impossible to divide the channels of linguistic research into a few clearly delineated branches, since there is constant overlapping. In this chapter we have tried to give some idea of the scope of language research. Some of the topics we have mentioned are developed more fully in later chapters of this book.

Suggested Reading

At the end of each chapter in this book there is a brief listing of works which discuss chapter topics in greater detail or which give views different from those found in the chapter. The works have been selected because their content and presentation are within the grasp of the beginning student. References to works found in the general bibliography at the end of this book are made by author and date only.

Bright, William, ed. *Sociolinguistics.* The Hague: Mouton, 1966.

Chomsky, Noam. "The Current Scene in Linguistics: Present Directions." *College English* 27 (1966): 587-95. Reprinted in Reibel and Schane, 1969.

Dinneen, Francis P. *An Introduction to General Linguistics.* New York: Holt, Rinehart and Winston, 1967.

Francis, W. Nelson. *The Structure of American English.* New York: Ronald Press Co., 1958. Chapter 1: "Language, Languages, and Linguistic Science."

Gleason, H. A., Jr. *Linguistics and English Grammar.* New York: Holt, Rinehart and Winston, 1965.

Marckwardt, Albert H. *Linguistics and the Teaching of English.* Bloomington. Indiana University Press, 1966.

Robins, R. H. *A Short History of Linguistics.* Bloomington. Indiana University Press, 1967.

Salus, Peter H., ed. *On Language: Plato to von Humboldt.* New York: Holt, Rinehart and Winston, 1969.

Saporta, Sol, ed. *Psycholinguistics.* New York: Holt, Rinehart and Winston, 1961.

Times Literary Supplement (London). 23 July 1970.

Waterman, John T. *Perspectives in Linguistics.* Chicago: University of Chicago Press, 1963, 1970.

CHAPTER TWO

English Sentence Structure

Man's achievements have often been spectacular. He has built machines which transport him across the surface of the earth, through the air, and even to the moon. He has developed techniques for combatting disease, for correcting certain birth defects, and for transplanting organs from one person to another. In other fields he has studied people of the past: neolithic man, the Egyptian pharoahs, the rulers of the Ming dynasty, Plato, Julius Caesar, Genghis Khan, Napoleon, and Catherine the Great. He has even acquainted himself with the unicorn and the phoenix and with people who have never had any physical existence: Ulysses, Don Juan, Ivanhoe, Little Red Riding Hood, and Agnes Gooch. No other animal has done any of these things, and man could not either if he did not have language. Most activities in which a person participates require interaction with other people, which in turn depends upon language.

Language should not be mistaken as a synonym for *communication.* Usually a person uses language to convey his ideas, but he has other means of communication available as well. By facial expressions he can register sympathy, sorrow, curiosity, amusement, shock, boredom, contempt, and several other emotions. With his arms, hands, fingers, feet, and other parts of the body he can make gestures that communicate ideas. He can make cooing, clucking, snarling, snorting, and smacking sounds with his mouth. Or he can pat another person on the shoulder or on the back. The number of ideas that can be conveyed without language is limited, but communication among all animals except man is restricted to these nonlinguistic devices. If man's need for communication did not go beyond ideas about self-protection, procreation, and the acquisition of food, these devices would be adequate for him as well; but the thoughts man may want to convey are limitless, and he is constantly creating new ones.

We know almost nothing about the physical composition of ideas beyond the fact that they have some kind of existence in the brain. With the possible exception of ESP, there are no extension cords for connecting the brains of different people for the transmission of ideas. A person, therefore, has to use other means if he is to pass on his thoughts. A person can communicate a few ideas by appealing to the other person's senses of sight, hearing, and touch. He can also employ sound beyond cooing and snorting and develop a more complex system for conveying ideas; that is, he can use language.

If the sounds a person makes are to carry meaning, they must be organized into some kind of system. When a person who understands this system hears the sounds, he will receive the idea. The process can be illustrated by Figure 2.1.

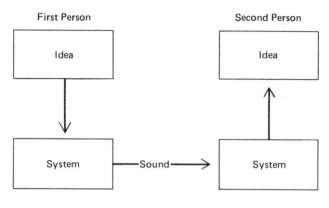

Figure 2.1

It is unlikely that the idea the second person receives is ever exactly the same as that which the first person intended. There may be external influences which affect the sound: Noise may drown out part of it, the two people may be so far apart that the signal is very weak when it reaches the second person, or other acoustical conditions may distort the sound. Also, the two systems may be quite similar, but they are never identical for any two people. In addition, the speaker may apply his system imperfectly in producing sound, just as a mathematician may carelessly make an error in adding. The speaker may cough or sneeze while he is speaking, or he may speak too rapidly, too loudly, or too softly. Fright, boredom, and other emotions may affect his speech; or he may become distracted and get words out of order. The listener may not be giving the message his undivided attention, or his past experiences and prejudices may influence his interpretation of what has been said. With all the features that can hamper the transmission of ideas, it is not surprising that communication is never perfect; what is surprising is that people understand one another's ideas as well as they do.

There are several possible systems a person could use to link his ideas with systematic patterns of sound. The simplest of these would contain one prearranged sound or combination of sounds for each idea:

Idea	Sound
1. Something disgusts me.	Ugh!
2. This is good.	Mmm!
3. I am surprised.	Gasping sound
4. Something stinks.	Pugh!

Each person does have a repertoire of conventionalized sounds such as these for certain ideas, but they obviously do not constitute a very large part of anyone's communication system.

Many people consider the communication system as nothing more than a pairing of words with meanings:

Idea	Sound
1. writing implement containing ink	pen
2. writing implement containing lead	pencil
3. organ of sight	eye
4. to motion with the hand	wave

Most people have several thousands of items such as these, but the system must contain something additional. If two people tried to restrict themselves to single word utterances to convey their ideas, the inadequacy of a communication system limited to pairings of ideas and words would rapidly become apparent. The words must be grouped together:

2.1   A salesman wrote my neighbor a letter.
2.2   The circus came to town.

Yet, all groupings are not possible:

2.3   *The a with yes.
2.4   *Miss Stanley occurred a truck.
2.5   *The rug laugh.
2.6   *In tree the black a cat was.

There must be some way that the system can form structures such as 2.1–2.2 but avoid those like 2.3–2.6. The asterisk is used to designate structures which the system rejects.

One possible method of accounting for which combinations are permitted would be a system in which ideas are not paired with individual words but rather with complete sentences. Each person would have a repertoire of sentences, and communication would involve finding and speaking the sentence that is paired with the idea to be transmitted. As remarkable as the human mind is, it is not capable of holding and manipulating the vast number of sentences required for even dull conversation. Furthermore, this kind of system would not permit a person to create or understand a new sentence. Yet except for a few stock expressions such as "It was nice meeting you," most of the sentences a person says and hears are new to him. That this is so can be shown by recording even a trivial conversation and counting the repeated sentences or by counting repetitions of sentences in a book. Since there are no limits on the new ideas a person may have, there must be new sentences for expressing them. A system consisting of nothing more than an inventory of prefabricated sentences would be inadequate for accounting for something as creative as human language.

A system less taxing on the memory and allowing for new sentences would be one containing sentence patterns rather than finished sentences. One such pattern would be like this:

2.7   The dog chased the cat.

We could keep the same framework but substitute other words for *the cat*: *the postman, my neighbor,* or *the mayor.* We could replace *chased* with *caught, frightened, bit,* or other verbs. Although this kind of system is more plausible than one containing an enormous list of memorized sentences, it also has its weaknesses. If a person started counting the number of patterns he would need to produce just the sentences on one page of a book, he would soon conclude that the number of patterns would be so high as to be unmanageable.

The system for linking ideas with sounds which we call language is obviously not just an inventory of prefabricated sentences or patterns. Rather, it probably consists of a group of processes which direct sentence formation. These processes can be directions for forming plurals or past tenses, or they can be directions for indicating the agent who performs an action as in 2.8 and 2.9:

2.8   *John* built the house.
2.9   The house was built by *John.*

We call these directions **rules** and the system which contains the rules a **grammar.** Each person, then, possesses an internalized grammar consisting of a system of rules which permit him to produce and understand the sentences of his language. If he speaks more than one language, he has more than one grammar. This grammar consists of a finite number of rules; the number must be finite because of the limitations of the mind. Yet it is capable of producing an infinite number of sentences.

What does the grammar look like? There is no way of knowing. We can study the sentences it produces and ask the speaker to comment on various sentences, such as whether 2.10–2.11 mean the same thing or not

2.10   The car which is parked in the driveway belongs to Ann.

2.11   The car parked in the driveway belongs to Ann.

or whether 2.12 is a possible sentence

2.12   Those girls saw car new your.

We may use information such as this to construct a theory about the speaker's internalized grammar. This theory is also called a grammar. So we are using *grammar* with two meanings: (1) the speaker's internalized system of rules which enable him to create and understand the sentences of his language, and (2) the linguist's attempt at describing these rules. The first is found in the minds of people, the second in books.

In studying language, we are more concerned with describing the internalized grammar than the individual sentences it produces. We refer to a person's knowledge of his language as his **competence**, and we call his actual production his **performance**. Our chief concern is with competence. Although a study of performance would be of interest, until we have a reasonable understanding of competence, no thorough analysis of performance is possible. It is probably obvious to everyone that deviant structures caused by distraction, mumbling, or a fit of coughing should play no part in an analysis of the grammar of a language. Less obvious are certain performance limitations. A person might argue that a very long sentence is impossible because no one would be able to remember the beginning by the time he got to the end. We can make a comparison to a person's competence in addition. His memory may make it impossible for him to add two very long numbers, yet if he is given paper and pencil he can add numbers of any length. Memory limitation is irrelevant to a person's competence in addition. Similarly, memory limitation definitely affects a person's linguistic performance but not his competence. Our goal in this chapter and in the rest of the book is to try to understand a native speaker's competence in English.

Surface Relationships

Anyone fluent in speaking English if asked to divide the sentence *The black dog was barking loudly* into two parts would probably make this division:

the black dog   was barking loudly

The words *the black dog* seem to cluster together, as do *was barking loudly*. Other divisions seem less probable:

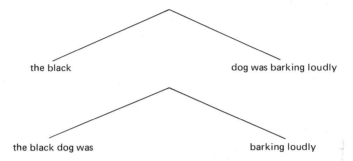

This intuition about division can be supported by various kinds of evidence which a native speaker unfamiliar with formal grammar can apply:

1. After *dog* is the only place at which one may pause and still have a sentence that sounds normal.
2. A single word can be substituted for *the black dog* (*it, he, Fred*) but not for *the black* or for *the black dog was*.

This division is the one traditional grammarians made between units they called *subject* and *predicate*.

A further breakdown of the sentence according to its words yields an analysis like this:

Using the criterion of substitution, we can replace *was barking* with *barked*, showing that *was barking* is a unit separate from *loudly* but that *was barking loudly* is a larger unit separate from *the black dog*.

We can analyze other sentences in a similar manner:

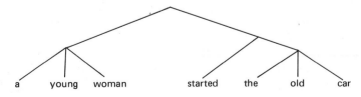

Because of the lines which "branch out," we call the structure we have drawn a
tree. We can recognize several units from the arrangement of the lines:

1. a young woman started the old car
2. a young woman
3. a
4. young
5. woman
6. started the old car
7. started
8. the old car
9. the
10. old
11. car

Some of these units, such as *a young woman* and *the old car,* seem to be very
much alike in that they can function in the same positions in a sentence:

2.13a   *A young woman* was in the garage.
   b   *The old car* was in the garage.
2.14a   We talked about *a young woman.*
   b   We talked about *the old car.*
2.15a   We saw *a young woman.*
   b   We saw *the old car.*

The other unit, *started,* seems to be quite different, since it will not substitute in
the above patterns:

2.13c   **Started* was in the garage.
2.14c   *We talked about *started.*
2.15c   *We saw *started.*

Both *a young woman* and *the old car* have nouns as part of the unit: *woman*
and *car.* The articles *a* and *the* may precede these nouns, but they may not appear as part of a unit such as *started*; **the started* is not a possible English structure. An adjective such as *young, pretty, happy,* or *exciting* may occur between
the article and the noun. The tree as we have it now does not show that *a young
woman* and *the old car* have anything in common as opposed to *started.* If we
label them both with the same name, **noun phrase (NP)**, we can show that they
are the same kind of structure.

   In like manner, within the noun phrase *woman* and *car* seem to be the same kind of structure since we could change them into the plural forms *women* and *cars* or let them substitute for each other in certain structures:

2.16   A *woman* was in front of the house.
2.17   A *car* was in front of the house.
2.18   *A *the* was in front of the house.
2.19   *A *young* was in front of the house.

As these examples show, *woman* and *car* are the same kind of structure, but *the* and *young* are different. We call *woman* and *car* **nouns (N)**. *Young* and *old* cannot show the difference between singular and plural, nor can they substitute by themselves for a word like *woman* or *car,* as sentence 2.19 shows; but they can be compared: *younger* and *older.* We call them **adjectives (Adj)**. *A* and *the* never change form. They are like *my, his,* and a few other words which we call **determiners (Det)**. The order determiner, then adjective, then noun is fixed for all English noun phrases. Any other arrangement is unacceptable:

2.20   *Young a woman* started the old car.
2.21   *Woman a young* started the old car.
2.22   *Young woman a* started the old car.

Of course, all noun phrases in English do not contain determiners or adjectives. In the sentence *Chuck ate spinach, Chuck* and *spinach* are still called noun phrases even though they contain only nouns.

For the unit *started the old car,* we use the term **verb phrase (VP)**. It contains a **verb (V)** and a noun phrase. We can now add our labels, using **S** as an abbreviation for **sentence** to mark the entire tree:

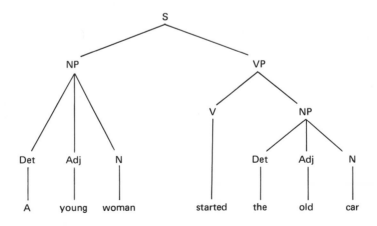

Underlying Structures

The trees we have drawn reveal much of the information the native speaker possesses about English sentences, but they still leave some ideas unexpressed. Notice the verbs in the following sentences:

2.23   Ethel *drove* the car.
2.24   Ethel *drives* the car.
2.25   She *walked* to work.
2.26   She *walks* to work.
2.27   She *talked* to herself.
2.28   She *talks* to herself.

If we draw trees of these six sentences, we wind up with six different verbs. The trees do not show that *walked* and *walks* or *talked* and *talks* are more alike than are *talked* and *walked*. There is obviously a generalization which we are not expressing but which the native speaker understands well: that the difference between *talked* and *talks* is one of **tense**. If our grammar is to contain the knowledge that the native speaker possesses, it must state this generalization. Here is one way of doing it:

past drive	past walk	past talk
present drive	present walk	present talk

These are to be read "the past form of *drive*," "the present form of *walk*," etc. By using the neutral form *drive,* we are not designating tense, but we are showing the identity linking *drives* and *drove*; by stating *past* and *present,* we are showing the difference. We are, furthermore, showing that the difference between *drives* and *drove* is the same one which exists between *walks* and *walked* or between *talks* and *talked.* Our goal is to make the grammar explicit enough that it does not depend upon a native speaker to interpret it.

We are now representing the verb on two levels with the surface form *talked* and the more abstract form *past talk* ("the past form of *talk*"). Such an abstraction is essential if we are to show the relationship between *talks* and *talked* and to show that this is the same one that exists between *eats* and *ate,* as well as similar pairs of verbs. This more abstract level of representation can be illustrated by a tree as follows:

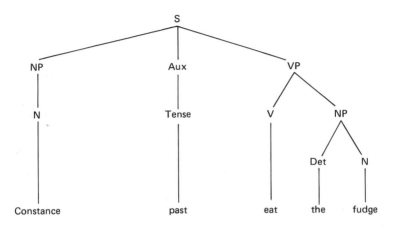

Tense is listed as part of the **auxiliary (Aux)**. The grammar will contain a section which tells us how to pronounce words and combinations of elements such as *past eat*. This will be discussed in Chapter Seven. One of these rules will state that the past form of *eat* is *ate*, and after we apply this rule our tree will be converted into the surface form:

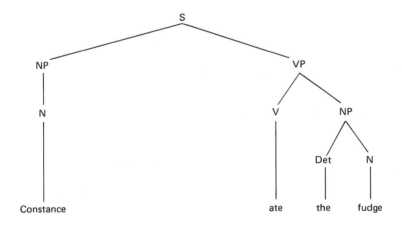

We say that *Constance past eat the fudge* **underlies** *Constance ate the fudge*, which we call a **surface structure**. For most structures there are even more abstract underlying forms going back in progression to the ultimate underlying form, which is called a **deep structure**. Our analysis of a sentence of English, then, looks something like this:

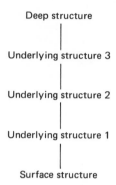

Deep structure

Underlying structure 3

Underlying structure 2

Underlying structure 1

Surface structure

The underlying structures between the deep structure and the surface structure are also called **intermediate structures.** The choice of five as the number of structures was made at random; each sentence has its own number. In the example, underlying structure one is more abstract than the surface structure; structure three is more abstract than two; the deep structure is the most abstract of all.

Let us see what other generalizations we can make about English by the use of underlying forms.

    2.29a   I let out the cat.
       b   I let the cat out.
    2.30a   I looked up the number.
       b   I looked the number up.

If we restrict ourselves to the surface forms given above, there is no convenient way to express the knowledge that the native speaker possesses: (1) that 2.29a and 2.29b mean the same thing, as do 2.30a and 2.30b, and (2) that 2.29a and 2.29b differ in the same way as 2.30a and 2.30b.

The tree for the structure underlying *I looked up the number* looks like this:

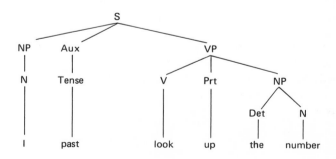

Prt stands for **particle**. *Up* is not an adverb in this sense, as it would be in *He looked up and saw a squirrel on the roof*; nor is it a preposition, as in *He ran up the hill.* It is part of the verb *to look up.* We can say that this same tree underlies *I looked the number up,* but for this sentence we have rearranged the structure:

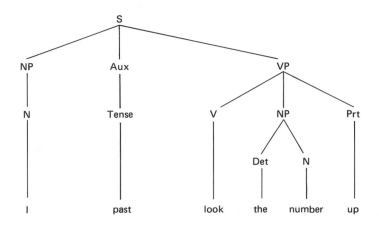

This rearrangement moves the particle after the noun phrase, but it does not alter the meaning of the sentence. Any action, such as rearrangement, which alters an underlying structure is called a **transformation**. Other transformations may add or delete parts of an underlying structure, but no transformation changes the meaning. We are now able to show why sentences 2.29a and 2.29b mean the same thing. They share the same underlying structure, but sentence 2.29b has undergone the **particle movement transformation**, whereas 2.29a has not.

Other pairs of related sentences include the following:

2.31a   Fred threw a pass to George.
   b   Fred threw George a pass.
2.32a   She baked a cake for me.
   b   She baked me a cake.

We can provide the same underlying structure for 2.31a and 2.31b:

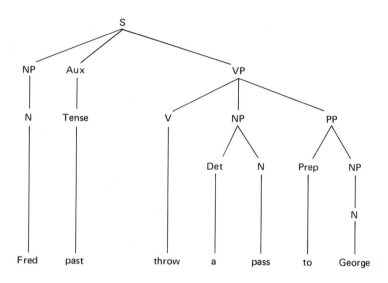

PP is the abbreviation for **prepositional phrase**. If we delete the preposition
(Prep) *to* and rearrange the structure so that the NP *George* precedes the NP
a pass, we derive the following structure:

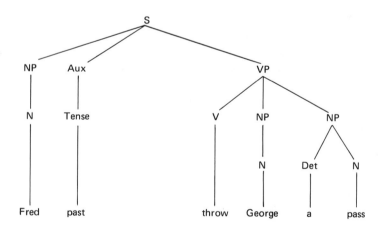

We call this the **indirect object transformation**. Sentences 2.31a and 2.31b share
the same underlying structure and, therefore, have the same meaning. Sentence
2.31a has not undergone the indirect object transformation, but 2.31b has. Sentences 2.32a and 2.32b are related in the same way.

Deep Structures

So far we have seen how underlying structures are transformed into less abstract forms, as the structure underlying *The man turned in his report* can be transformed into the one underlying *The man turned his report in.* The underlying structures we have examined have been very close to surface structures. A traditional grammarian could easily recognize the same parts of speech and the same functions of subject and direct object in both structures.

Now let us look at some more sentences:

2.33   The secretary opened the door with a key.
2.34   The secretary opened the door.
2.35   A key opened the door.
2.36   The door opened.

With the kind of underlying structures we have been using so far, these are four unrelated sentences with four separate deep structures. *Open* has to be listed in the dictionary with two or possibly three meanings: the intransitive meaning of sentence 2.36 and the transitive meanings of the other three sentences; probably it needs to distinguish between the meaning of sentence 2.34, with a human subject, and sentence 2.35, with an inanimate subject. Obviously this interpretation is missing a generalization, since the meaning of *open* is the same for all the sentences, and the noun phrases—*the secretary, the door, a key*—maintain a constant semantic relationship to *open* and to one another in all four sentences. It seems that the differences in structure may be of the same nature as that between *I gave a rose to Susan* and *I gave Susan a rose.*

Nor is *open* the only verb that presents a problem:

2.37a   Someone burned the house.
   b   The house burned.
2.38a   Something tore the page.
   b   The page tore.
2.39a   Something froze the water.
   b   The water froze.

There are a great many verbs in English which share this kind of relationship. The object of the transitive verb can appear as the subject of the same verb used intransitively. Sentence 2.37a can be paraphrased as *Someone caused the house to burn*; some grammars call *burn* in 2.37a a **causative verb**, as they do the verbs in 2.38a and 2.39a. We need some way to show that the relationship between *house* and *burn* is the same for both 2.37a and 2.37b.

As linguists have studied transformational grammar, they have discovered that deep structures are much more abstract and remote from surface structures than they had originally thought. Structures which they at one time thought were deep structures turned out to be merely intermediate structures. All earlier studies of transformational grammar have worked with deep structures that have fixed word order designating such functions as subject and object, no doubt because most of them were written by scholars whose native language is English. There are languages such as Russian, Latin, and Old English, however, in which syntactic relationships are expressed primarily by the forms of the words. These languages make use of word order, but it is only of secondary importance in showing these relationships. If all languages share the same deep structures, as some linguists believe, it seems highly unlikely that deep structures express such concepts as subject and object rather than some more general concepts with semantic meaning. Such functional relationships as subject and object are undeniable in surface structures, but their presence in deep structures is questionable. Also, such parts of speech categories as noun, verb, and adjective seem to be categories of the surface but not of deep structures. The deep structures that are currently being recognized are very close to semantic structures and are possibly the same for all languages. Each language has its own vocabulary and transformational rules for deriving surface structures from these deep structures.

One of the most promising proposals for deep structures is found in the studies of **case grammar**, originally proposed by Charles J. Fillmore. (See the suggested readings at the end of this chapter.) A modified version of this proposal is presented in this chapter. According to this system, deep structures contain constituents called **modality (M)** and **proposition (Prop)**. The modality constituent contains such elements as tense, negation, and question. The proposition contains a verb and one or more **case categories**. By *case* we are not referring to such surface properties as nominative, possessive, and objective, but rather to the semantic relationships that exist among the basic elements of the sentence in the deep structure. We can illustrate case with the following sentences:

2.40   Bill cracked the mirror with a hammer.
2.41   Bill cracked the mirror.
2.42   A hammer cracked the mirror.
2.43   The mirror cracked.

Bill in 2.40 and 2.41 instigated the cracking. A noun designating a human or animal that instigates an action is known as an **agent (A)**. *Bill,* then, is the deep-structure agent, and it does not matter whether the surface structure is that of sentences 2.40 and 2.41 or that of the sentence *The mirror was cracked by Bill.* We are concerned solely with the semantic relationship between *Bill* and *cracked,* not the surface syntactic relationship. *A hammer* is an **instrument (I),** the inanimate object used to bring about the action or state of the verb. In sentences 2.40 and 2.42, *a hammer* has the same relationship to *cracked* even though the surface forms are quite different. We can contrast agent and instrument by examining sentences 2.41 and 2.42. A human or an animal can bring about an action by its own force, but an inanimate object, such as a hammer, cannot. Rather, a hammer or other inanimate object has to be moved by some other force. Finally, in all four sentences *mirror* is a **patient (P)**, the noun which is affected by the action or state of the verb.

We can represent the deep structure of *Bill cracked the mirror with a hammer* on a tree:

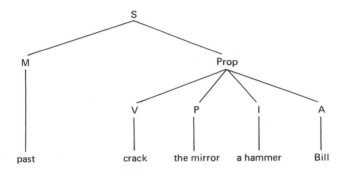

Associated with each deep-structure case is a preposition. For a universal grammar it would be more accurate to say that underlying the preposition is an abstract element which is eventually realized as a preposition or (for certain languages other than English) as preposition and case ending. Since English has only prepositions for this element, we are simplifying by calling it just **preposition**. Also, determiners do not belong in deep structures, but since their derivation is not relevant to our purpose in this chapter, we are placing them in our trees. For that matter, the deep structure lexical representations such as *mirror* and *crack* should be more abstract than we are presenting them here. These simplifications are normally found both in textbooks and in articles in technical journals which are intended primarily for specialists.

From the surface structure we can see that the preposition associated with instrument is *with,* but for agent we see no preposition. However, in the sentence *The mirror was cracked by Bill,* we can see that the preposition for agent is *by.* There are no prepositions normally associated with patient; we, therefore, give it a zero preposition, written **∅**. After adding the prepositions, we change the tree as follows:

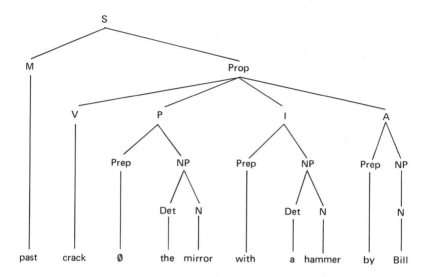

Although linguists differ in their beliefs about the order of cases, we are following the assumption that in the deep structure the ordering of the cases is irrelevant. The verb comes first, but there is no intended ordering of other elements in the proposition. For a language such as English, in which surface word order is rigidly fixed, there are transformational rules which order the elements. The first transformation moves the agent to the beginning of the sentence into subject position:

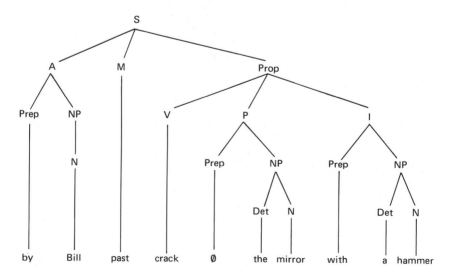

Now that the agent NP is in subject position, another transformation deletes the preposition before it, and with it the case label:

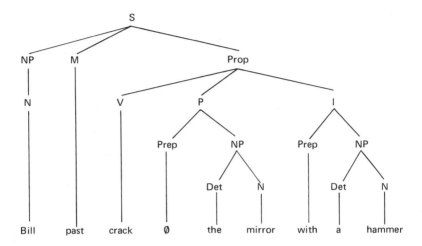

Next a transformation moves patient to the direct object position, immediately after the verb. If patient is already there, the transformation applies vacuously. Another transformation deletes the preposition before the NP in object position and the case label. If we now substitute *Aux* for *M*, *VP* for *Prop*, and *PP* for *I*, we have a surface structure tree like those we worked with at the beginning of this chapter:

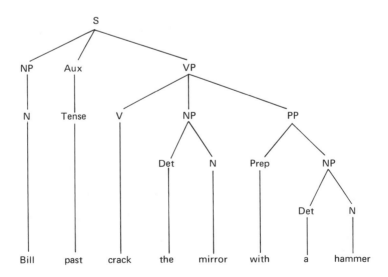

Finally, phonological rules apply to give *Bill cracked the mirror with a hammer.* We have applied the following rules:

1. Subject placement
2. Deletion of subject preposition
3. Object placement
4. Deletion of object preposition
5. Phonological rules

Let us now see what happens to a sentence that contains no agent in the deep structure.

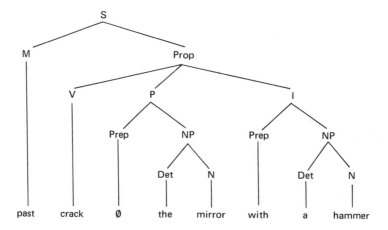

If there is no agent, then instrument is moved into subject position:

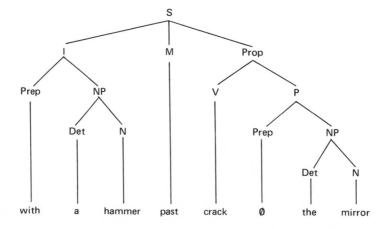

Second, the subject preposition *with* is deleted and with it the case label *I*. Third, patient is moved into object position; it is already there. Fourth, the object preposition and case label are deleted. After the application of phonological rules, the sentence is *A hammer cracked the mirror.*

Finally, let us look at a sentence with neither agent nor instrument in the deep structure:

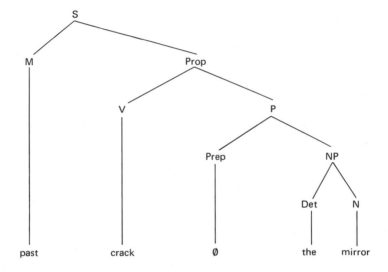

Since only one case category is in the deep structure, it becomes the subject:

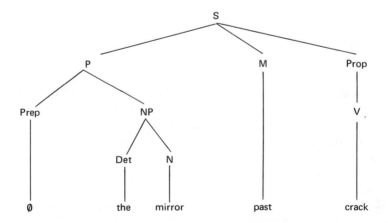

The subject preposition and case label are deleted. After the application of phonological rules, we have the sentence *The mirror cracked.*

The selection of which case category is to be the subject is restricted. When agent is present, it becomes the subject. (Sentences such as *The mirror was cracked by Bill* are discussed later in this chapter.) Other choices produce ungrammatical sentences:

2.44   Bill cracked the mirror with a hammer.
2.45   *A hammer cracked the mirror by Bill.
2.46   *The mirror cracked with a hammer by Bill.

If there is no agent, but there is an instrument, it becomes the subject:

2.47   A hammer cracked the mirror.
2.48   *The mirror cracked with a hammer.

If there is neither agent nor instrument, the patient becomes the subject:

2.49   The mirror cracked.

The ordering for subject selection, then, is (1) agent, (2) instrument, (3) patient. The first of these cases that is present becomes the subject. If either agent or instrument is present to become the subject, then patient becomes the object.

For the kind of grammar that we are presenting, we need a special dictionary, or **lexicon**, which will be similar to those dictionaries now in existence but which will differ in some respects. Part of the entry for *crack* in this dictionary will be the cases that the verb permits. There are four possibilities:

[*crack*: Patient, Instrument, Agent]
[*crack*: Patient, Instrument]
[*crack*: Patient, Agent]
[*crack*: Patient]

We have a way of combining these four statements: [*crack*: P (I) (A)]. Patient must be present for *crack*; it is, therefore, not in parentheses. Since instrument and agent may or may not be present, they are placed in parentheses; either or both of them may be selected. We call a representation such as [*crack*: P (I) (A)] a **case structure** for the verb. Some other verbs that share the same case structure as *crack* are *open, close, break, bend, snap, rip, tear, grow, shrink, melt, cook,* and *fry.*

All verbs that take three case categories do not necessarily have the same case structure as *crack.* Notice *tickle* in the following sentences:

2.50   Tom tickled Ruby with a feather.

2.51   Tom tickled Ruby.
2.52   A feather tickled Ruby.
2.53   *Ruby tickled.

As with *crack,* the verb *tickle* must have patient. It may not, however, have patient as the only case; either agent or instrument must also be present. That is, only these possibilities exist:

[*tickle*: Patient, Instrument, Agent]
[*tickle*: Patient, Instrument]
[*tickle*: Patient, Agent]

To show that at least one of the cases instrument and agent must be selected, we use linked parentheses: [*tickle*: P (I)(A)] This means that patient must be selected; both of the other cases or only one of them may be selected. We may not omit both instrument and agent. Other verbs with the case structure [___ : P (I)(A)] are *hit, slap, thump, kick, strike,* etc.

There is, then, a syntactic difference between verbs like *crack* with the case structure [___ : P (I) (A)] and those like *tickle* with [___ : P (I)(A)]. Verbs like *tickle* cannot function as intransitive verbs with patient as the subject, but verbs like *crack* may. In addition to this syntactic difference, there is also a semantic difference. The action denoted by verbs like *crack* changes the patient from one state to another. If we say, *John cracked the mirror,* we are saying that the mirror was changed as a result of the action from an uncracked to a cracked state. Or the mirror may already have been cracked and he cracked it some more; this would still change the object. We call verbs like *crack* **change of state verbs.** Verbs like *tickle,* on the other hand, name an action that does not change the patient from one state to another. If we say, *Tom tickled Ruby with a feather,* we are not indicating any change that occurred to Ruby as a result of the tickling. Verbs like *tickle* are called **surface contact verbs.** Because surface contact verbs do not specify an action that actually changes anything, the case label *patient* is probably inaccurate for *Ruby* in *Tom tickled Ruby with a feather.* Some other term such as **location** may be more accurate.

Some clear uses of the case category *location* are these:

2.54   The dog ran *in the yard.*
2.55   Fred lives *at home.*
2.56   The ball is *under the car.*
2.57   The ball is *behind the car.*
2.58   The ball is *on top of the car.*
2.59   The ball is *beside the car.*
2.60   The ball is *in front of the car.*

Unlike the prepositions used with patient, agent, and instrument, those for location are not predictable. The agentive *by* and the instrumental *with* are empty semantically; they have no real meaning in themselves, but rather serve to signal syntactic functions. The prepositions used with location, however, do have meaning in addition to that of indicating syntactic function, as is shown in sentences 2.56 through 2.60. Some of these prepositions are idiosyncratically determined by the verb or the noun; for example, one lives *in* a city, *on* a certain street, *at* a particular address. One blames a person *for* something but blames something *on* a person. Prepositions for location are selected from the lexicon, either because of their own semantic content or because of idiosyncratic features of the noun or verb.

Another case is that which we call **dative (D)**, the person or animal affected by the action or state named by the verb, as in the following sentences:

2.61   The supervisor wrote a letter to *Lucas.*
2.62   Ann baked a cake for *her neighbor.*
2.63   It seemed to *John* that he had been cheated.
2.64   *John* thought that he had been cheated.

We can illustrate the use of the dative in a case structure for the verb *give*:
[*give*: P, D, A]. The sentence *He gave the child a sandwich* illustrates the cases.

With the listing of five cases (agent, patient, instrument, dative, and location), we have by no means covered all of the possibilities for a language such as English, nor have we given all of the details and problems involved with these five cases. The material given has been selected to give an indication of the way cases operate in deep structure. These are also the cases that are needed for the transformations used in this chapter and in the ones that follow.

Transformations

We have seen several examples of transformations. The particle movement and the indirect object transformations as well as the subject and object placement transformations rearrange structures. But rearrangement is not the only process that a transformation can perform. Some transformations add elements that were not in the deep structure, such as *that* when added to the structure underlying *We know he is going* becomes *We know **that** he is going.* When *for* and *to* are added to the underlying structure *he would like (you leave)*, the structure becomes *He would like for you to leave.* A third transformational process is deletion. We have seen this process delete subject and object prepositions. Also, repeated words are often deleted, as the underlying structure *He can't **play the piano**, and she can't **play the piano** either* becomes *He can't play* *the piano, and she can't either*; the repeated VP *play the piano* has been deleted. A fourth process is substitution. For example, we may substitute pronouns for noun phrases that are repeated:

2.65   When Ann saw Bill, *Ann* kicked *Bill.*
2.66   When Ann saw Bill, *she* kicked *him.*

Normally transformations do not affect the meaning of the deep structure.

Now that we have described a deep structure as a modality element and a proposition containing a verb and one or more case categories, let us reexamine the indirect object construction. We may have the following underlying structure:

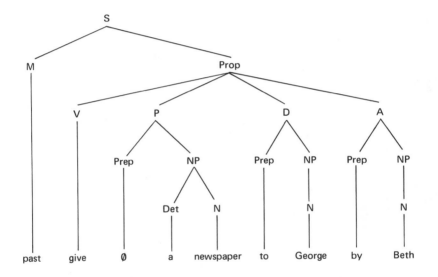

We can apply transformations in the following order:

1. Subject placement of agent
2. Deletion of subject preposition
3. Object placement of patient
4. Deletion of object preposition

After the application of phonological rules, the sentence is *Beth gave a newspaper to George.* Let us now examine another possibility of object placement. After subject placement and deletion of subject preposition, the structure looks like this:

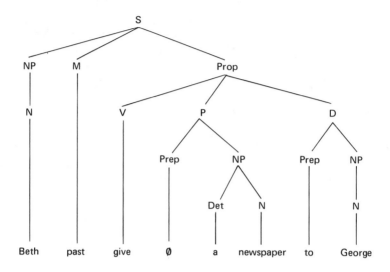

Instead of selecting patient as the object, we may select dative:

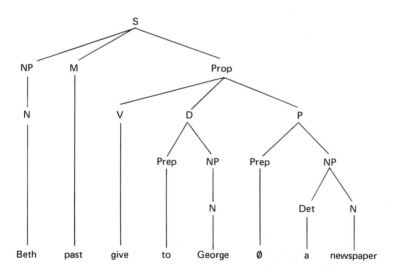

The object-deletion rule will delete *to,* and another rule will delete any segments—
prepositions or other elements—that are zero. This will give the sentence *Beth
gave George a newspaper.* The sentences mean the same thing, whether we select
patient or dative as the object:

2.67   Beth gave a newspaper to George.
2.68   Beth gave George a newspaper.

With a deep structure expressed in terms of cases rather than structures with subjects and objects, no special indirect object transformation is needed. Both of the above sentences are derived by transformations that are needed in the grammar for other structures as well. We may, then, select either dative or patient for the object.

.In some sentences we have a choice of cases for the subject as well. Here is a deep structure that permits this choice:

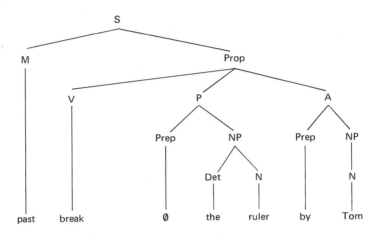

By selecting agent as the subject and patient as the object, we obtain the sentence *Tom broke the ruler,* after deletion of prepositions and application of phonological rules. It is also possible to select patient as the subject. After subject placement of patient and deletion of subject preposition, we have the following structure:

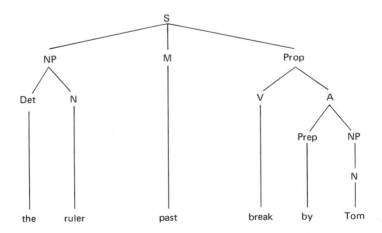

A restriction will state that agent cannot become an object; hence, neither object placement nor deletion of object preposition is applicable. The agent *by Tom* will remain as it is. The normal choice of subject is always agent, but in this case we are not making the normal choice. To indicate this deviation, we add *be* to the modality constituent and the past participial form to the verb. The past participial form will change the verb *break* to *broken* as in *was broken*. The past participial form of *eat* is *eaten,* that of *see* is *seen,* that of *drop* is *dropped,* that of *hit* is *hit,* etc. We use *en* as an abbreviation for "past participle of." After this addition, our structure looks like this:

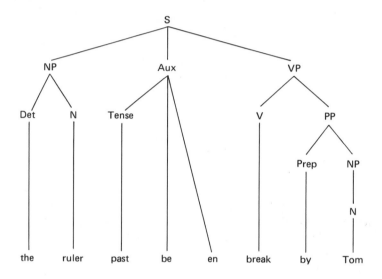

There are phonological rules that tell us how to pronounce combinations such as *past be* and *en break.* These will tell us that the past form of *be* is *was* or *were* and that the *en* form of *break* is *broken.* After the application of all rules, the sentence is *The ruler was broken by Tom.*

By the use of transformations we are able to convert deep structures containing semantic case categories into surface structures with such syntactic functions as subject and object. A deep-structure case category may appear on the surface in various syntactic functions, depending upon the transformations that have been applied. Here are some examples:

Deep Structure *agent*
2.69   *The thief* stole her costume jewelry.
2.70   Her costume jewelry was stolen by *the thief.*
Deep Structure *instrument*
2.71   He cut his finger with *an axe.*
2.72   *An axe* cut his finger.

Deep Structure *patient*
2.73   Walter gave *the shoe* to Michael.
2.74   *The shoe* was given to Michael by Walter.
2.75   Michael was given *the shoe* by Walter.
Deep Structure *dative*
2.76   Walter gave the shoe to *Michael*.
2.77   Walter gave *Michael* the shoe.
2.78   *Michael* was given the shoe by Walter.

These are the surface syntactic functions that traditional grammar called *subject* (2.69, 2.72, 2.74, 2.78), *direct object* (2.73), *retained object* (2.75), *indirect object* (2.77), and *object of a preposition* (2.70, 2.71, 2.76). The same deep cases and surface functions exist whether the sentence is short or longer and more complex, such as those we will be examining in the next chapter.

Exercises

I. Surface Relationships
    A. What evidence can you provide to show that the italicized groups of words are or are not the same kind of structure?
        1. *Those silly girls* were laughing at *the woman in the red hat*.
        2. *Alice* looked *very silly in the red hat*.
    B. Provide evidence to show that the italicized words are or are not nouns:
        1. That *dog* is Ralph's *mother*.
        2. This *furniture* is *expensive*.
    C. Draw trees for the following surface structures:
        1. An old tree fell.
        2. We found the treasure.
        3. The new secretary opened the package.
II. Underlying Structures
    A. Draw two trees for this sentence: A student bought the chair. Show (1) the underlying structure in which tense is separate from the verb (such as *past eat*) and (2) the surface structure in which tense is incorporated in the verb (such as *ate*).
    B. Perform the particle movement transformation:
        1. He read through the report.
        2. We hurried up the typist.
    C. Use the particle movement transformation as evidence for showing whether *up* is the same kind of structure in the following sentences:
        1. He ran up the bill.
        2. He ran up the hill.
    D. From the following sentences determine the conditions under which

particle movement is optional and those under which it is obligatory
for certain verb-particle combinations:
1. The clerk read out the names.
2. The clerk read the names out.
3. *The clerk read out them.
4. The clerk read them out.
5. He turned down the offer.
6. He turned the offer down.
7. *He turned down it.
8. He turned it down.

E. Use trees to show how these sentences are related:
1. Someone handed the note to the announcer.
2. Someone handed the announcer the note.

III. Deep Structures

A. Read the different meanings listed for *crack* in a good dictionary, pay-
ing special attention to the intransitive meaning as in *The mirror
cracked* and the transitive meaning as in *Bill cracked the mirror.* Do
the two meanings show a difference in the verb or in the selection of
the subject?

B. Why does a grammar need underlying structures as well as surface
structures?

C. Draw deep structure trees for the following sentences and perform the
transformations (subject placement, etc.) needed for deriving the surface structures:
1. Janet slapped Ralph.
2. The fish fried.
3. The knife cut his arm.

D. In the following pairs of sentences, one is ungrammatical because it
violates a restriction on which case may become the subject or the
object. Explain why one of the sentences is ungrammatical but the
other grammatical.
1a. The janitor opened the door with a key.
 b. *A key opened the door by the janitor.
2a. The glass broke.
 b. *The glass broke with a bat.
3a. John cut his arm with a knife.
 b. *John cut a knife his arm.

E. Classify the following verbs as change of state or as surface contact,
using both syntactic evidence and meaning: *lock, tap, shove, move,
destroy.*

IV. Transformations

A. Show that the following sentences are derived from the same deep
structure but with a different selection of cases for the object:

     1. The manager sent the money to me.

     2. The manager sent me the money.

B. Give the deep structure for these sentences and show which transformations have been applied:

     1. Mike wrote the letter.

     2. The letter was written by Mike.

C. Use sentences 2.69–2.78 to show why it is inadequate to define the subject of a sentence as "the one that performs the action." How would you define the term *subject*?

D. Explain the following: *deep structure, surface structure, underlying structure, intermediate structure, transformation, deep-structure case.* Why does the grammar contain the concepts named by these terms?

Suggested Reading

Chafe, Wallace L. *Meaning and the Structure of Language.* Chicago: University of Chicago Press, 1970.

Fillmore, Charles J. "The Case for Case" in Bach and Harms, 1968.

_____. "The Grammar of *Hitting* and *Breaking*" in Jacobs and Rosenbaum, 1970.

_____. "A Proposal Concerning English Prepositions" in Dinneen, 1966. Revised as "Toward a Modern Theory of Case" in Reibel and Schane, 1969.

Fraser, Bruce. "Some Remarks on the Verb-Particle Construction in English" in Dinneen, 1966.

Halle, Morris. "Questions of Linguistics" in Reibel and Schane, 1969.

Huddleston, Rodney. "Some Remarks on Case-Grammar." *Linguistic Inquiry* 1 (1970): 501–11.

Langendoen, D. Terence. *Essentials of English Grammar.* New York: Holt, Rinehart and Winston, 1970. Chapter 4: "Roles and Role Structure."

Postal, Paul. "Underlying and Superficial Linguistic Structure" in Reibel and Schane, 1969.

CHAPTER THREE

Conjoined and Embedded Structures

Anyone who has learned a language well enough to converse freely in it has acquired an impressive amount of knowledge. Even people with little formal education have learned several thousand words, although they do not use all of them with the same frequency. But impressive as a person's vocabulary is, it is relatively uninteresting in comparison to other knowledge he has about his language, namely his ability to produce literally an infinite number of structures in which these words can be used. Since even the mind of a genius has definite limitations, the rules which permit a person to produce and understand the sentences in his language must be finite in number.

Every fluent speaker has an internalized grammar of his language, and he knows more about his language than is contained in the most voluminous descriptions of the language in print. It would seem that there is no point in studying language if every speaker already has such a vast knowledge of it. The problem is that this knowledge is implicit rather than explicit. An illiterate adult with normal intelligence could answer a number of questions like the following:

1. Do these sentences mean the same thing, or are they different in meaning?

    3.1a   The salesman handed the wrench to Joe.
       b   The salesman handed Joe the wrench.
    3.2a   He was declared to be insane.
       b   He was declared insane.
    3.3a   What did you send your children for Christmas?
       b   Did you send your children something for Christmas?

2. In the following sentence, what is it that I will do?

    3.4   Leslie won't help you, but I will.

3. In the following sentences, who does the cheating and who is cheated?

    3.5   Tom is hard to cheat.
    3.6   Tom is ready to cheat.

4. Can *he* mean *Allen* in both of the following sentences?

3.7   The possibility that *he* might win excited Allen.

3.8   *He* was excited by the possibility that Allen might win.

Provided that the directions are made clear enough, a native speaker of English with no formal education can answer these questions as well as a linguist can. But there is a major difference: The illiterate, intelligent adult cannot explain *why* he answers the questions as he does, whereas the linguist can discuss one sentence in relation to other sentences. Most linguists feel that they know why the answers to the above questions are what they are, although there are a great many more questions that they cannot answer.

No one has ever been able to point to a particular brain cell and say that therein is contained the person's knowledge of the passive, negative, or indirect object. We are unable to read directly the internalized grammar of a person's language. Realizing this limitation, we do the next best thing: We use a person's answers to questions like those above to help us construct an artificial grammar of the language. This second kind of grammar is the one that we find in books. Generally, when a person talks about a grammar, this is the kind he means.

The grammar that we are describing in this book begins with forms that we call **deep structures**. Possibly our deep structures will some day be revised so that they will be **semantic** or **conceptual structures**; our knowledge of how people think and assign meaning to utterances is still too limited for us to write structures that we are convinced are real semantic structures. By a series of processes that we call **transformations**, we convert deep structures into **surface structures**; after we apply phonological rules to the surface structures, we have **surface phonetic structures**, which are very close to what we usually think of as sentences of English. These surface phonetic structures will, of course, be altered by individual stylistic preferences and by performance features; and, if they are written, they will be subjected to rules for spelling, punctuation, and other writing conventions. Because of the importance of transformations in this grammar, we call it a **transformational grammar**. Figure 3.1 gives a diagram of the composition of the grammar. Although it may be very similar to an individual's internalized grammar, no one claims that it is a model of how people produce and understand sentences. That is, no one says that a person with an idea he wants to communicate first turns this idea into a deep structure and then subjects it to subject placement, deletion of subject preposition, and other transformations to produce sound waves so that someone else can receive the sound and work in reverse order from phonological rules back through the transformations to a deep structure and the idea the speaker had. What we are saying is that a transformational grammar provides us with a means of analyzing given sentences, as do many other grammars. But it goes beyond this in predicting which unobserved sentences

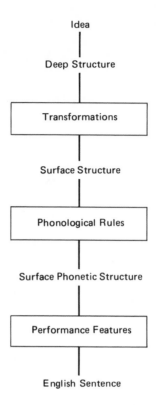

Figure 3.1

will be possible and in providing an explanation for much of the knowledge a
native speaker has about his language, such as the questions we asked at the beginning of this chapter. Although there is still much to be explained, transformational grammar has gone farther than any other grammar in providing these
explanations. A further goal of this grammar is to provide a means of evaluating
alternate rules or grammatical descriptions and to provide a metatheory for
grammars in general.

Conjoined Structures, Pro Forms, and Deletion

In the last chapter we saw that underlying each surface structure are a deep
structure and several intermediate structures. Each deep structure consists of
a modality element and a proposition; the proposition consists of a verb and one

or more case categories. Underlying the surface structure *Susan screamed* is this deep structure:

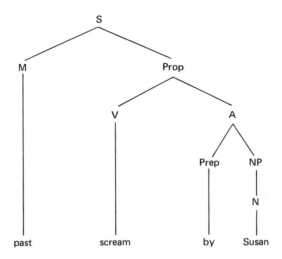

After the application of subject placement, deletion of subject preposition, and phonological rules, we have the sentence *Susan screamed.* Some deep structures consist of not just one sentence, but of two or more joined together, as shown in the following tree:

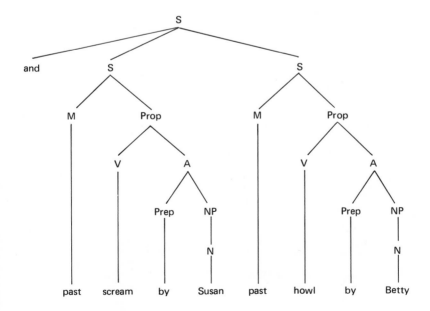

The deep structure *past scream by Susan* will be transformed into the surface structure *Susan screamed. Past howl by Betty* will be transformed into *Betty howled.* Finally, a conjunction movement transformation will place *and* between the two sentences to give *Susan screamed and Betty howled.* The tree shows that *Susan screamed* is a sentence, as is *Betty howled.* It also shows that the larger unit *Susan screamed and Betty howled* is a sentence. Two or more sentences joined together in this fashion constitute a **compound sentence.**

A compound sentence may consist of more than two simple sentences, as 3.9 shows:

> 3.9   Susan screamed, Betty howled, Ann laughed, Agnes fainted, and Donna ran away.

In theory there is no limit to the number of sentences that can be joined together in this fashion. Of course, stylistic preferences and performance features such as memory limitation will restrict excessive conjoining, but the syntactic rules contain no such restriction. The deep structure for 3.9 looks like this:

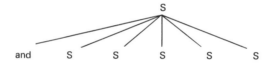

A transformation will copy *and* before each *S*:

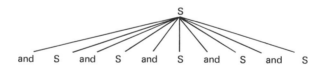

A second transformation will delete the first *and*:

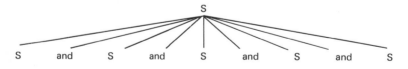

If no further transformations of this nature are performed, 3.9a is the result:

> 3.9a   Susan screamed, and Betty howled, and Ann laughed, and Agnes fainted, and Donna ran away.

There is also an optional transformation which deletes all except the last *and*:

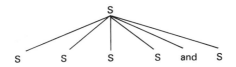

By this process we derive 3.9:

3.9   Susan screamed, Betty howled, Ann laughed, Agnes fainted, and Donna ran away.

Now returning to our original sentence, suppose that both acts of screaming and howling are performed by Susan. In our tree we will have *Susan* instead of *Betty* in the second sentence, and we will derive the structure *Susan screamed and Susan howled.* Although this is a grammatical sentence, most speakers of English find the repetition of *Susan* irritating. When a sentence contains two identical noun phrases, we usually substitute a pronoun for the second one. The two noun phrases must refer to the same person or object; that is to say, they must have the same **referent.** In the sentence we are discussing, both occurrences of *Susan* must refer to the same person, and not one of them to Susan Smith and the other to Susan Black. The pronoun that is substituted for the second noun phrase must agree with it in person, number, and gender. We must select *she* to replace the second pronoun: *Susan screamed and she howled.* The following sentences illustrate this restriction:

3.10   Susan screamed and *I* howled. (different person)
3.11   Susan screamed and *they* howled. (different number)
3.12   Susan screamed and *he* howled. (different gender)

All of the above sentences are grammatical, but none of them means *Susan screamed and Susan howled.* Also, if both noun phrases are to be understood as referring to the same person, we normally may not substitute a pronoun for the first one. *She screamed and Susan howled* would be interpreted as meaning that *Susan* and *she* are different people. Later in this chapter we will see a few cases in which the first noun phrase may be pronominalized, but the sentences we are considering now do not fulfill the requirements for this process.

We can see other uses of pronominalization in the following sentences:

3.13a   *Thomas* will be sick when *Thomas* learns that *Thomas* has been drafted.
   b   *Thomas* will be sick when *he* learns that *he* has been drafted.

3.14a   *Those children* heard you calling *those children,* but *those children* didn't answer.

b   *Those children* heard you calling *them,* but *they* didn't answer.

Pronouns are not the only words that substitute for others to prevent repetition:

3.15a   We arrived *in Seattle* at 10:00 and stayed *in Seattle* until noon.

b   We arrived *in Seattle* at 10:00 and stayed *there* until noon.

3.16a   I received the book *at ten o'clock,* but I didn't read the book *at ten o'clock.*

b   I received the book *at ten o'clock,* but I didn't read it *then.*

In each of these sentences we are substituting a general word for a more specific one. *Susan* is the name of a specific girl; *she* is a general word for any girl or woman. *In Seattle* is a specific place; *there* is a general word that can designate any place. These general words such as pronouns, *then,* and *there* are collectively called **pro forms.** When we substitute one of them for a specific word or phrase, we are applying the **pro form transformation.** This transformation applies only when two or more words or phrases have the same referent, as in the sentences we used as examples.

The pro form transformation allows us to avoid repetition, but this is not the only means available to us. An alternate choice is **deletion:**

3.17a   *Susan* screamed and *Susan* howled.

b   *Susan* screamed and   howled.

Deletion, like other transformations, does not affect meaning. The only elements that may be deleted are those which are clearly understood by the listener. For the deletion process which we are considering here, only repeated elements may be deleted. **Screamed and Susan howled* is not possible, since this structure would show deletion of the first noun phrase. We are unable to delete anything from *Susan screamed and Betty howled. Susan screamed and howled* means that Susan performed both acts; it would not allow us to know that Betty did the howling. The following sentences show that noun phrases are not the only structures that may be deleted:

3.18a   *We went* to Montana, and *we went* to Idaho.

b   We went to Montana and to Idaho.

3.19a   Janice can't *type well,* but I can *type well.*

b   Janice can't type well, but I can.

Sometimes deletion makes other transformations necessary:

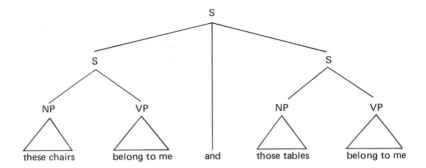

Whenever we wish to simplify a tree by not giving a complete analysis of some part, we use a triangle. The fact that *these chairs* is placed under NP shows that it is a noun phrase. The triangle shows that we are not concerned with showing the constituents. First we perform deletion:

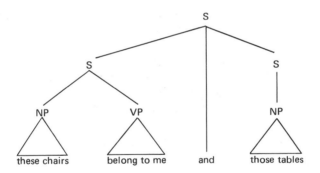

There are other transformations which rearrange the structure so that *and those tables* is brought within the same noun phrase as *these chairs*:

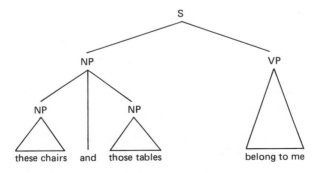

Most conjoined structures in English are ultimately derived from conjoined sentences; pro form and deletion transformations remove repeated structures. Sometimes rearrangement follows the deletion transformation.

For some conjoined noun phrases there is no possible underlying conjoined sentence:

> 3.20a   The ball rolled between the fence and the road.
>   b   *The ball rolled between the fence, and the ball rolled between
>   the road.
> 3.21a   Louise mixed mustard and sugar together.
>   b   *Louise mixed mustard together, and she mixed sugar together.

A few noun phrases, such as these, are conjoined in the deep structure; they are not derived from underlying conjoined sentences.

When we encounter a compound noun phrase in a surface structure, how are we to know what kind of structure it is derived from? We have several tests.

1. Those derived from underlying conjoined sentences can be paraphrased by surface conjoined sentences:

> 3.22a   Don and John knew your name.
>   b   Don knew your name, and John knew your name.
> 3.23a   Bill and Hugh conferred.
>   b   *Bill conferred and Hugh conferred.

2. Those derived from underlying conjoined sentences can be preceded by *both*:

> 3.22c   Both Don and John knew your name.
> 3.23c   *Both Bill and Hugh conferred.

3. Those derived from underlying conjoined noun phrases may be followed by *together*:

> 3.22d   *Don and John knew your name together.
> 3.23d   Bill and Hugh conferred together.

4. Those derived from underlying conjoined noun phrases may be paraphrased by *with* constructions:

> 3.22e   *Don knew your name with John.
> 3.23e   Bill conferred with Hugh.

Hence, the deep structure of 3.22 has a conjoined sentence, that of 3.23 a conjoined noun phrase.

Sometimes a surface structure meets all four of the above criteria:

3.24a   Rudy and Alice sang songs.
  b   Rudy sang songs, and Alice sang songs.
  c   Both Rudy and Alice sang songs.
  d   Rudy and Alice sang songs together.
  e   Rudy sang songs with Alice.

Since 3.24b and 3.24c do not mean the same thing as 3.24d and 3.24e, sentence 3.24a must be ambiguous. If we restricted ourselves to surface structures, we would have no way of accounting for this ambiguity apart from appealing to the native speaker to apply his internalized grammar. With a grammar that contains deep structures and transformations as well as surface structures, we can show precisely how the ambiguity occurs. Two or more different deep structures may have the same form on the surface, as shown in Figure 3.2.

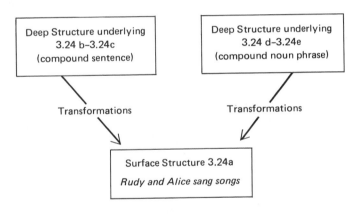

Figure 3.2

Our grammar also permits the reverse situation: One deep structure may be converted into two or more synonymous surface structures through a different choice of transformations. This is illustrated in Figure 3.3.

It would be a mistake to think that the only reason for setting up deep structures is to explain ambiguous and synonymous sentences. Our real goal is to describe the native speaker's competence, and much of the knowledge which constitutes this competence is not obvious on the surface. By means of deep structures and transformations, we are able to account for certain kinds of

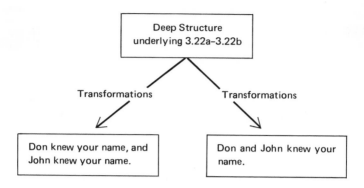

Figure 3.3

synonymy and ambiguity, but we are able to account for much more as well. Although there is still much about English and language in general that no one understands, the kind of grammar we are discussing seems promising as a means for accommodating added knowledge.

Relative Constructions

So far the only components of noun phrases that we have examined are determiners and nouns. In surface structures there are other possibilities as well, such as in the following sentence:

  3.25 The man who was whistling hit me.

The structure *the man who was whistling* is the subject of *hit,* and it must be derived from a deep structure agent. We can easily show that this structure is a noun phrase, since it can undergo pronominalization:

  3.26 The man who was whistling chased me, and *the man who was whistling* hit me.
  3.27 The man who was whistling chased me, and *he* hit me.

Or if we had selected patient instead of agent for the subject, the sentence would have been

  3.28 I was hit by the man who was whistling.

The noun phrase consists of the determiner *the,* the noun *man,* and the structure *who was whistling.* This structure must be derived from a sentence in the deep structure since it contains all of the components of a sentence: tense, verb, and a case category. *Who* is a pro form for the noun phrase *the man.* A simplified tree for an underlying structure of *The man who was whistling hit me* looks like this:

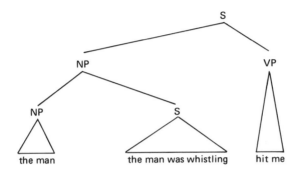

We say that the sentence *the man was whistling* is **embedded** in a noun phrase. The pro form transformation substitutes *who* for *the man* to prevent repetition. The surface structure *who was whistling* is called a **relative clause.**

We can illustrate other uses of the relative clause in the following sentences:

3.29   I don't know the people *who live next door.*
3.30   We looked at the coin *which you had found.*
3.31   The milk *that you bought yesterday* already smells bad.

The relative clauses are derived from the following underlying structures:

3.29a   *the people* live next door.
3.30a   you had found *the coin*
3.31a   you bought *the milk* yesterday

There must be more to forming relative clauses than just using the pro form transformation, or the above underlying structures would become

3.29b   *who* live next door
3.30b   you had found *which*
3.31b   you bought *that* yesterday

We need a transformation that will move the relevant noun phrase to the begin-

ning of its sentence. We call this transformation the **relative transformation.**
Our relative clauses, then, are formed by the following sequence of transformations from their underlying (not deep) structures:

> 3.29a   *the people* live next door
> relative: *the people* live next door
> pro form: *who* live next door
> 3.30a   you had found *the coin*
> relative: *the coin* you had found
> pro form: *which* you had found
> 3.31a   you bought *the milk* yesterday
> relative: *the milk* you bought yesterday
> pro form: *that* you bought yesterday

The need for the relative transformation in sentence 3.29a is not obvious since it does not affect the word order; however, it is easier to say that the relative transformation applies to all of these structures—even though it may apply vacuously in some cases—than to specify the cases for which it does not apply.

Since the choice of pronouns is different from that normally used in pronominalization, we should look at them. There are three: *who, which,* and *that.* Does it matter which one we use? The following sentences will provide evidence:

> 3.32a   I haven't met the people *who* live next door.
>   b   I haven't met the people *that* live next door.
>   c   *I haven't met the people *which* live next door.

Obviously we may use *who* or *that* to refer to humans but not *which.* Some people prefer *who* instead of *that,* and others prefer *that,* but both are grammatical. Since there are restrictions as to which pronouns may be used for noun phrases designating humans, we should next see whether there are also restrictions as to those which may be used for noun phrases designating nonhumans:

> 3.33a   We looked at the coin *which* you had found.
>   b   We looked at the coin *that* you had found.
>   c   *We looked at the coin *who* you had found.
>   d   *We looked at the coin *whom* you had found.

Who may be used only for humans, *which* only for nonhumans, and *that* for either. In the following sentence either *who* or *whom* may be used, depending upon the formality of the situation:

> 3.34a   The people *who* we met are friendly.
>   b   The people *whom* we met are friendly.

Sometimes the noun that is pronominalized in a relative clause is preceded by a preposition, as shown in these intermediate structures:

3.35a   the people *you were talking with the people* are strangers
3.36a   the hammer *he broke the dish with the hammer* is new

If we shift just the noun phrase without the preposition and then apply the pro form transformation, we derive the following structures:

3.35b   The people *who you were talking with* are strangers.
c   The people *whom you were talking with* are strangers.
d   The people *that you were talking with* are strangers.
3.36b   The hammer *that he broke the dish with* is new.
c   The hammer *which he broke the dish with* is new.

But if we shift the preposition along with the noun phrase, our choice of pronouns is restricted:

3.35e   *The people *with who you were talking* are strangers.
f   *The people *with that you were talking* are strangers.
g   The people *with whom you were talking* are strangers.
3.36d   *The hammer *with that he broke the dish* is new.
e   The hammer *with which he broke the dish* is new.

In this case, only *whom* may be used for humans and *which* for nonhumans.

In a sentence such as *Carol saw me, but Carol didn't speak,* we have seen that the second instance of *Carol* can be replaced by the pronoun *she,* or it can be deleted. Let us now see whether relative clauses have this same option of pronominalization or deletion. After the relative transformation we have the following structures:

3.37   the house *they built the house* needs painting
relative: the house *the house they built* needs painting
pro form: The house *which they built* needs painting.
                          or
deletion: The house *they built* needs painting.
3.38   the problems *they were talking about the problems* were minor
relative: the problems *the problems they were talking about* were minor
pro form: The problems *that they were talking about* were minor.
                          or
deletion: The problems *they were talking about* were minor.

Deletion is indeed possible. Let us now examine some more sentences to see whether it is always possible or whether there are restrictions on its application:

3.39   the girl *the girl sang* is his fiancee
 relative: the girl *the girl sang* is his fiancee
 pro form: The girl *who sang* is his fiancee.

         or

 deletion: *The girl *sang* is his fiancee.

3.40   we overlooked the package *the package lay there*
 relative: we overlooked the package *the package lay there*
 pro form: We overlooked the package *that lay there.*

         or

 deletion: *We overlooked the package *lay there.*

3.41   the problems *they were talking about the problems* were
       minor
 relative: the problems *about the problems they were talking* were
       minor
 pro form: The problems *about which they were talking* were minor.

         or

 deletion: *The problems *about they were talking* were minor.

3.42   the people *he was speaking with the people* are from
       Belgium
 relative: the people *the people he was speaking with* are from
       Belgium
 pro form: The people *that he was speaking with* are from Belgium.

         or

 deletion: The people *he was speaking with* are from Belgium.

3.43   the people *he was speaking with the people* are from
       Belgium
 relative   the people *with the people he was speaking* are from
       Belgium
 pro form: The people *with whom he was speaking* are from Belgium.

         or

 deletion: *The people *with he was speaking* are from Belgium.

As these sentences show, a subject noun phrase may not be deleted in a relative clause; pronominalization is the only choice. An object of a preposition may be pronominalized or deleted if the preposition is not shifted to the beginning of the clause. In case the preposition is shifted along with the noun phrase, only pronominalization is possible.

Since the subject noun phrase in a relative clause may not be deleted, we may not delete *the car* in the following structure:

3.44a   the car *the car is in the garage* isn't mine

    b   *the car *is in the garage* isn't mine

We may, of course, use the pro form transformation:

3.44c   The car *that is in the garage* isn't mine.

However, there is another structure that means the same thing as *that is in the garage*:

3.44d   The car *in the garage* isn't mine.

According to the concept of grammar that we are presenting, synonymous sentences should share the same deep structure. We would like, then, to see a common deep structure for sentences 3.44c and 3.44d. We could delete *the car, tense,* and *be* from the underlying structure *the car is in the garage* and derive *in the garage,* and this would permit a common deep structure for sentences 3.44c and 3.44d and account for their differences in surface forms. To distinguish this deletion transformation from the one that deletes just repeated structures, we can call it the **relative deletion transformation.**

If we developed transformations for individual sentences, we could eventually have as many transformations as there are sentences in the language: an infinite number. Obviously this would tell us nothing about English. Rather than provide transformations that are applicable to only one sentence, we want to provide those which will apply to large numbers of sentences and which will express generalizations about the language. We also want our transformations to be as applicable to sentences we have not yet examined as they are to the ones we have considered. If we use relative deletion to account for just one sentence, there is no point in having the transformation. On the other hand, there is nothing wrong with starting with observations about one sentence and then bringing in other sentences to see how these observations affect them. Let us do this with our proposed relative deletion transformation:

3.45a   the dog *the dog was under the house* was barking loudly

    b   The dog *under the house* was barking loudly.

3.46a   John doesn't see the woman *the woman is looking at him*

    b   John doesn't see the woman *looking at him.*

3.47a   funeral services were held for the man *the man was killed in the accident*

    b   Funeral services were held for the man *killed in the accident.*

3.48a   the people *the people are outside* are angry

    b   The people *outside* are angry.

3.49a   the rhinoceros *the rhinoceros is in the living room* is very rude
   b   The rhinoceros *in the living room* is very rude.

These sentences show that there is a need for the relative deletion transformation since it applies to a great many sentences containing a variety of structures, including previously unobserved sentences such as 3.49. It also accounts for synonymy:

3.45b   The dog *under the house* was barking loudly.
   c   The dog *that was under the house* was barking loudly.
3.46b   John doesn't see the woman *looking at him.*
   c   John doesn't see the woman *who is looking at him.*
3.47b   Funeral services were held for the man *killed in the accident.*
   c   Funeral services were held for the man *who was killed in the accident.*
3.48b   The people *outside* are angry.
   c   The people *who are outside* are angry.
3.49b   The rhinoceros *in the living room* is very rude.
   c   The rhinoceros *that is in the living room* is very rude.

In addition to explaining synonymous sentences, the relative deletion transformation accounts for some ambiguous surface structures, such as the following one:

3.50   I painted the picture in the den.

In the den could be derived through the relative deletion transformation and be synonymous with

3.51   I painted the picture which is in the den.

Or it could be derived from the deep structure case *location,* meaning where I painted the picture rather than which one. Another example of ambiguity in surface structure is seen in the following sentence:

3.52   The man standing at the door wouldn't say what he wanted.

This sentence can mean the same thing as either of the following sentences:

3.53   The man who *is* standing at the door wouldn't say what he wanted.
3.54   The man who *was* standing at the door wouldn't say what he wanted.

Since tense is deleted by the relative deletion transformation, two deep structures—one with past tense and the other with present—are represented by identical surface forms.

We have formulated a rule that goes beyond describing one sentence. It describes many sentences in English, it will describe new sentences that we may want to create, and it will contain some of the knowledge that a native speaker possesses in explaining the source of ambiguity and synonymy in certain sentences. We still need to test our rule on other structures, preferably structures different from the ones we have already examined. Let us consider the following ones:

3.55a   the positions *the positions are remaining* will be filled soon
    b   The positions *remaining* will be filled soon.
3.56a   the apartment *the apartment is upstairs* is for rent
    b   The apartment *upstairs* is for rent.
3.57a   the people *the people are here* are friendly
    b   The people *here* are friendly.
3.58a   the child *the child was curious* asked me my age
    b   *The child *curious* asked me my age.
3.59a   we bought a chair *a chair was brown*
    b   *We bought a chair *brown*.

The last two sentences present a problem. We have already seen enough cases in which relative deletion is valid for us not to drop the transformation altogether. We could restrict the transformation so that it does not apply to structures like those in sentences 3.58 and 3.59, where only an adjective follows *be*. This solution would prevent the ungrammatical sentences 3.58b and 3.59b, but we would still have to account for the following pairs of synonymous sentences:

3.60a   The child *that was curious* asked me my age.
    b   The *curious* child asked me my age.
3.61a   We bought a chair *which was brown*.
    b   We bought a *brown* chair.

These pairs of sentences seem to share the same relationship as do those such as 3.55a and 3.55b.

An alternative to restricting relative deletion so that it is inapplicable to structures with only an adjective following *be* is to add another transformation that moves the adjective in front of the noun, the **adjective movement transformation**:

3.59a   we bought a chair *a chair was brown*
    relative: we bought a chair *a chair was brown*

relative deletion: we bought a chair *brown*
adjective movement: we bought a *brown* chair

This transformation is obligatory for some structures, such as adjectives. For other structures it is optional:

3.55b   The positions *remaining* will be filled soon.
  c   The *remaining* positions will be filled soon.
3.56b   The apartment *upstairs* is for rent.
  c   The *upstairs* apartment is for rent.
3.62a   The books *leftover* will soon be sold.
  b   The *leftover* books will soon be sold.
3.63a   The room *downstairs* should be painted.
  b   The *downstairs* room should be painted.

For a few structures the transformation is inapplicable:

3.64a   The people *here* are friendly.
  b   *The *here* people are friendly.

We now have two transformations which produce a large number of structures and which account for much of the knowledge possessed by native speakers of English.

In formulating rules, we want to make sure that they apply not to just one or two sentences but rather to a sizable number, including new sentences that we have not yet examined or created. In addition, as far as possible, the rules should account for the knowledge that a native speaker possesses and should express generalizations about the language that are not always obvious on the surface.

Complement Constructions

In this chapter so far, we have seen two different ways that sentences can be expanded. A sentence may be added to another, in which case we say the sentences are **conjoined**:

3.65   Susan insulted me, and I left.

Or a sentence may be **embedded** inside another one:

3.66   The girl *who spoke* didn't know me.

Let us examine embedding further, as seen in the following sentences:

3.67   The belief *that he professed* was frightening.
3.68   The belief *that he would win* was frightening.

On the surface both of the embedded sentences appear to be relative clauses. *That he professed* in sentence 3.67 has an underlying structure *he professed the belief*. The relative transformation rearranges this to *the belief he professed*, and the pro form transformation changes *the belief* to *that*. The other sentence, 3.68, cannot be derived in this manner. **He would win the belief* is not a possible underlying structure, since one cannot *win* beliefs. Nor is **the belief which he would win* synonymous with *the belief that he would win*. In this sentence *that* is not a pro form; in fact, it has no lexical meaning at all. *He would win* is the underlying structure for *that he would win,* and neither the relative nor the pro form transformation has been applied. In addition to the syntactic differences between *that he professed* and *that he would win,* there are semantic differences as well. *That he would win* tells what the belief is, whereas *that he professed* does not. Some traditional grammarians classified *that he would win* as an appositive, like *Tom* in *My brother Tom graduated last year.* Although 3.67 and 3.68 on the surface appear to have the same kind of embedded structures, closer inspection shows that this resemblance is only superficial.

To indicate that the structure *that he would win* is not a relative clause, we need to show a different tree structure from the one for *that he professed.* Here is a tree after several transformations have already been applied:

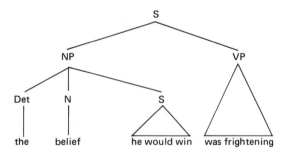

We call *he would win* a **noun phrase complement**. The *that* **transformation** adds the semantically empty word *that* to produce *that he would win.* Here are some more noun phrase complements after the *that* transformation has been applied:

3.69   We considered the possibility *that we would be late.*
3.70   We were horrified by the idea *that we might be late.*
3.71   We didn't believe his claim *that he would prevent the strike.*

There are other structures to which the *that* transformation has been applied but which differ from those we have been examining:

3.72   Susan dreamed *that she could fly.*
3.73   Janice thinks *that she is pretty.*
3.74   Most people believe *that mosquitoes are a nuisance.*

These embedded sentences are obviously noun phrases, since a different selection of deep structure cases for the subject position would have yielded the following passive sentence:

3.74a   *That mosquitoes are a nuisance* is believed by most people.

The surface structure tree for sentence 3.74 is as follows:

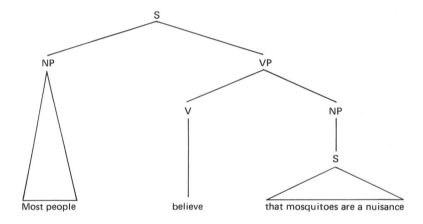

There is actually very little difference between this sentence and the kind we were considering previously:

3.74   Most people believe *that mosquitoes are a nuisance.*
3.74b   Most people believe the statement *that mosquitoes are a nuisance.*

The difference is that in 3.74b the sentence is embedded in a noun phrase that also contains a determiner and a noun; in 3.74 the embedded sentence is the only element in its noun phrase.

Determining that the embedded sentences are noun phrases and that they permit the *that* transformation is only part of our inquiry. We next must examine more sentences to see whether there are restrictions on the processes we have discovered. Before the *that* transformation, we have the following intermediate structures:

3.75a   I promised John *I would go to the store*
3.76a   we assume *you are going*
3.77a   I would like *you come with us*
3.78a   *he visits us* would be pleasant
3.79a   I intended *Janice went with you*

After application of the *that* transformation, we derive the following structures:

3.75b   I promised John *that I would go to the store.*
3.76b   We assume *that you are going.*
3.77b   *I would like *that you come with us.*
3.78b   **That he visits us* would be pleasant.
3.79b   *I intended *that Janice went with you.*

Certain verbs such as *promise* and *assume* may have *that* structures; others obviously may not, as sentences 3.77b–3.79b show. These three do permit other surface structures, however:

3.77c   I would like *for you to come with us.*
3.78c   *For him to visit us* would be pleasant.
3.79c   I intended *for Janice to go with you.*

Some verbs permit the *for-to* structure but not the *that*; others permit *that* but not *for-to*:

3.80a   We realize *that we have made a mistake.*
   b   *We realize *for us to have made a mistake.*
3.81a   I thought *that you were happy.*
   b   *I thought *for you to be happy.*

Some verbs permit either *for-to* or *that*:

3.82a   I preferred *that they go alone.*
   b   I preferred *for them to go alone.*

We next need to inquire how the *for-to* structure is formed:

3.83	Underlying:	you	present	come
	Surface:	for you	to	come
3.84	Underlying:	he	present	visit us
	Surface:	for him	to	visit us
3.85	Underlying:	Janice	past	go with you
	Surface:	for Janice	to	go with you

From this comparison we can see that the *for-to* **transformation** deletes tense and adds *for* before the NP and *to* before the verb.

Let us now examine some more sentences with different verbs:

3.86a   We knew that you were unhappy at camp.
   b   *We knew *for you to be unhappy at camp.*
3.87a   *We love *that she helps us.*
   b   We love *for her to help us.*
3.88a   *We objected to *that she closed the door in our faces.*
   b   *We objected to *for her to close the door in our faces.*
3.89a   *They protested against *that William made the first speech.*
   b   *They protested against *for William to make the first speech.*

As sentences 3.88a–3.89b show, some verbs do not permit either *that* or *for-to*. Do these verbs not permit embedded sentences, or is there yet some other structure that we have not examined? The following sentences indicate the latter:

3.88c   We objected to *her closing the door in our faces.*
3.89c   They protested against *William's making the first speech.*

There is, then, a third kind of surface structure. To derive it we need a transformation which deletes tense and adds *possessive* (**poss**) to the first noun phrase (*William's, her, his, our, Mary's,* etc.) and *ing* to the verb (*closing, making, eating, seeing,* etc.).

3.88d   Underlying: she   past close   the door in our faces
        Surface: she poss   close ing   the door in our faces
3.89d   Underlying: William   past make   the first speech
        Surface: William poss   make ing   the first speech

We call this the ***poss-ing* transformation.** The elements *poss* and *ing*, as well as *for, to,* and *that,* are called **complementizers.**

As we saw earlier with compound and relative structures, it is often possible to derive several surface structures, all with the same meaning, from one deep structure. This situation exists as well with the complement construction, as illustrated in Figure 3.4.

Most verbs do not permit all three complement constructions. Since the determination of which complementizers, if any, are accepted is apparently idiosyncratic, a complete lexicon would include features for each verb, telling whether it permits complementizers and if so which ones.

It should also be noted that the complementizers *that, for, to, poss,* and *ing* have no real semantic content, but rather serve to indicate structural relationships.

Deep Structure

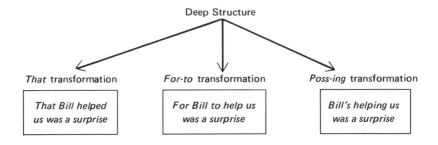

That transformation	For-to transformation	Poss-ing transformation
That Bill helped us was a surprise	*For Bill to help us was a surprise*	*Bill's helping us was a surprise*

Figure 3.4

This adds support to our introduction of them by transformational rules rather than by inclusion in the deep structure.

Extraposition

Sometimes complement constructions appear in different positions from those which we have been examining:

3.90a   The possibility *that you could be wrong* delighted Ann.
  b   The possibility delighted Ann *that you could be wrong.*

The derivation of 3.90a presents no problem. In 3.90b, however, the position of *that you could be wrong* is new to us. Meaning shows that there is no unit **Ann that you could be wrong* and that there are not three deep structure cases underlying (1) *the possibility,* (2) *Ann,* and (3) *that you could be wrong. That you could be wrong* is obviously part of the semantic unit to which *the possibility* belongs. Since both 3.90a and 3.90b have the same meaning, we would like to find some way of deriving both of them from the same deep structure. A possibility is that at some point in the derivation we add a rule which shifts the embedded sentence to the end. Using simplified trees, we can illustrate the process as follows:

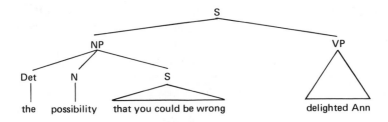

The embedded sentence is then moved:

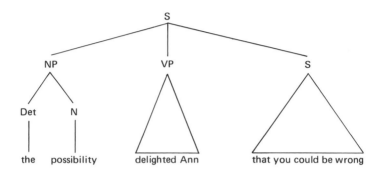

This simplified tree should not lead one to think that sentence 3.90b is derived from 3.90a. They are both derived from the same deep structure, but 3.90b has undergone a transformation that 3.90a has not experienced.

In discussing relative deletion, we argued against devising ad hoc rules which apply to only one sentence. Only rules which express significant generalizations about entire classes of structures have any value. We should see, then, whether there are other pairs of sentences such as 3.90a and 3.90b in which an embedded sentence in one member of the pair has been moved to the end. If there are, we should then determine which refinements of our proposed rule, if any, are in order. If there are no other sentences to which our rule would apply, then we should forget about it and look for a different rule. The following sentences provide examples:

3.91a   The idea *that it might snow* pleased the children.
    b   The idea pleased the children *that it might snow.*
3.92a   The realization *that we had missed the plane* was appalling.
    b   The realization was appalling *that we had missed the plane.*
3.93a   The decision *that no one would receive a raise* was announced by the Dean.
    b   The decision was announced by the Dean *that no one would receive a raise.*

These sentences follow the same pattern as 3.90a-3.90b. In each of the *b* sentences, the embedded structure has been moved to the end of the sentence in which it is embedded. This process is called **extraposition.**

Having determined that extraposition is applicable not to just one sentence, we next should decide whether it is applicable only to structures like those we have been considering. The following pairs of sentences need to be considered:

3.94a   *That you are sick* is a shame.
   b   It is a shame *that you are sick.*
3.95a   *That he was so honest* surprised me.
   b   It surprised me *that he was so honest.*
3.96a   *For you to volunteer to help her* would be a mistake.
   b   It would be a mistake *for you to volunteer to help her.*
3.97a   *For her to be so tall* seems strange.
   b   It seems strange *for her to be so tall.*

For each pair, the sentences have the same meaning and, therefore, share the same deep structure. Extraposition will account for the differences in placement of the embedded sentences. Sentences 3.96 and 3.97 show that extraposition is applicable to *for-to* structures as well as to those that have undergone the *that* transformation. Normally *poss-ing* structures do not undergo extraposition. The only problem with these sentences is the presence of *it.* Although superficially like the pronoun *it* in *He saw it,* this *it* has no semantic content, but rather is used to provide syntactic information in the same way as *for* and *to.* Many traditional grammarians referred to *it* in this use as an **expletive.** There are two possibilities for its existence: (1) It is not present in the deep structure but is added by a transformational rule after extraposition has occurred; (2) it is present in the deep structure and is deleted in case extraposition does not occur. Following possibility one, the following sequence of transformations is needed:

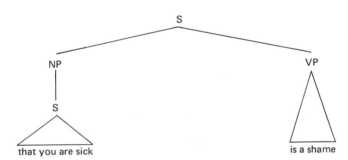

Extraposition:

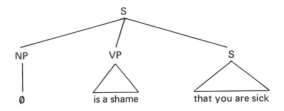

It addition:

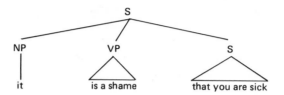

Hence, two more transformations are needed for deriving *It is a shame that you are sick* than are needed for *That you are sick is a shame.* The second possibility would require the following transformations:

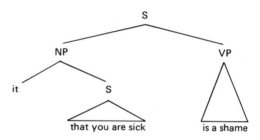

Extraposition:

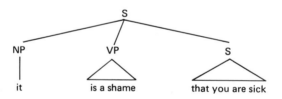

Or if extraposition is not performed, *it* deletion must be:

It deletion:

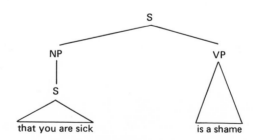

The two solutions are of equal complexity as far as transformations are concerned. Both require the extraposition transformation; and one requires *it* deletion, whereas the other requires *it* addition. From the standpoint of the transformational component of the grammar, there is no reason to prefer one solution over the other. But since all parts of the grammar are related, we would like to examine the effects on other components to see what influence our specific choice of solutions would have. There is no reason to believe that our choice would affect the phonological component of the grammar, but it might affect the lexicon or the rules which produce the deep structure. Until we know more about semantic structures, no one can give the rules for producing deep structures, and there are still many unanswered questions regarding the form of the lexicon. Since many linguists believe that deep structures should not contain semantically empty elements, we are rejecting the inclusion of *it* in the deep structure and are accepting the *it* addition rule. This *it* is only a filler with no lexical meaning, unlike the pronoun *it* in *She found it in the drawer,* which does have lexical meaning. The addition of *it* by a transformational rule parallels that of the addition of the complementizers and certain prepositions, i.e., elements which show syntactic structure but which are semantically empty.

One point should be clear by now. No statements about English grammar should be accepted as absolute truths, regardless of which books contain them or how many linguists believe them. The discovery of new information often causes the rejection of some previously accepted ideas and the alteration of others. Since there is still more that is not known about language than that which is known, we can expect future discoveries to continue to produce changes in linguistic grammars.

The *it* insertion rule may be part of a more general rule in English which demands some element in the subject position. Normally a noun phrase will be in this position as a result of the subject placement transformation, but if the noun phrase has been moved from this position, as in the case of extraposition, the expletive *it* is added. There are other reasons for a vacant subject position which require *it* insertion. A few verbs such as *to rain* and *to snow* do not require case categories in the deep structure; hence, there will be no noun phrase in subject position at the stage that *it* insertion is applicable, and structures like the following will result:

3.98   *It* is raining.
3.99   *It* is snowing.

Still another use of the expletive *it* can be found in sentences with location as the only case, as in this structure:

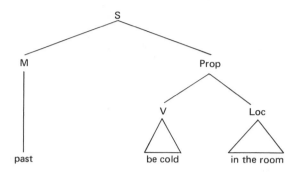

A complete grammar would not have forms of *be* in deep structures but would insert them transformationally. The place in the ordering of transformations for *be* insertion is not yet clear; we are arbitrarily placing it before subject placement for the purpose of clarity. Also, *cold* will later be designated as an adjective. If subject placement and preposition deletion occur, the structure will eventually become

3.100   The room was cold.

Subject placement is optional under certain conditions when location is the only case category. If it does not occur in the above sentence, 3.101 will result:

3.101a   *Was cold in the room.

But *it* insertion is applicable, and 3.101b is produced:

3.101b   *It* was cold in the room.

In a number of cases *it* insertion is applicable for filling an empty subject position.

For the sentences which we have examined so far, extraposition has been optional. Only stylistic reasons will cause a person to prefer 3.102 or 3.103:

3.102   That you are embarrassed is obvious.
3.103   It is obvious that you are embarrassed.

There are other sentences in which extraposition is obligatory, as in the following intermediate structure:

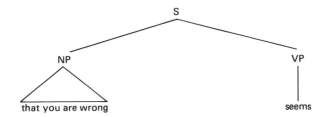

If extraposition were always optional, 3.104a would be grammatical:

 3.104a *That you are wrong seems.

After extraposition and *it* insertion, a grammatical sentence results:

 3.104b It seems that you are wrong.

Other examples can easily be found:

 3.105a *That you are right happens.
   b It happens that you are right.
 3.106a *That we are late appears.
   b It appears that we are late.

For most verbs, then, extraposition is optional, but for a few it is obligatory.
 Earlier we saw that some verbs permit both *that* and *for-to* structures, whereas others permit one but not the other. It appears that the verbs in sentences 3.107–3.109 do not permit *for-to*.

 3.107a *For you to be wrong seems.
   b *It seems for you to be wrong.
 3.108a *For you to be right happens.
   b *It happens for you to be right.
 3.109a *For us to be late appears.
   b *It appears for us to be late.

But there are similar sentences which are grammatical:

 3.107c You seem to be wrong.
 3.108c You happen to be right.
 3.109c We appear to be late.

In each case a noun phrase in the embedded sentence has been raised into the subject position of the main sentence. We call this the **subject raising transformation**. If subject raising occurs before *it* insertion, there will be no reason to add *it,* since the subject position will be filled already. The ordering, then, must be

1. Extraposition
2. Subject raising
3. *It* addition

There may be other intervening transformations, but these three will hold this order in relation to one another.

The transformations needed for 3.107c are the following:

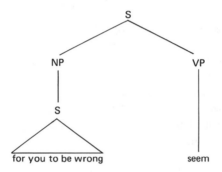

Extraposition:

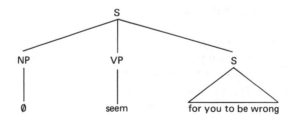

Subject raising:

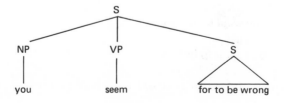

For deletion:

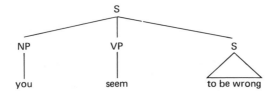

For is deleted whenever it immediately precedes *to*. It can be in this position because the subject of the embedded sentence has been moved or deleted.

Subject raising helps to account for a type of surface structure that is common today:

3.110   George began to read the letter.
3.111   George started to read the letter.
3.112   George continued to read the letter.
3.113   George began reading the letter.
3.114   George started reading the letter.
3.115   George continued reading the letter.

The derivation of structures such as these can be explained by the transformations we have already examined:

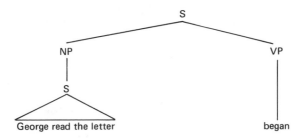

For-to:

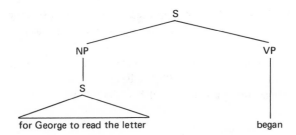

Extraposition:

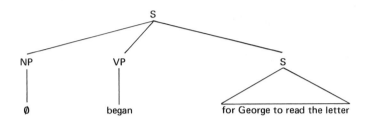

Subject raising:

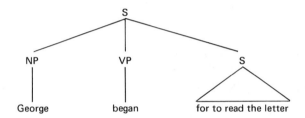

For deletion:

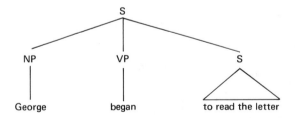

As 3.113–3.115 show, this process is not restricted to *for-to* structures. The same transformations are involved in deriving these sentences as are for *George began to read the letter.*

The process of embedding sentences may be **recursive.** That is, an embedded sentence may have a sentence embedded in it, and the latter may also contain an embedded sentence, giving a structure such as the following:

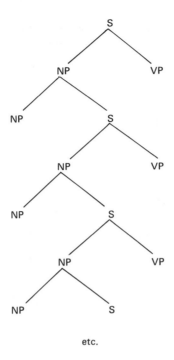

etc.

The degree of embedding is theoretically unlimited. A sentence with only limited embedding of relative clauses is 3.116:

3.116   The woman who owns the cat that chased your dog which has the funny bark sounded perturbed.

We can also find the process of recursion in complement constructions. Suppose that sentence 3.110 is embedded as the subject of the verb *seem*:

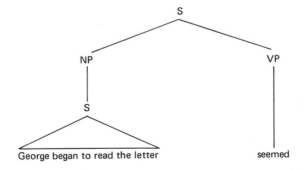

For-to:

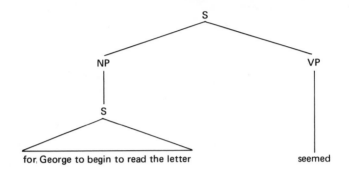

Extraposition:

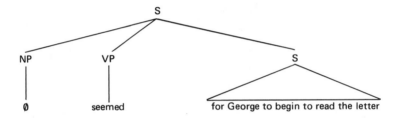

Subject raising:

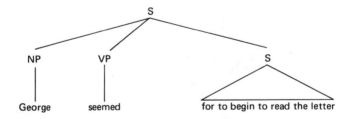

For deletion:

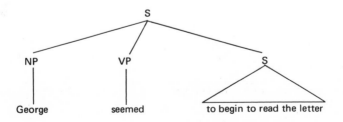

If we had to restrict ourselves to surface structures, *George seemed to begin to read the letter* would present several problems for analysis. How do the three verbs *seem, begin,* and *read* relate to one another? And this sentence is by no means exceptional, as an examination of almost any newspaper will show. A grammar which contains deep as well as surface structures can account for sentences such as this with only a few transformational rules.

Deletion Transformations

It seems clear that all complement constructions are derived transformationally from underlying sentences, as illustrated by the following structures:

3.117a   *That Harold is stupid* is true.
    b   It is true *that Harold is stupid.*
3.118a   *For her to act unselfishly* would be a surprise.
    b   It would be a surprise *for her to act unselfishly.*
3.119   We objected to *their playing the radio.*
3.120a   It happens *that Doug is her husband.*
    b   Doug happens *to be her husband.*

Sentences 3.117a–b have undergone the *that* transformation; 3.117b has also undergone extraposition and *it* addition. The embedded sentence clearly is derived from *Harold is stupid.*[†] Similarly, 3.118a–b have the embedded structure *for her to act unselfishly,* which is derived from *she acts unselfishly* by the *for-to* transformation. *Their playing* the radio in 3.119 is derived from *they played the radio* by the *poss-ing* transformation. In 3.120a–b, *Doug is her husband* is the underlying structure for the embedded sentence, although it is less apparently so in *b* than in *a* since subject raising and *for* deletion have been performed.

There are other embedded structures which look similar to the complement constructions we have been examining, but they lack subjects:

3.121   It is impossible *to get along with Irma.*
3.122   *Daydreaming during an interview* is bad manners.

The embedded structure of 3.121 looks as though it may have been derived from a structure like the following, in which *NP* is used for a noun phrase whose iden-

---

[†]A more accurate statement would be "is derived from the structure which underlies *Harold is stupid,*" and the same holds true for the sentences that follow. Such a statement is cumbersome, and a series of such statements, as would be necessary in the sentences that follow, would be distracting to the reader.

tity we will consider presently: *NP gets along with Irma.* Similarly, the embedded structure in 3.122 seems to be derived from something like *NP daydreams during an interview.* In both sentences we understand the noun phrase to be a human. Furthermore, these sentences seem similar to 3.123–3.124 except for the noun phrase:

> 3.123   It is impossible *for Jean* to get along with Irma.
>
> 3.124   *Sam's* daydreaming during an interview is bad manners.

In 3.121 and 3.122 we do not understand the subjects of *get* and *daydream* to be anything so specific as *Jean* or *Sam*; in fact, the subjects refer to people in general. 3.121 and 3.122 are understood to mean the same thing as 3.125 and 3.126:

> 3.125   It is impossible *for anyone* to get along with Irma.
>
> 3.126   *Anyone's* daydreaming during an interview is bad manners.

It would be impossible to delete *Jean* or *Sam* in 3.123–3.124 and not lose meaning. It is, however, possible under certain circumstances to delete a very general word such as *anyone* or *someone.* Evidence for this statement can be found in the native speaker's understanding of 3.121–3.122 as meaning the same thing as 3.125–3.126, but not the same thing as 3.123–3.124. We call the transformation which deletes *anyone* or *someone* **indefinite deletion.** The derivation of *to get along with Irma* in 3.121 is as follows:

Intermediate:	anyone gets along with Irma is impossible
For-to:	for anyone to get along with Irma is impossible
Extraposition:	is impossible for anyone to get along with Irma
Indefinite deletion:	is impossible for to get along with Irma
For deletion:	is impossible to get along with Irma
It addition:	It is impossible to get along with Irma.

Similarly in 3.122:

Intermediate:	anyone daydreams during an interview . . .
Poss-ing:	anyone's daydreaming during an interview . . .
Indefinite deletion:	's daydreaming during an interview . . .
Poss deletion:	daydreaming during an interview . . .

In our derivation of 3.121 before *it* addition we could have applied subject raising:

Intermediate: is impossible for to get along with Irma
For deletion: is impossible to get along with Irma
Subject raising: Irma is impossible to get along with.

Now *it* addition is inapplicable. As this sentence shows, it is not only the subject of the embedded sentence that may be raised. Other examples are readily found:

3.127   This shirt is easy to iron.
3.128   He is hard to get to know.
3.129   That mountain looks impossible to climb.

With extraposition, *it* addition, and subject raising, we are able to show that certain very different surface structures are actually quite similar:

3.127   This shirt is easy to iron.
3.127a   It is easy to iron this shirt.
3.127b   To iron this shirt is easy.

We are thus able to account for the native speaker's knowledge that these sentences are synonymous.

In this book we have been following the practice of many linguists by saying that sentences which differ no more in meaning than 3.127, 3.127a, and 3.127b are synonymous. It seems that if the three sentences are really identical in meaning, no one would ever have reason to prefer one over the others; any choice would be like flipping a coin. Yet there are situations in which each of these sentences is preferable to the other two because 3.127 gives prominence to the shirt, 3.127a gives prominence to ease, and 3.127b gives prominence to the act of ironing. None of the sentences need be given emphatic stress to achieve these slight differences. Differences in degree of prominence can be seen in other so-called synonymous sentences:

3.130a   Wanda washed the car.
    b   The car was washed by Wanda.
3.131a   He gave the assignment to Mike.
    b   He gave Mike the assignment.
3.132a   The door will open with this key.
    b   This key will open the door.

Most "optional" transformations produce differences such as these. Possibly someone in the future will discover a way to incorporate a concept of prominence in deep structures, and this concept will direct the choice of certain transformations which now appear to be purely optional.

Let us return now to the indefinite deletion transformation to see whether it applies to structures different from those we have been examining:

3.133a   Brenda was writing *something.*
3.134a   The carpenters are eating *something.*
3.135a   He read *something* all afternoon.

We may delete the indefinite *something*:

3.133b   Brenda was writing.
3.134b   The carpenters are eating.
3.135b   He read all afternoon.

As these sentences show, indefinite deletion is not restricted to the human indefinites *someone* and *anyone.*

Another use of indefinite deletion can be seen in agents in passive sentences:

3.136   The money has been found (by someone).
3.137   The door was slammed (by someone).
3.138   The cake has already been eaten (by someone).

By using indefinite deletion along with other transformations, we can derive the following sentence:

Intermediate:	he is crooked is known by someone
For-to:	for him to be crooked is known by someone
Extraposition:	is known by someone for him to be crooked
Indefinite deletion:	is known for him to be crooked
Subject raising:	he is known for to be crooked
For deletion:	He is known to be crooked.

This is the derivation of 3.139; by a different choice of transformations we can derive 3.140 from the same deep structure.

3.139   He is known to be crooked.
3.140   It is known that he is crooked.

In addition to indefinites, certain other noun phrases may be deleted when they are obvious.

3.141   Luella was given a speeding ticket (by the patrolman).
3.142   The mail was delivered early today (by the mail carrier).
3.143   The defendant was found guilty (by the jury).

The agents in these sentences are obvious because the listener knows who normally gives speeding tickets, delivers mail, and finds defendants guilty, not because of any linguistic information contained in the sentence. Also, reflexive pronouns are often deleted after certain verbs:

    3.144a   Alfred forgot to shave (himself) this morning.
    3.145a   I bathed (myself) before going to bed.
    3.146a   The students prepared (themselves) for the exam.

These verbs, of course, may have other noun phrases following them:

    3.144b   Alfred forgot to shave *his paralyzed brother* this morning.
    3.145b   I bathed *my foot* before going to bed.
    3.146b   The students prepared *us* for the exam.

Whenever the noun phrase following these verbs is deleted, it is understood to be the reflexive pronoun. Many verbs do not permit deletion of reflexives:

    3.147   The cook cut *himself.*
    3.148   Alice hurt *herself.*
    3.149   The monkey saw *himself* in the mirror.

Deletion of reflexives is restricted to only a few verbs.
    In compound sentences we saw another use of deletion, with repeated elements:

    3.150a   *Dorothy* raved and *Dorothy* screamed.
        b   Dorothy raved and screamed.

It is possible to have repeated elements in embedded as well as in conjoined structures:

    3.151a   It seemed obvious to Betty that *Betty* had lost.
        b   *It seemed obvious to Betty that had lost.
        c   It seemed obvious to Betty that *she* had lost.
    3.152a   Fred didn't know that we had seen *Fred.*
        b   *Fred didn't know that we had seen.
        c   Fred didn't know that we had seen *him.*

As the *b* sentences show, deletion of repeated noun phrases in *that* clauses is not possible; pronominalization is the only possible means of avoiding repetition. We should next see whether this restriction applies to other complement constructions as well.

3.153a   Bill would like for Tom to go with you.
    b   *Bill would like for Bill to go with you.
    c   Bill would like for him to go with you.
    d   Bill would like to go with you.

Sentence 3.153c is grammatical, but it cannot mean the same thing as the *b* or *d* sentences; *him* clearly does not mean *Bill*. It can mean the same thing as 3.153a. In the *d* sentence *Bill* is understood as the subject of *go*; no other subject is possible. Hence, deletion of the subject noun phrase in a *for-to* structure is obligatory if it has the same referent as a noun phrase in the higher sentence. Pronominalization is not possible. The same is true for the *poss-ing* structure:

3.154a   Eloise was amused at Roberta's finding the dead woman.
    b   *Eloise was amused at Eloise's finding the dead woman.
    c   Eloise was amused at her finding the dead woman.
    d   Eloise was amused at finding the dead woman.
    e   Finding the dead woman amused Eloise.

In the *c* sentence, *her* cannot mean Eloise; in the *d* and *e* sentences *Eloise* is the understood subject of *finding*. Deletion of the subject of a *for-to* or *poss-ing* structure because it has the same referent as a noun phrase in the higher sentence is known as the **Equi-NP deletion transformation.** In conjoined structures only a repeated NP can be deleted, never the first one. No such restriction holds for Equi-NP deletion, as 3.154e shows. The only requirement is that the subject noun phrase in the complement construction must be identical to a noun phrase in the higher sentence. This noun phrase may be the subject in the higher sentence (3.154d), but it does not have to be (3.154e).

A rather common type of structure to which Equi-NP deletion applies is found in the following sentences:

3.155   I encouraged Bob to drive Marie to the airport.
3.156   I encouraged Marie to be driven to the airport by Bob.

The only difference between the two sentences appears to be whether the passive structure is used in the embedded sentence or not, but this similarity is only superficial. Here is an intermediate structure for 3.155:

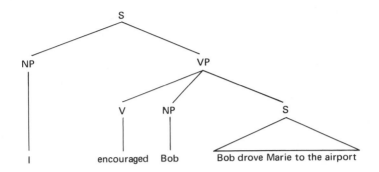

For-to: I encouraged Bob for Bob to drive Marie to the airport
Equi-NP deletion: I encouraged Bob for to drive Marie to the airport
For deletion: I encouraged Bob to drive Marie to the airport.

Sentence 3.156 has a different noun phrase following the verb:

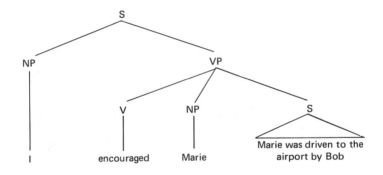

For-to: I encouraged Marie for Marie to be driven . . .
Equi-NP deletion: I encouraged Marie for to be driven . . .
For deletion: I encouraged Marie to be driven . . .

Close inspection of underlying structures shows that these two sentences are different, although on the surface they look alike except for the choice of the passive structure.

On the surface, 3.157 and 3.158 look like 3.155 and 3.156 except for a difference in word choice: *want* for *encourage.*

3.157   I wanted Bob to drive Marie to the airport.

3.158   I wanted Marie to be driven to the airport by Bob.

Since we have learned that surface structures often are deceptive, we should examine these sentences more closely. 3.155 and 3.156 do not mean the same thing, and the trees show that their underlying structures are different. Sentences 3.157 and 3.158, on the other hand, do mean the same thing in spite of their surface differences, and they should share the same deep structure:

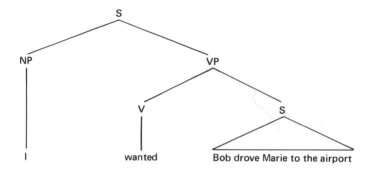

The native speaker, of course, in some way understands these differences. Our grammar is able to give an explicit account of them.

Pronominalization in Embedded Sentences

We have seen that deletion is possible in English when one structure repeats another one or when a noun phrase is vague or otherwise obvious to the listener:

3.159a   *Judy* was ready for *Judy* to leave, but *Judy* didn't look bored.
     b   Judy was ready to leave but didn't look bored.
3.160a   *Someone's* being slapped by *someone* is unpleasant.
     b   Being slapped is unpleasant.

Under certain conditions a pro form may be substituted for the repeated structure:

3.159c   Judy was ready to leave, but *she* didn't look bored.

We should now look at pronominalization in more detail.
   Except for the conditions under which Equi-NP deletion is applicable, any repeated noun phrase may be replaced by a pronoun:

Compound Sentence
3.161a   *Donna* saw you coming, and *Donna* hid in the closet.
     b   *Donna* saw you coming, and *she* hid in the closet.

That clause

3.162a *Bill* said that *Bill* would be late.
  b *Bill* said that *he* would be late.

For-to structure (other than subject)

3.163a Fred waxed *the car* to make *the car* shine.
  b Fred waxed *the car* to make *it* shine.

Poss-ing structure (other than subject)

3.164a *The Jacksons* were disturbed by your criticizing *the Jacksons'* son.
  b *The Jacksons* were disturbed by your criticizing *their* son.

Relative clause

3.165a *The old woman* kicked the girl who helped *the old woman.*
  b *The old woman* kicked the girl who helped *her.*

In each of these sentences it is also possible to pronominalize the first noun phrase, but then the two noun phrases are not understood to refer to the same person or thing:

3.161c *She* saw you coming, and *Donna* hid in the closet.
3.162c *He* said that *Bill* would be late.
3.163c Fred waxed *it* to make *the car* shine.
3.164c *They* were disturbed by your criticizing *the Jacksons'* son.
3.165c *She* kicked the girl who helped *the old woman.*

In each of these sentences the pronoun refers to a person or thing that was mentioned in a previous sentence or that is physically present and under observation by both speaker and listener. We can form a rule, then, saying that repeated noun phrases may be pronominalized except under the conditions for which Equi-NP deletion is applicable.

In view of the sentences which we have been examining, it seems that we should make our rule stronger so that it will prevent the pronominalization of the first occurrence of all noun phrases. Before imposing this restriction, however, we should examine some additional sentences.

3.166a That *Lucy* might get caught didn't bother *Lucy.*
  b That *Lucy* might get caught didn't bother *her.*
  c That *she* might get caught didn't bother *Lucy.*
3.167a For you to give *Tony* a present would please *Tony.*
  b For you to give *Tony* a present would please *him.*
  c For you to give *him* a present would please *Tony.*
3.168a Mary's sending *the children* her picture delighted *the children.*

3.168b   Mary's sending *the children* her picture delighted *them.*
   c   Mary's sending *them* her picture delighted *the children.*

Each of the *c* sentences is ambiguous. *She, him,* and *them* can refer to someone mentioned in a previous sentence, or to *Lucy, Tom,* and *the children.* Sentences 3.161c–3.165c show that in some instances the first occurring noun phrase cannot be pronominalized, but sentences 3.166c–3.168c show that in other instances it can be. We should try to determine the systematic difference between those sentences which permit the first noun phrase to be pronominalized and those which do not.

We can sometimes gain insight into a system by comparing sentences which share the same deep structure but which have not undergone the same transformations. The following sentences differ from the corresponding *a, b,* and *c* sentences above in the selection or rejection of extraposition:

3.166d   It didn't bother *Lucy* that *she* might get caught.
   e   It didn't bother *her* that *Lucy* might get caught.
3.167d   It would please *Tony* for you to give *him* a present.
   e   It would please *him* for you to give *Tony* a present.

In the *d* sentences, in which the second noun phrase is pronominalized, both *Lucy* and *she,* as well as *Tony* and *him,* may mean the same person. In the *e* sentences, however, *her* and *Lucy* mean different people, as do *him* and *Tony.* Since extraposition affects the position of an embedded sentence, let us see if the sentences in which either noun phrase can be pronominalized share some positional characteristic not found in the sentences which permit pronominalization only of the second noun phrase. In the *a, b,* and *c* versions of 3.166–3.168, the embedded sentence occurs first, whereas in the *d* and *e* versions it occurs last.

We can formulate the following tentative rules:

Rule 3.1   Equi-NP deletion: If the subject NP in a *poss-ing* or *for-to* structure has the same referent as an NP in the higher sentence in which the structure is embedded, this subject NP is deleted.

Rule 3.2   (Optional): If an NP in an embedded sentence has the same referent as an NP in the higher sentence, the NP in the embedded sentence may be pronominalized, regardless of whether it occurs before or after the NP in the higher sentence.

Rule 3.3   The second of two NPs with identical referents is pronominalized.

These rules apply in the order given. If the conditions for Equi-NP deletion are met, Rule 3.1 applies. Rules 3.2 and 3.3 are linked together so that if 2 has been applied, 3 is inapplicable.

To test rules 3.1–3.3, we should examine some additional sentences. In each of the following examples, the first noun phrase is in an embedded sentence; we should, therefore, be able to pronominalize either the first or the second NP without altering the referents.

3.169a   When *Bob* looked out the window, *he* saw that it was snowing.

   b   When *he* looked out the window, *Bob* saw that it was snowing.

3.170a   Whoever helps *that woman* will be rewarded by *her*.

   b   Whoever helps *her* will be rewarded by *that woman*.

3.171a   The possibility that *Edna* might not graduate didn't disturb *her*.

   b   The possibility that *she* might not graduate didn't disturb *Edna*.

Each of these sentences is ambiguous, but for one reading both NPs have the same referent. If our rules are accurate, the *c* sentences below should allow the two NPs to have the same referent, but the *d* sentences should not:

3.169c   *Bob* saw that it was snowing when *he* looked out the window.

   d   *He* saw that it was snowing when *Bob* looked out the window.

3.170c   *That woman* will reward whoever helps *her*.

   d   *She* will reward whoever helps *that woman*.

3.171c   *Edna* wasn't disturbed by the possibility that *she* might not graduate.

   d   *She* wasn't disturbed by the possibility that *Edna* might not graduate.

These additional sentences lend support to our rules.

Conclusion

In this chapter we have been examining the syntactic component of a transformational grammar. In this examination we have discussed several transformations which convert deep structures into surface structures: relativization, *for-to*, deletion, pronominalization, and others. Although these transformations give an illustrative rather than a complete picture of the syntactic component of the grammar, they are representative and all of them are important.

We have shown in several places that transformations are applied in a prescribed order in relation to one another. For example, extraposition must precede subject raising, which in turn must precede *it* addition. In addition, it seems probable that some transformations apply **cyclically**. To give some idea of the notion of the cycle, we can consider an abbreviated structure:

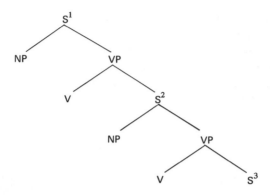

If there were no cyclical rules, all transformations would apply to all parts of the sentence (S^1, S^2, S^3) simultaneously. That is, at the time that extraposition or subject raising is applicable, the transformation is applied to all parts, including S^1, S^2, and S^3, which meet the requirements of the rule. If rules apply cyclically, on the other hand, the rules are applied first to the most deeply embedded sentence (S^3 in this case). After all possible rules for the cycle have been applied, we move up to the next sentence (S^2) and repeat the cycle. After this cycle is completed, we move up to S^1 and work through the rules again. In addition to cyclical rules, there are those which are **precyclical** (applying before those in the cycle) and others which are **postcyclical** (applying after those in the cycle). The transformations needed for the structure described by the above tree would be applied in the following order:

    1. Precyclical rules
    2. Cyclical rules
        a. Cycle 1 (S^3)
        b. Cycle 2 (S^2)
        c. Cycle 3 (S^1)
    3. Postcyclical rules

At present linguists are divided as to which transformations are cyclical and which ones are postcyclical. We have, therefore, not given examples from syntax, but in Chapter Seven the concept of the cycle will be discussed in regard to phonological rules.

Exercises

    I. Compounding
        A. Draw two trees for the following sentence, one for the deep structure

and one for the surface structure: *Frank killed the snake with a stick, and Trudy sat in the car.*

B. Paraphrase the following sentences with other surface structures to which deletion has not been applied:
   1. The man saw the accident but didn't stop.
   2. We found six stamps and three envelopes in the drawer.
   3. The pecan tree and the mimosa grew while we were away.

C. In the following sentence, what is it that I will do? *Leslie won't help you, but I will.* How do you know?

D. Explain why sentence three is a paraphrase of sentence one but not of sentence two:
   1. We bought a new paino, and we bought a new bed.
   2. We bought a new piano, and they bought a new bed.
   3. We bought a new piano and a new bed.

E. Paraphrase the following sentences with other surface structures without pro forms:
   1. Kate was tickled, but she didn't laugh.
   2. At six o'clock I will see Joan, and I will remind her then.

F. Explain why two but not three is a possible paraphrase for sentence one:
   1. My aunt saw us, and my aunt waved.
   2. My aunt saw us, and she waved.
   3. My aunt saw us, and we waved.

G. Give evidence to show whether the following structures are derived from underlying compound sentences or compound noun phrases:
   1. Dorothy and Joan are stupid.
   2. Dorothy and Joan met in St. Louis.

H. Some of the following sentences are ambiguous, but others are not. Explain how this can be.
   1. Fred and Roberta danced at the party.
   2. Fred and Roberta sneered at me.
   3. The man and his son listened attentively.
   4. Tom and Ruth came to the party.

II. Relative Constructions
   A. Perform the relative and pro form transformations:
      1. do you know the name of the poem *Ann is reading the poem*
      2. the girl *the girl spoke* is a senior
      3. he told the story to the people *he was riding with the people*
   B. Explain why the following sentences are not grammatical:
      1. *He didn't know the girl which opened the door.
      2. *The people with that she lives are out of town.
      3. *The pen with whom I am writing cost less than a dollar.

4. *The pen with I am writing cost less than a dollar.
5. *The boy sneezed has a bad cold.

C. Explain why the grammar does not permit adjectives in noun phrases in deep structures. That is, why do we go through the lengthy process of relativization, relative deletion, and adjective movement to produce *the ugly duckling* instead of permitting *ugly* to be in this position in the deep structure?

D. Use deep (or intermediate) structures and transformations to account for the synonymy of the following groups of sentences:
1a. The man that she is dancing with is her husband.
 b. The man with whom she is dancing is her husband.
 c. The man she is dancing with is her husband.
2a. The man who was waiting in line didn't see the laughing woman.
 b. The man waiting in line didn't see the woman who was laughing.

E. Account for the ambiguity in the following sentence: *Did you open the package in the kitchen?*

F. Explain how a person who has not studied formal grammar can recognize synonymous, ambiguous, and ungrammatical sentences. What can you say about these sentences that a person who has not studied formal grammar cannot?

G. Explain what is wrong with devising rules applicable to only one or two sentences.

H. Which structures in the following sentences are derived from underlying embedded sentences through the relative and other transformations?
1. The old car parked in the garage belonged to the people who used to live here.
2. The frowning receptionist at the desk insulted the people waiting for the doctor.

III. Complement Constructions and Extraposition
A. Perform the *that* transformation:
1. He dreamed *he went to class in his underwear.*
2. Janice thinks *she is pretty.*

B. Perform the *poss-ing* transformation:
1. *John agreed with our suggestion* was a shock
2. we resented *she kept us waiting*

C. Perform the *for-to* transformation:
1. we would like *he goes with us*
2. they slowed down *we caught up with them*

D. Determine which complementizers the following verbs permit: *assert, love, deny, intend, prefer, like, realize, maintain, recommend, welcome.*

E. Perform the following transformations: (1) *that* or *for-to*, (2) extraposition, (3) *it* insertion, if applicable.

     1. *their new house is ugly* is true
     2. the possibility *they might be married* seems strange
     3. *he walks without help* is hard

F. Give evidence to show that the following sentences are only superficially alike:
     1. The suggestion that she made was preposterous.
     2. The suggestion that she cheated was preposterous.

G. From the following sentences determine when *that* may be deleted:
     1a. That you left without telling anyone seemed strange.
      b. It seemed strange that you left without telling anyone.
     2a. That she can't add is true.
      b. It is true that she can't add.
     3. We thought that you would be late.
     4. They know that you will help them.

H. Explain specifically what extraposition does. Is it applicable to all complement constructions?

I. When is extraposition optional, and when is it obligatory?

J. Use underlying structures and transformations to show how the following sentences were derived:
     1. It appears that they are early again.
     2. They appear to be early again.
     3. Bill continued to ignore us.
     4. It began to rain.

IV. Deletion and Pronominalization

A. Perform the *for-to* or *poss-ing* transformation and, where applicable, Equi-NP deletion:
     1. we would like *you help us*
     2. we would like *we help you*
     3. Amos enjoyed *Lucille sang*
     4. Amos enjoyed *Amos sang*
     5. I promised Bob *I helped Bob*

B. Use underlying structures and transformations to show how the following sentences were derived:
     1. It is important to know how to drive.
     2. This door is hard to open.
     3. Reading the entire paper is not necessary.
     4. He wrote all morning.
     5. She dressed and ate breakfast.
     6. He was discovered to be lying.
     7. It disturbed him that we left early.
     8. Perry regretted telling the lie.

C. Account for the ambiguity in the following sentences:

    1. Burning buildings can be dangerous.

    2. Miss Peabody takes delight in cursing men.

D. Show how *He seemed to be sad* is derived. Now look at *He seemed sad*. We could provide a rule which deleted *to be* and thereby account for the synonymy of the two sentences. Try to determine whether such a rule would be justified for the grammar as a whole.

E. In each of the following groups, two of the sentences are synonymous but the third is not. Determine which two are synonymous and account for the synonymy; then explain why the third must have a different meaning.

    1a. This question is hard to understand.

      b. It is hard for Bill to understand this question.

      c. It is hard to understand this question.

    2a. Sam enjoyed Tom's cooking.

      b. Sam enjoyed his cooking.

      c. Sam enjoyed cooking.

    3a. She screamed when Ann found the dead rat.

      b. Ann screamed when she found the dead rat.

      c. When she found the dead rat, Ann screamed.

F. Provide evidence to show that the following pairs of sentences do or do not have the same deep structures, apart from the different choice of words.

    1a. The man at the door said for Sam to park the car.

      b. The attendant at the garage said for you to leave the keys.

    2a. I expected Marie to be accompanied by Tom.

      b. She persuaded Alice to be accompanied by Fred.

    3a. It disturbs Susan that Frank is slow.

      b. Frank's being slow worries Susan.

    4a. That he was late worried Tom.

      b. It bothered him that Sam was early.

G. Explain what is meant by the following: *deep structure, surface structure, underlying structure, intermediate structure, transformation, deletion, pronominalization, relative clause, complement construction, Equi-NP deletion.*

H. Give several reasons for including both deep and surface structures in a grammar instead of relying on surface structures alone.

Suggested Reading

Allen, J. P. B., and Van Buren, Paul, eds. *Chomsky: Selected Readings.* London: Oxford University Press, 1971.

Chomsky, Noam. *Aspects of the Theory of Syntax.* Cambridge, Mass.: M.I.T. Press, 1965.

Jacobs, Roderick A., and Rosenbaum, Peter S., eds. *Readings in English Transformational Grammar.* Waltham: Ginn and Co., 1970.

Katz, Jerrold J., and Postal, Paul M. *An Integrated Theory of Linguistic Descriptions.* Cambridge, Mass.: M.I.T. Press, 1964.

Postal, Paul M. "On Coreferential Complement Subject Deletion." *Linguistic Inquiry* 1 (1970): 439-500.

Reibel, David A., and Schane, Sanford A., eds. *Modern Studies in English: Readings in Transformational Grammar.* Englewood Cliffs, N.J.: Prentice-Hall, 1969.

Rosenbaum, Peter S. *The Grammar of English Predicate Complement Constructions.* Cambridge, Mass.: M.I.T. Press, 1967.

Smith, Carlota S. "A Class of Complex Modifiers in English." *Language* 37 (1961): 342-65.

_____. "Determiners and Relative Clauses in a Generative Grammar of English." *Language* 40 (1964): 37-52.

CHAPTER FOUR
Syntactic Change

In the last two chapters we examined the syntactic component of English grammar. Except for an occasional reference to individual variation, we treated syntax as a uniform subject. Such an approach is useful in discovering systematic relationships in the language, but if we are to obtain a true picture of English, we need to broaden our investigation. The system that exists among some speakers of the language is not identical to that of all others, nor is the system found at one period of time the same as that of an earlier or a later period.

There are two possible approaches for studying language with regard to time. The first of these concentrates on a language at a single point in time and disregards earlier and later developments. This is called a **synchronic** approach. If a person studies present-day plural formations in English from a synchronic viewpoint, he describes the pattern of the regular *s* plural, showing when it is pronounced [s] as in *gates* and *lips,* when it is pronounced [z] as in *rags* and *lids,* and when it is pronounced as a vowel and [z] as in *watches* and *badges.* He will not be concerned with the forms of the plural in earlier stages of English, nor will he explain the origins of such plurals as *feet, deer, oxen, children,* and *larvae.* From a purely synchronic viewpoint these are merely exceptions. Synchronic studies are not restricted to present-day English and other languages. A person could make a study of Spenser's language, for example, and describe it without reference to earlier or later periods. If a person decides to compare aspects of a language at different points in time, he is making a **diachronic** study. Following this approach, a person could compare plural formations in Old English with those of today, or negative constructions in Chaucer's English with those in Shakespeare's. In the last two chapters we followed a synchronic approach in studying Modern English syntax. In this chapter we will compare various syntactic features of earlier English with those of today.

Examples of Change

Around 1385, when Geoffrey Chaucer was writing *Troilus and Criseyde,* he

reminded his readers that customs change in the course of time. In the prologue
to Book Two, he compared changing conventions in love with changes in language:

> Ye knowe ek that in forme of speche is chaunge
> Withinne a thousand yeer, and wordes tho
> That hadden pris, now wonder nyce and straunge
> Us thinketh hem, and yet thei spake hem so,
> And spedde as wel in love as men now do;
> Ek for to wynnen love in sondry ages,
> In sondry londes, sondry ben usages.

Although only 600 years have passed since these lines were written, a person
does not have to be a linguist to conclude that Chaucer was right about change
in language. To the person first encountering Middle English, the spelling of
many words looks peculiar: *knowe, speche, chaunge, wel.* But spelling changes
are trivial in comparison to the other differences.

Let us start with syntax. An underlying structure of *for to wynnen love*
(line 6) is *for someone to win love,* as in Modern English. *Someone* is deleted by
the indefinite deletion transformation. If this were Modern English, *for* would
now have to be deleted since it immediately precedes *to.* But in Chaucer's English, deletion of *for* was not an obligatory rule, and he could write *for to wynnen
love,* "for to win love." An even more unusual structure is *now wonder nyce
and straunge us thinketh hem* (lines 3-4). The verb *thinketh,* "seems," has no
surface subject. Both *us* and *hem* are objective in form and plural in number;
the *-eth* ending of *thinketh* is third person singular. With both direct (*hem*) and
indirect (*us*) objects, the structure is hard to paraphrase in Modern English. "It
seems them to us" is meaningless, so the passage is usually translated something
like "they seem to us." Verbs like *thinketh* with no subject are often called
"impersonal" verbs. We find this one surviving into the Renaissance as *methinks,*
"it seems to me," as in Gertrude's "The lady doth protest too much, methinks"
(*Hamlet,* III, ii, 240). Modern English is so adamant about having surface subjects that we add the semantically empty *it* in sentences such as *It is raining* or
It seems to me that you are lying. For Chaucer, *it* addition was an optional
rule, and he normally did not use it with verbs like *thinken,* "to seem."

More numerous than differences in syntax between twentieth-century English
and the language of Chaucer are those in morphology, especially in inflections.
In the fourteenth century, *yeer,* "years," (line 2) still showed no difference in
form between singular and plural, like *sheep* and *deer.* Since then, it has lost its
exceptional marking and forms the plural by rule: *years.* The verb forms, also,
are different from those of the twentieth century. The *-eth* ending on *thinketh*
(line 4) reminds us of such forms as *goeth* and *eateth* from Shakespeare and the

King James Bible, an ending that has since been replaced by *-s* as in *thinks*. The *-en* ending on *hadden* (line 3) denotes plural number. Except for forms of *be* (*are, were*), verbs no longer have a special form to designate plurality (*he had, they had*). In line 6, *to wynnen*, "to win," has the Middle English infinitive ending *-en*, which is no longer in use. *Ben* (line 7) has now been replaced by *are*. Even the pronouns have changed since Chaucer's day. *Ye* (line 1) was originally the subject form and *you* the object form; during the seventeenth century, *ye* died out and *you* came to serve as both subject and object. Chaucer's *thei* (line 4) became Modern English *they*, but *hem* (line 4) was later replaced by *them*.

There are also differences in vocabulary and meaning between Chaucer's English and our language today. The word *ek*, "also," though disguised in *nickname* (*an ek name*) is obsolete today. *Pris* (line 3) meant "esteem, worth"; *nyce*, "nice," (line 3) meant "foolish"; *spedde*, "sped," (line 5) meant "succeeded."

The most extensive changes in English during the last 600 years have been in pronunciation. Many of these changes are not indicated by the spelling. *Us* and *love* probably had the vowel of Modern English *hood*; *nyce* probably sounded like Modern English *niece*, and *pris* rhymed with it; *yeer* probably rhymed with Modern English *care*; the first vowel in *thousand* and *now* was probably that of Modern English *mood*; the *k* of *knowe* was pronounced. Only a few words—*in, forme, a, yet, wel, for*—remain unchanged in pronunciation.

As these lines from *Troilus and Criseyde* show, all aspects of language change: syntax, morphology, phonology, semantics, vocabulary. We could easily compare features of fourteenth-century English with those of the twelfth century and see that Chaucer's English had developed from an earlier, still different form. In fact, we could compare specimens of English from 800, 1100, 1400, 1700, and 2000 (in round numbers the language of today) and see definite progressions of change. If we are to judge the future from the past, we can expect that there will be continuing changes by 2300, 2600, and 2900. If mechanical recordings of our speech survive until 2300, twentieth-century English will no doubt sound quaint; by 2900 it will probably be unintelligible except to scholars. Of all the past and present languages about which we have very much information, the only ones that have stopped changing are those that are no longer spoken either because of the extermination of all the speakers or their adoption of another language.

Divisions of the English Language

If we had all the relevant data concerning changes in the English language during the last fifteen centuries, we would probably see a continuous development with no clear dividing points. If we are discussing only Chaucer's English, we can comfortably speak of London English during the last half of the fourteenth century, but usually we need to work within a broader scope when studying divisions of the language. Since there are no natural breaking points in most languages, any division is necessarily somewhat arbitrary. People do not stop speaking in one way on December 31 of a year and start speaking in another way the next morning on January 1. One way of dividing the fifteen hundred years of English would be according to centuries, but fifteen periods are more than we can comfortably keep track of; worse, this kind of division would be entirely arbitrary, having no more significance to linguistic developments than if we randomly selected, say, 1217, 1538, and 1807 as dividing points. Or we could select significant political or literary events: 899 (the death of Alfred the Great), 1066 (the Battle of Hastings), 1400 (the death of Chaucer), 1623 (the publication of the First Folio of Shakespeare's plays), 1660 (the restoration of Charles II), 1784 (the death of Samuel Johnson), 1914 (the outbreak of World War I). With the exception of the Battle of Hastings, none of these events had any real impact upon the English language.

More significant criteria for division can be found in linguistic developments than in political and literary events. During the first few centuries of its development, English relied only partially upon word order to express such surface syntactic relationships as subject, direct object, and indirect object; these relationships were also expressed by characteristic inflectional suffixes and by the forms of modifiers. The words *se blaca hund*, "the black dog," furnish an example:

> Nominative: se blaca hund
> Genitive: þæs blacan hundes
> Dative: þæm blacan hunde
> Accusative: þone blacan hund

The letter þ was called *thorn* and represented the sound now spelled *th* in *thorn*; æ was the spelling for the vowel in Modern English *cat*. Unlike today, when we have only one form for *the*, the definite article changed forms according to the gender and number of the noun it was modifying and according to how the noun was used in the sentence (i.e., according to its surface case). If the noun was a subject, the nominative form was used: *Se blaca hund arn*, "The black dog ran." If the noun was a possessive, the genitive was used: *gebeorc þæs blacan hundes*, "barking of the black dog." An indirect object was expressed by the dative: *He geaf þæm blacan hunde þæt ban*, "He gave the black dog the bone." A direct object was expressed by the accusative: *Ic sloh þone blacan hund*, "I killed the black dog." Each of the cases expressed other functions as well, but those given are sufficient for illustrating the principle under discussion.

A few centuries later we find only one form of the definite article, *the*, and the adjectival endings are all *-e* (except where there are no endings):

Nominative: the blacke hound
Genitive: the blacke houndes
Dative: the blacke hounde
Accusative: the blacke hound

At this time form alone was not sufficient for distinguishing cases, especially nominative and accusative. During the earlier period syntactic relationships were expressed primarily by inflections and only secondarily by word order. During the later period the situation was reversed: Syntactic relationships were expressed primarily by word order and only secondarily by inflectional suffixes. The transition from the earlier period to the later was gradual; but written records from the tenth century and before reflect the circumstances of the earlier period, whereas those of the twelfth century and after reflect those of the later. We, therefore, select a round number in between as a dividing point: 1050, 1100, or 1150. For purely arbitrary reasons, we are selecting 1100 as the dividing point between the earlier period, which is called **Old English,** and the later, which is called **Middle English.** The changes in inflections and syntax were accompanied by others in phonology and vocabulary, thereby making the division between Old and Middle English more significant than if it were based on one feature alone.

We now need to consider the date for the beginning of the Old English period. From some unknown time until the middle of the fifth century, the ancestors of the modern English, Germans, Dutch, Flemings, and Frisians lived between the Elbe and Rhine, speaking mutually intelligible dialects of the same language. Farther north in Scandinavia other dialects of this language were spoken, dialects that were later to become separated into different languages: Danish, Norwegian, Swedish, and Icelandic. And east of the Elbe as well as to the south were still other speakers of this language: the Visigoths, the Ostrogoths, and others. We do not know what these people called their language, but today it is known as **Proto-Germanic** or **Teutonic.** The prefix *Proto-* is used to designate any language which is not actually attested in written documents, but about which we can reconstruct hypothetical information based on languages which evolved from it. It is impossible to tell whether all of the dialects of this language were still mutually intelligible by the fifth century; probably they were not. Except for a few inscriptions and a fourth-century translation of part of the Bible into Gothic, we have no written records from any Germanic language until several centuries later, when they were distinct languages rather than dialects of one language. Around the middle of the fifth century, some of these people living between the Elbe and the Rhine—Angles, Saxons, Frisians, and probably others—began immigrating to Britain. No doubt the language of the first generation or two living on the island was scarcely distinguishable from that of their relatives who remained on the continent; but by the time of our first written records in the language, 200 years later, there were enough differences for us to speak of it as a separate language. The word they were later to use most frequently in referring to their language was *Englisc* or *Anglisc* (i.e., the language of the Angles), the *-isc* suffix (pronounced *-ish*) being the same as we find in *Spanish* and *Swedish*. Later developments in pronunciation and spelling have since changed this to *English*. There is no question about referring to the language in England after the seventh century as Old English; but before then, without written records, there is no way of accurately saying when we should stop calling it Proto-Germanic and when to start saying Old English: 450? 500? 550? 600? 650?

Having examined the beginning and ending of the Old English period, let us now consider the Middle English period, which began around 1100. The changes which are usually given to mark the end of the period are the loss of final *-e* and the Great Vowel Shift. During the early Middle English (or late Old English) period most of the vowels in unstressed syllables had changed to [ə], the final vowel sound heard today in *sofa, China,* and *Cuba.* This vowel, spelled *e,* is all that remained of most Old English inflectional endings. By the latter part of the fourteenth century, final [ə], spelled *e,* was probably no longer pronounced by most speakers, although in poetry it was still used for metrical purposes. Using this feature, we could give 1400 as the end of the Middle English period. The other event, known as the Great Vowel Shift, had a major impact on about half of the vowels in the language. Middle English *bete,* "beet," had the vowel sound of Modern English *wait;* as a result of the vowel shift it changed to the modern pronunciation. The vowels in *bite, beet, beat, bout, boot,* and *boat* all became what they are in Modern English as a result of the Great Vowel Shift; they were all different in Middle English. This change occurred to these vowels regardless of which word they were in. The main changes effected by the vowel shift were carried out during the course of the fifteenth century, making 1400–1500 something of a transitional period. Some scholars have elected to place this century with the Modern English period, giving 1400 as the dividing date; others have used 1500, placing the fifteenth century with the Middle English period. Still others have compromised and placed it at 1450.

By using rather arbitrary dates based upon linguistic criteria, we can divide the English language into three historical periods:

c. 500–c.1100   Old English
c. 1100–c. 1450   Middle English
c. 1450–the present   Modern English

The abbreviations *OE* and *ME* for *Old English* and *Middle English* are standard. Sometimes Old English is called *Anglo-Saxon* and abbreviated *AS.* The abbreviation for *Modern English* is something of a problem, since *ME* has already been reserved for *Middle English.* The two usual solutions are *MnE* and *NE* (for *New English*). Some scholars subdivide the Modern English period into

Early Modern English and *Late Modern English*, using the middle of the eighteenth century (c. 1750) as the dividing date. These are abbreviated *EMnE* and *LMnE* or *ENE* and *LNE*.

Some further words of caution regarding the divisions are in order. It would be erroneous to think of English or any other language as being relatively stable for several centuries and then undergoing rapid, abrupt changes which shove it into another period. All spoken languages are constantly in the process of change. Although it may appear that certain centuries in the past witnessed more rapid linguistic developments than others, this may be an illusion which would be dispelled if we had more information. For example, even a cursory comparison of documents from 1600 with those from 1750 would reveal a great many changes in the language; a comparison of those from 1750 with documents from 1900, another 150 year period, would reveal very few changes. We know that the appearance of stability during the second period is the result of a conservative spelling system which does not reflect changes in speech. The two periods may have witnessed about the same number of linguistic changes, but those of the first period are reflected in the writing system, whereas those of the second are not.

Another factor often overlooked in dividing a language into periods is variation among speakers of the language. Just as there has never been a spoken language which has not changed with time, there has never been a language which all speakers used uniformly. There are always differences among people from different geographical areas and among those from different social classes. The common form of language used by a group of people from the same geographical location or social class is known as a **dialect**. Each language is composed of several dialects. If the people of one region or social group become more important than those from other regions and social classes, usually for economic or cultural reasons, then their dialect becomes a **prestige dialect** or the **standard language**. If a change in the language spreads uniformly through all the dialects, it becomes a historical change for the language as a whole. Some changes, however, affect certain dialects but not others; these changes are the sources of differences among dialects of the language. Most changes do not occur in all dialects at the same time, even if they eventually affect all of them. This situation complicates our division of a language into periods, since a change which we are using as a criterion for division may have occurred a century apart in two dialects and not have occurred at all in a third. Our information about some dialects of the past is very scant, and for many we have no information at all. Evidence for dividing a language into periods is almost always derived exclusively from the prestige dialect, but we should remember that this is only one part of the language.

There are many reasons for distrusting all dates which have been given for marking periods of any language, but probably no one would reject the division of English into at least three periods: Old English, Middle English, and Modern English.

Rule Formation in Adult and Child Grammars

So far we have been speaking of changes in language in a rather general manner with no specific attention to what it is in a language that changes. We now need to look more closely at the subject. The most common and the least significant kind of change is that which affects only a single lexical entry in the grammar of an individual or even in the grammars of many people. In the course of a century several thousand words are added to the lexicons of speakers of any language. In recent times, English has witnessed the addition of such words as *television, escalator, to escalate, astronaut,* and *cinerama.* At the same time, other words have been dropped: *surrey, whiffletree, galluses.* Or some part of a lexical entry changes, such as the pronunciation of the first vowel in *either,* or the meaning of a word such as *nice* changes from "foolish" to "pleasing." Each of these changes affects only a single lexical entry; in no case is there any influence on rules in the grammar: relativization, subject placement, deletion, plural formation, etc.

Of greater significance is a change affecting a rule in the grammar, since rules change entire classes of structures. One such change is the addition of a new rule. In developing his internalized grammar, each speaker of English forms a rule for assigning surface case forms to the personal pronouns. Since this rule is based on the usage to which the person has been exposed, all speakers of English do not develop exactly the same rule. For many people the rule becomes something like the following:

Rule A   For pronouns in subject position, assign subject forms; for all others assign object forms.[†]

Subject position is designated by the syntactic rule of subject placement. Rule A accounts for these surface structures:

4.1a   *He* left.
4.2a   *We* saw *her.*
4.3a   This is *him.*
4.4a   These are *them.*

[†]In a complete grammar this rule would probably do nothing more than add an abstract symbol, such as *obj,* to the pronoun that is to be an object form, leaving the others unmarked. Later rules would give each pronoun its phonetic form, changing *I + obj* to *me, she + obj* to *her, he + obj* to *him, we + obj* to *us, they + obj* to *them, it + obj* to *it,* and *you + obj* to *you.*

4.5a   *She* and *I* talked to Bill and *him.*

4.6a   Tom and *she* sent Ann and *me* a Christmas card.

There are other people who develop a slightly different rule:

Rule B   For uncompounded pronouns in subject position, assign subject
         forms; for all others assign object forms.

For these people sentences 4.1–4.4 are the same as for those who have Rule A;
however, instead of 4.5a and 4.6a, they produce 4.5b and 4.6b:

4.5b   *Her* and *me* talked to Bill and *him.*

4.6b   Tom and *her* sent Ann and *me* a Christmas card.

Still others develop a third rule:

Rule C   For pronouns in subject position and after forms of *be* assign
         subject forms; for all others assign object forms.

This rule will assign the following surface forms:

4.1c   *He* left.

4.2c   *We* saw *her.*

4.3c   This is *he.*

4.4c   These are *they.*

4.5c   *She* and *I* talked to Bill and *him.*

4.6c   Tom and *she* sent Ann and *me* a Christmas card.

The fact that some people have Rule A, whereas others have B and still others
have C does not change the language. People form their rules according to the
speech of the people with whom they come in contact. Rules such as these reveal a person's linguistic environment.

So long as a person who has Rule A, B, or C associates primarily with other
people who have the same rule, he will feel linguistically secure and probably
give no thought to pronoun case forms. But if a person begins associating with
another group, either professionally or socially, he will sound like an outsider.
Reactions to his speech will vary: Other people may look surprised, or they
may smile. Other people may not invite the outsider to dinner or to visit with
them. For whatever reason, the newcomer may find it advantageous to talk like
his new associates.

Let us assume that the person who changes environments is moving from associates with Rule C to those with Rule B. Since people are not conscious of their

rules, he is not able to compare them directly, but rather must rely on the sentences produced by those rules. Here is what he will hear:

	From Rule B			From Rule C
4.1b	*He* left.		4.1c	*He* left.
4.2b	*We* saw *her.*		4.2c	*We* saw *her.*
4.3b	This is *him.*		4.3c	This is *he.*
4.4b	These are *them.*		4.4c	These are *they.*
4.5b	*Her* and *me* talked to Bill and *him.*		4.5c	*She* and *I* talked to Bill and *him.*
4.6b	Tom and *her* sent Ann and *me* a Christmas card.		4.6c	Tom and *she* sent Ann and *me* a Christmas card.

If the speaker with Rule C is astute enough in his observations, he will make a generalization which will enable him to produce the same sentences as his new friends do. Seemingly the only way an adult can change the rules of his grammar is through addition of a few new rules, not through revision of a rule that already exists. He will, therefore, retain his earlier rule:

Rule C   For pronouns in subject position and after forms of *be* assign subject forms; for all others assign object forms.

After it he will add his new rule:

Rule D   Change all pronouns except those in uncompounded subject position to object forms.

Rule C will continue to function:

4.1c   *He* left.
4.2c   *We* saw *her.*
4.3c   This is *he.*
4.4c   These are *they.*
4.5c   *She* and *I* talked to Bill and *him.*
4.6c   Tom and *she* sent Ann and *me* a Christmas card.

Rule D will now apply to change the pronouns as follows:

4.1b   *He* left.
4.2b   *We* saw *her.*
4.3b   This is *him.*
4.4b   These are *them.*

4.5b   *Her* and *me* talked to Bill and *him.*

4.6b   Tom and *her* sent Ann and *me* a Christmas card.

We have, of course, simplified the process. Neither rule is applied to finished sentences, but rather both are applied to more abstract intermediate structures that still require further transformations which are irrelevant to the assignment of pronoun case forms.

Let us assume that this person who has added Rule D remains in his new environment and becomes a parent. His children will hear the same sentences and form their own generalizations. There is no reason to assume that they will develop rules C and D; rather, they will develop the much shorter, more direct Rule B. They will then be producing the same sentences as their parent but by means of a different rule.

The subject of rule formation in child and adult grammars deserves further explication. Except in the most severe cases of mental retardation, all children are born with the capacity for learning the language or languages to which they are exposed. For most other things the child learns, he is given special instruction: to tie his shoes, to use knife and fork, to read, to write, to add, to play a musical instrument. Without instruction he will learn none of these activities; also, he will not learn them if the instruction is weak or learning conditions are poor. Language learning is entirely different. No one is tuaght his first language; and because of the number of faulty sentences which he hears undifferentiated from grammatical sentences, learning conditions are almost always poor. Yet, in spite of the absence of instruction and the presence or poor learning conditions, every child except in the most unusual cases learns a language.

Exactly how much linguistic sophistication a child is born with is a subject that no one can answer at present, but opinions range from a great deal of innate knowledge to none at all. We do know that the exact nature of the rules which comprise his grammar is determined by the form of language to which he is exposed. He will make generalizations based on the sentences he hears and develop rules which will enable him to speak intelligibly and to understand others' sentences. He will start with a few simple rules and gradually expand his grammar by the addition of new rules and revisions of those he has previously formulated. By the time he is five or six, most of his rules will be in their final form. Until about the time he reaches puberty, he will still be able to make major revisions in his rules, and he will continue to make these revisions as he encounters new structures or if he moves into a new regional or social environment in which his friends employ rules different from his. By the beginning of adolescence, his ability to revise the rules of his grammar deteriorates sharply. The only changes adults make to their grammars seem to be the addition of a few rules. Of course, people of all ages are capable of learning new words, but the addition of a new word to the lexicon does not affect the grammar.

During the first eleven or twelve years of life, then, a person has a great capacity for adding new rules to his grammar and for revising those previously formed. Also, in adding or revising rules he is guided in the direction of those rules which are the simplest and the most efficient. The exact meaning of *simplicity* is a subject which linguists are still investigating, but among all of its aspects, one is economy. If two possible rules are identical in the generalizations they express and in the structures they predict but one is longer than the other (i.e., requires more words or symbols), then the shorter rule is preferred. In our examples given earlier, Rule B is shorter than the combination of C and D; the child will, therefore, select it rather than the combination of rules from his parent's grammar.

Let us now return to our three hypothetical groups of speakers with Rules A, B, and C. If a person with Rule B moves into an environment in which his new associates have Rule A, he may want to make a change in pronoun forms. Like the child, he will analyze the sentences he hears; he will also make some kind of comparison between these and the ones his grammar produces.

	From Rule B		From Rule A
4.1b	*He* left.	4.1a	*He* left.
4.2b	*We* saw *her.*	4.2a	*We* saw *her.*
4.3b	This is *him.*	4.3a	This is *him.*
4.4b	These are *them.*	4.4a	These are *them.*
4.5b	*Her* and *me* talked to Bill and *him.*	4.5a	*She* and *I* talked to Bill and *him.*
4.6b	Tom and *her* sent Ann and *me* a Christmas card.	4.6a	Tom and *she* sent Ann and *me* a Christmas card.

If he makes the correct analysis, he will add a new rule which will change the forms in 4.5b and 4.6b to those in 4.5a and 4.6a. His children will have the ability to revise rules and will develop the more economical Rule A rather than the combination of B and the new rule.

There is also the possibility that the adult will make a faulty generalization and add Rule E:

Rule E Change all compounded pronouns to subject forms.

Applying Rule E after Rule B, he will derive

4.5d   *She* and *I* talked to Bill and *he.*
4.6d   Tom and *she* sent Ann and *I* a Christmas card.

He will in effect be overcorrecting his grammar and not producing sentences like those of his new associates. There will be a great many cases, however, in which Rule E will give the desired result: *She and I laughed.*

Changes in Questions in English

We have been examining one process of linguistic change: A person or a group of people add a rule to their grammars, thereby changing the forms of the sentences they produce. The members of the next generation develop new rules based on the sentences they hear. It should be understood that the principles involved are usually more complex than the above examples suggest. A child by no means forms his generalizations about language exclusively from the speech of his parents unless these are the only people he is allowed to hear. The average child encounters language from television and from other children and adults as well as from his parents. If there is a contrast between the speech of his parents and that of his friends, he will usually make his rules conform to those of his friends. He is not in danger of losing his parents' love if he does not sound like them, but he may lose the acceptance of his friends if his speech greatly differs from theirs. Also, a person does not have to move to a new environment to encounter change. He may remain with his former associates, among whom a change may be spreading. He will then consciously or unconsciously add a rule to his grammar.

Let us now examine some rule additions which eventually spread to all speakers of English. In all languages of the world there are sentences which make statements and others which ask questions. An examination of the ways in which English has formed questions during various periods will give us insight into some of the ways in which a grammar can change.

In Modern English it is possible to form a question by using a special intonation pattern while leaving the rest of the sentence unchanged. The only difference between the *a* and *b* sentences below is the intonation pattern, represented in writing by a question mark.

    4.7a   You can go.
       b   You can go?
    4.8a   They've already left.
       b   They've already left?

More often this intonation pattern is accompanied by an inversion of certain parts of the sentence:

    4.7c   Can you go?
    4.8c   Have they already left?

Possibly both types of questions, with and without inversion, were possible in earlier stages of English, but before the modern period there is little evidence for the type without inversion. We will, therefore, limit our investigation to sentences like 4.7c and 4.8c.

For most questions in Modern English, the verb which contains tense is placed before the subject noun phrase:

4.9   *Were* you listening?
4.10   *Had* she already heard the news?
4.11   *Should* we have answered the telephone?
4.12   *Are* they cold?

The verb which contains tense may be an auxiliary (4.9–4.11) or a form of *be* (4.12). It is neither the entire verb unit nor the entire auxiliary which goes before the subject, but just the one that contains tense. The auxiliary may be any of the following:

1. a modal: *may, might, can, could, shall, should, will, would, must*
2. a form of *have*: *have, has, had*
3. a form of *be*: *am, is, are, was, were, be, been, being*

Or it may be a combination of these, as 4.11 shows.

If tense is carried by a verb other than an auxiliary or *be*, only tense is placed before the subject noun phrase:

Intermediate structure: they past find it
Question transformation: past they find it

Another rule adds *do*, a word void of semantic content, to carry tense, since it cannot be attached to the pronoun *they*:

Do insertion: past do they find it
Phonological rules: Did they find it?

Verbs other than *be* and the auxiliaries have their own procedure for forming questions.

Let us next compare two surface structures, a question and an affirmative sentence.

4.13   Are you afraid?
4.14   You are afraid.

Since the sentences do not mean the same thing, their deep structures should not be the same. The difference in meaning results from the fact that 4.13 is a question, whereas 4.14 is not. To indicate this difference, let us include the abstract element **Q** in the deep structure of a question.

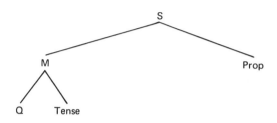

The kind of question we have been considering so far is normally answered with *yes* or *no*. There are others which require different answers:

4.15   What did Bob break?
4.16   What should he open it with?
4.17   Who hit you?
4.18   To whom have you given the message?
4.19   Where are they living?
4.20   When will you return?

With the exception of 4.17, we see an inversion of the verb which contains tense and the subject noun phrase: *did Bob, should he, have you, are they, will you.* In addition there is a question word at the beginning of each sentence: *what, who, whom, where, when.* Since they all begin with the letters *wh*, we call these **WH words.** In addition to those in the above sentences, there are a few others: *why, how, which, whose. How,* of course, does not begin with *wh*, but is still part of the classification. In each of these sentences we do not know the identity of the WH word; that is the reason for asking the question. We can see, though, that each one is derived from a deep structure case: patient (4.15), instrument (4.16), agent (4.17), dative (4.18), location (4.19), time (4.20).
An abbreviated tree of the deep structure for 4.15 looks like this:

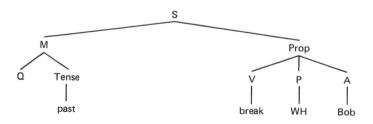

Instead of giving full semantic information for patient, which would enable us to select an entry from the lexicon (*mirror, cup, chair*), the deep structure gives merely *WH*. Subject placement applies, along with deletion of the preposition and case designation:

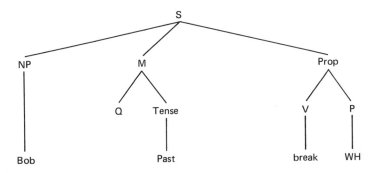

Object placement and deletion of the object preposition make no changes. Next the question transformation applies, deleting *Q* and moving *tense* before the subject noun phrase:

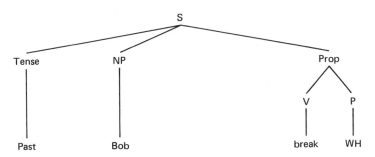

A rule now moves any *WH*, regardless of its case, to the beginning of the sentence:

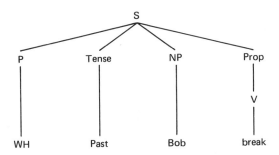

The *do* transformation is now applicable, since tense cannot be attached to *Bob*:

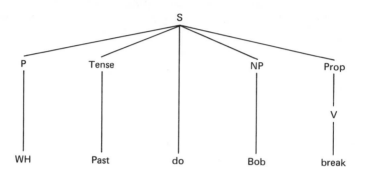

Phonological rules replace *WH* with *what* and perform other operations to give
What did Bob break?

Let us now examine questions in earlier periods of English. Starting with sentences with auxiliaries, we find structures like 4.21 in Old English:

               canst   thou   in discourse   words   command

4.21   Meaht þu   meðelcwidum worda gewealdan? (*Guthlac*, 1015)
      "Can you speak?"

For this kind of sentence, the *yes/no* question is formed the same way as it is in Modern English. The auxiliary which contains tense is placed before the subject noun phrase. The same procedure is followed in WH questions which contain auxiliaries:

               how   can   we   so   hide

4.22   Hu   magon   we   swa   dygle ... (*Daniel*, 130) "How can we hide?"

               (*for*) *what   shall   I   labor*

4.23   Hwæt sceal   ic   winnan? (*Genesis*, 278) "Why should I work?"

In Middle English we find the rule unchanged:

4.24   "Gode sir," quoþ Gawan, "woldez þou go . . ." (*Sir Gawain and the Green Knight,* 811) "Good sir," said Gawain, "would you go. . ."

4.25   Haf I prys wonnen? (*Sir Gawain and the Green Knight*, 1379) "Have I won praise?"

4.26   How may ye slepen al the longe day? (*The Miller's Tale*, 3438)
        "How can you sleep all the day long?"

4.27   What sholde I moore unto this tale sayn? (*The Nun's Priest's Tale*, 4236) "What more should I say about this tale?"

And it continues into Early Modern English:

4.28   But shall we wear these honors for a day? (*Richard III*, IV, ii, 5)

4.29   Why should we go in? (*The Merchant of Venice*, V, i, 50)

There has been no change, then, in the rules for forming questions with sentences containing auxiliaries. For both *yes/no* and WH questions, the rule has continued unchanged since Old English times.

Sentences with *be* and no auxiliary also show unchanged rules. In Old English we find sentences like the following, with tense and *be* placed before the subject noun phrase:

	art	*thou*	*the*	*Beowulf*	*who against*	*Breca*	*strove*
4.30	Eart	þu	se	Beowulf,	se þe wið	Brecan	wunne?

(*Beowulf*, 506) "Are you the Beowulf who competed against Breca?"

	which	*was*	*more*	*than*	*he*
4.31	Hwylc	wæs	mara	þonne	se?

(*Guthlac*, 400) "Who was greater than he?"

	what	*are*	*you*
4.32	Hwæt	syndon	ge . . .

(*Beowulf*, 237) "What are you?"

The same process continued into Middle English:

4.33   Is no tyme bet than oother in swich cas? (*The Man of Law's Tale*, 311) "Is no time better than another in such a case?"

4.34   Sire olde kaynard, is this thyn array? (*The Wife of Bath's Prologue*, 235) "Sir old dotard, is this your state of affairs?"

4.35   What is þat? (*Sir Gawain and the Green Knight*, 1487) "What is that?"

4.36   Where is she? (*The Summoner's Tale*, 1797)

And in Early Modern English we find sentences such as the following:

4.37   Is all our company here? (*A Midsummer Night's Dream*, I, ii, 1)

4.38   Where's my cousin Cressid? (*Troilus and Cressida*, IV, ii, 24)

So far we see no differences in the rules for question formation at any time in the recorded history of English.

But with verbs other than *be* and the auxiliaries, we do find differences. As we saw earlier, in Modern English if a sentence contains no auxiliary and a verb other than *be*, as in *She saw us*, the question is not formed by moving the verb which contains tense before the subject noun phrase, as **Saw she us?* Rather, only tense is moved and *do* is added: *Did she see us?* In Old English a different system existed:

	Hearest	*thou*	*seafarer*	*what*	*this*	*folk*	*says*
4.39	Gehyrst	þu	sælida	hwæt	þis	folc	segeð?

("The Battle of Maldon," 45) "Do you hear, seafarer, what these people say?"

	Knowest	*thou*	*lord*		*how*	*this*	*sickness*	*shall*	*end*	*set*
4.40	Wast	þu	freodryhten	hu	þeos	adle		scyle	ende	gesettan?

(*Guthlac*, 1021) "Do you know, lord, how this sickness shall come to an end?"

	where	*came*	*of*	*angels*	*glory*
4.41	Hwær	com	engla		ðrym

(*Christ and Satan*, 36) "Where has the glory of the angels gone?"

	what	*catchest*	*thou*	*in*	*(the)*	*sea*
4.42	Hwæt	fehst	þu	on		sæ?

(Ælfric's *Colloquy*, 105) "What do you catch in the sea?"

For this period of the language we do not find structures such as *Did she see us?* but only those like *Saw she us?*

This system continued through the Middle English period:

4.43   What! Alison! herestow nat Absolon? (*The Miller's Tale*, 3366) "What! Alison! Hearest thou not Absolom?"

4.44   Have ye no mannes herte? (*The Nun's Priest's Tale*, 4110) "Have you no man's heart?"

4.45   Hou fares thy faire doghter and thy wyf? (*The Reeve's Tale*, 4023) "How are your fair daughter and your wife?"

4.46   Wher rydestow under this grene-wode shawe? (*The Friar's Tale*, 1386) "Where ridest thou under this greenwood grove?"

And it is found as late as the Early Modern English period:

4.47   Looks he not for supply? (*I Henry IV*, IV, iii, 3)
4.48   Wither wander you? (*A Midsummer Night's Dream*, II, i, 1)

Through the Early Modern English period, then, the following two rules existed to account for questions:

Question Transformation: Move the verb which contains tense before the subject noun phrase.
WH Transformation: Move *WH* to the beginning of the sentence.

The WH transformation was the same as in Late Modern English, but the question transformation was different. Unlike in Late Modern English, there was no difference between auxiliaries and *be* on one hand and other verbs on the other. If this rule had remained unchanged, the following sentences would be possible today:

4.49   Can you help us?
4.50   Is she the librarian?
4.51   *Saw she the librarian?

The verb which contains tense is placed before the subject noun phrase, regardless of the kind of verb it is.

By 1600 another rule had been added to the grammar:

Do insertion: If there are no auxiliary verbs, add *do* after tense. (Optional)

So far as we can tell now, this rule was applied whimsically, and *do* had no syntactic or semantic meaning. Hence, we find the following surface structures:

4.52a   The winds did sing it to me. (*The Tempest*, III, iii, 97)
4.53a   They do abuse the king that flatter him. (*Pericles*, I, ii, 38)
4.54a   They do offend our sight. (*Henry the Fifth*, IV, vii, 56)

Apparently the following sentences without *do* could have been selected as well:

4.52b   The winds sang it to me.
4.53b   They abuse the king that flatter him.
4.54b   They offend our sight.

In case it is applied to a structure containing Q, *do* will be the verb containing tense and will be moved before the subject:

4.55a   Fair lady, do you think you have fools in hand? (*Twelfth Night*, I, iii, 60)

4.56a   Do you mark this, Reynaldo? (*Hamlet*, II, i, 15)
4.57a   Why dost thou so oppress me with thine eye? (*Troilus and Cressida*, IV, v, 241)
4.58a   When did I see thee so put down? (*Twelfth Night*, I, iii, 75)

These sentences could also have been

4.55b   Fair lady, think you that you have fools in hand?
4.56b   Mark you this, Reynaldo?
4.57b   Why oppressest thou so me with thine eye?
4.58b   When saw I thee so put down?

At this time *do* could have been selected or not.

We can illustrate the effect of the *do* insertion transformation in Early Modern English as follows:

4.59a   Intermediate: Ann past sing your song
        Do: (not selected)
        Phonological: Ann sang your song.

Or alternatively,

4.59b   Intermediate: Ann past sing your song
        Do: Ann past do sing your song
        Phonological: Ann did sing your song.

This sentence is not possible today unless we give emphatic stress to *did*, but during the seventeenth century it would have been a perfectly acceptable alternate to *Ann sang your song*. Let us now look at some questions:

4.60a   Intermediate: Ann Q past sing your song
        Do: Ann Q past do sing your song
        Question: past do Ann sing your song
        Phonological: Did Ann sing your song?

In case the *do* transformation is not selected, the following derivation results:

4.60b   Intermediate: Ann Q past sing your song
        Do: (not selected)
        Question: past sing Ann your song
        Phonological: Sang Ann your song?

Around 1600, sentences 4.60a and 4.60b apparently had the same meaning. Similarly with the WH question, either *What did Ann sing?* or *What sang Ann?* was possible. In Early Modern English, then, there were two ways of forming questions with sentences containing verbs other than auxiliaries and *be*: with or without *do*.

There is a tendency in language to separate synonymous structures. If two words, such as *bucket* and *pail*, are in use in a given region, most speakers will not use both words interchangeably to refer to the same object. They may use one of the words exclusively although they understand the other one when other people use it. Or they may use both words with specialized meanings, distinguishing a *bucket* from a *pail* according to its size, the material from which it is made, or its function. Some people use *bucket* for the general term and *pail* only in such compounds as *lunch pail* and *sand pail*. The same tendency is true for syntactic structures. If there are two synonymous types of sentences such as *Did she sing your song?* and *Sang she your song?* chances are that one will be dropped or they will develop different meanings. Eventually the alternate with *do* became the only possible form, and such questions as *Sang she your song?* are no longer found.

The loss of a structure such as *Sang she your song?* effected a change in some of the rules:

> Question: Move the auxiliary or form of *be* which contains tense before the subject noun phrase; if there is no auxiliary verb or form of *be*, move just tense.
>
> *Do* insertion: If tense precedes a structure to which it cannot be attached, add *do* after tense.

The *do* transformation is no longer optional, but applies now under well defined conditions. Also it now follows the question transformation, whereas earlier it preceded it. The question transformation does not apply uniformly to all verbs, but distinguishes between auxiliaries and *be* on one hand and other verbs on the other. The WH transformation was not altered. This change in the rules for forming questions eventually spread to all parts of the English-speaking world.

Changes in Negation in English

In the course of time the rules of a grammar change. A new rule may be added, such as *do* insertion in Shakespeare's English. Or a rule may be lost. Some rules become modified, optional rules becoming obligatory or vice versa. Further examples of modification of a rule can be seen in the *do* insertion rule.

Finally, the ordering of rules may be altered. In Shakespeare's English, *do* insertion preceded the question transformation, whereas in Late Modern English it follows it. Keeping in mind these changes, let us next examine negation in English.

All languages have processes for negation, but they do not necessarily use the same processes. One which is frequently encountered is that of inserting a special negative particle, such as *not* in English, in some prescribed position in the sentence, which may vary from language to language. There are also other means of forming negatives. In English, for example, in addition to *She does not know anything* we have *She knows nothing*. It is also possible to add certain negative prefixes: *impossible, unable.* In addition, there are a number of other devices by which we can construct sentences which are interpreted as negatives. We will limit our investigation to the particle *not* and to such negative forms as *nothing* and *never* and see how the rules regulating their occurrence have changed since Old English times.

The deep structures of negative sentences differ from those of positives in the inclusion of an element abbreviated *neg.* In the deep structure this element appears within the modality constituent:

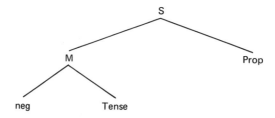

Transformational rules move *neg* to its proper place in each sentence, and later rules give it a phonetic form.

Before we look at negation in earlier periods of English, it will be useful for us to see how the process operates in Modern English. From the following sentences we can see where the negative particle *not* appears in surface structures:

4.61   They were *not* happy.
4.62   They are *not* singing.
4.63   They were *not* chosen.
4.64   They had *not* eaten.
4.65   They have *not* been reading.
4.66   They have *not* been seen.
4.67   They will *not* go.
4.68   They would *not* have told you.
4.69   They must *not* have been listening.

4.70a *They *not* answered.
    b *They answered *not*.
    c They did*n't* answer.

As sentences 4.61–4.69 show, *not* is placed after the auxiliary or form of *be* that carries tense. If it is a verb other than an auxiliary or *be* which carries tense, *not* is placed between tense and the verb: *tense + not + verb*. *Do* insertion then applies to carry tense, since it cannot be attached to *not*. The ungrammatical 4.70a and 4.70b show that for verbs other than auxiliaries and *be* a simple placement of *not* is not enough. The **negative transformation** will, then, position *neg* as follows:

    4.61 Intermediate: they neg past be happy
            Negative: they past be neg happy
            Phonological: They were not happy.

The derivation of 4.70c is as follows:

    4.70c Intermediate: they neg past answer
             Negative: they past neg answer
             Do: they past do neg answer
             Phonological: They didn't answer.

Modern English has other negative structures as well:

    4.71a Tony has *not* said anything.
       b Tony has said *no*thing.
    4.72a They are *not* discussing it with anyone.
       b They are discussing it with *no* one.
    4.73a Louise will *not* be going anywhere.
       b Louise will be going *no*where.
    4.74a She has*n't* ever thanked me.
       b She has *n*ever thanked me.

Sentences 4.71a and 4.71b are paraphrases of each other, as are the other pairs. In the *a* sentences the negative *not* occurs in the same position as it does in 4.61–4.69. In the *b* sentences we find *nothing, no one, nowhere, never*. These can easily be analyzed as *neg* and a morpheme that we call a **quantifier**: *some, any*, etc. Later we will have more to say about the rules which place *neg* in its proper position. At present all we are illustrating is two means for showing negation in surface structures in Modern English: with *not* and with negative quantifiers.

In Old English we find the following surface structures, with the negative particle *ne* appearing directly before the verb which contains tense:

	1	*not*	*did*
4.75	Ic	ne	dyde.†	"I did not do [it]."

	beware	*that*	*you*	*that*	*not*	*do*
4.76	Warna	ðæt	ðu	ðæt	ne	do.	"Beware that you do not do that."

	Not want	*1*	*ever*	*hence*	*out*	*(to) go*
4.77	Nylle	ic	æfre	hionan	ut	witan.	"I do not ever want to depart from here."

	Not have	*1*	*sin*	*committed*
4.78	Næbbe	ic	synne	gefremed.	"I have not committed a sin."

	Not is	*allowed*
4.79	Nis	alyfed.	"It is not allowed."

In 4.77–4.79 we see the contracted forms *nylle, næbbe,* and *nis* from *ne wylle, ne hæbbe,* and *ne is* (cf. Modern English *don't, can't, hasn't* from *do not, can not, has not*). The positioning of the negative particle in Old English is different from that of Modern English, but it is not complicated: It remains before tense and the verb or auxiliary to which it is attached.

In addition to sentences with *ne* as the only element of negation, there were those with negative quantifiers:

	never	*1*	*more*	*saw (of)*	*earls*	*over*	*earth*
4.80	Næfre	ic	maran	geseah	eorla	ofer	eorþan.	"I have never seen a greater leader on earth."

	there	*none*	*is*	*night*	*in*	*summer*
4.81	Ðær	nængu	biþ	niht	on	sumera.	"There is no night there in summer."

	Andrew	*not at all*	*you*	*sinned*
4.82	Andreas	nænigwuht	ðu	gefirnodest.	"Andrew, you have sinned not at all."

	no	*more*	*man*	*was*	*begotten*
4.83	Nan	mærra	man	wurde	acenned.	"No greater man was begotten."

	because	*it*	*is*	*nothing*
4.84	Forðy	hit	is	nauht.	"Because it is nothing."

---

†The Old English examples in this section are from Joseph Bosworth and Northcote Toller, *An Anglo-Saxon Dictionary* (London: Oxford University Press, 1898).

These are similar to structures in Modern English with negative quantifiers. The phonetic shape, of course, is different:

ne + æfre ——➤ næfre, "not ever," "never"
ne + ænig ——➤ nænig, nængu, "not any," "none"
ne + ænig wiht ——➤ nænigwiht, "not anything," "nothing"
ne + an ——➤ nan, "not one," "none"
ne + awiht ——➤ nawiht, nauht, "nothing"

The negative quantifiers are clearly contracted forms of the negative particle *ne* and a quantifier.

Unlike most dialects of Modern English, an Old English sentence was not limited to one negative particle:

never   since   Romans   not   ruled   in   Britain
4.85   Næfre   siðan   Romane   ne   ricsodon   on   Bretone.
"Never since Romans ruled in Britain."

no   man   not   dared   slay   another   man   not had   he
4.86   Nan   man   ne   dorste   slean   oðerne   man,   næfde   he
never   so   much   done   against   the   other
næfre   swa   mycel   gedon   wiþ   ðone   oðerne. "No man dared to kill another man, however much he had done against the other."

he   never   none   divine   angels   not had
4.87   He   næfre   nænige   godcunde   englas   næfde. "He never had any divine angels."

not   none   of them   one   not is   no   less   than   all   the trinity
4.88   Ne   nan   heora   an   nis   na   læsse   ðonne   eall   seo þrynnys.
"No one of them is less than all the trinity."

he sought his weapons but he not saw   them nowhere
4.89   He sohte   his wæpnu   ac   he ne   geseah hi   nahwær.
"He looked for his weapons, but he didn't see them anywhere."

In these sentences all quantifiers are made negative in addition to the verb.

It is also possible to find sentences with negative verbs but no negative element in the quantifiers:

not was there any   toil
4.90   Næs   ðær   ænigum gewin. "There was no toil for anyone."
any   not may the skill   desert
4.91   Ængum   ne   mæg se   cræft losian. "The skill may not desert anyone."

kin   ever   not   may   one   turn aside
4.92   Sibb   æfre   ne   mæg   wiht   onwendan. "Nothing can ever
turn aside kinship."

Although these are much less common than the other types, they do exist and
must be included in any account of negation in Old English.
We have examined four kinds of negative sentences:

1. Those with no quantifier, in which the verb is preceded by *ne*:
   4.75–4.79
2. Those in which the quantifiers are preceded by *ne* but the verb is not:
   4.80–4.84
3. Those in which both the verb and the quantifiers are preceded by *ne*:
   4.85–4.89
4. Those in which the verb is preceded by *ne* but the quantifiers are not:
   4.90–4.92

We could end our examination here with this collection and organization of data.
But as we saw in Chapters Two and Three, we are more concerned with the rules
that account for sentences than we are with the individual sentences themselves.
In this way when we proceed to later periods of English, we will see how the
rules change. By studying changes in the rules of grammars, we gain more insight
into the development of a language than if we stopped with sentence classification. We have already stated that each negative sentence has *neg* in the deep
structure modality constituent. To derive the sentences we have been examining,
we need two rules:

Neg Copying: Copy *neg* before all quantifiers. (Optional)
Neg Deletion: If neg copying has been applied, delete *neg* before the
    verb. (Optional)

There is no transformation needed to place *neg* before the verb, since it precedes
tense in the deep structure. None of the transformations we examined in Chapters
Two and Three moved tense from its deep structure position; only case constituents were moved. If a complete grammar of Old English should contain rules
which move tense, the negative particle would be moved along with it. There is no
special negative transformation needed for sentences such as 4.75 and 4.78:

4.75   Ic ne dyde. "I did not do [it]."
4.78   Næbbe ic synne gefremed. "I have not committed a sin."

If a sentence contains quantifiers, we may copy *neg* before all of them. By *copying* we are not moving *neg* from its original position before tense; we are merely duplicating it elsewhere. Ignoring transformations not related to negation, we can apply *neg* copying to an intermediate structure underlying one of the sentences we have already examined:

4.87   Intermediate: he æfre ænige godcunde englas neg hæfde
        Neg copying: he *neg* æfre *neg* ænige godcunde englas neg hæfde
        Phonological: He næfre nænige godcunde englas næfde.
                       "He never had any divine angels."

To derive sentence 4.83, we apply both optional rules:

4.83   Intermediate: an mærra man neg wurde acenned
        Neg copying: *neg* an mærra man neg wurde acenned
        Neg deletion: neg an mærra man wurde acenned
        Phonological: Nan mærra man wurde acenned. "No greater man
                       was begotten."

Finally, sentences 4.90–4.92 are derived without the application of the optional *neg* copying rule. If *neg* copying is not selected, then *neg* deletion is inapplicable:

4.90   Intermediate: neg wæs ðær ænigum gewin
        Phonological: Næs ðær ænigum gewin. "There was no toil for
                       anyone."

With two optional rules we are able to account for all four types of surface structures.

Some linguists are suspicious of optional rules, and perhaps justifiably so. Yet no one has yet been able to account for what governs the different choices in the following pairs of synonymous sentences:

4.93a   Someone told the secret to Betty.
    b   Betty was told the secret.
4.94a   The man who is driving the black car looks familiar.
    b   The man driving the black car looks familiar.

If the choices leading to passives and reduced relatives remain optional for Modern English, a language for which we have living speakers who can comment on the grammaticalness of sentences, how can we hope to be more specific about a language with no living speakers? It may well be that *neg* copying and deletion were not optional at all, but rather obligatory under certain specified conditions.

If so, some scholar in the future may discover what those conditions were; but at present the best we can do is assume that those rules were optional.

In writing grammars of languages spoken today, the goals of transformationalists are rules which explain the native speaker's competence in his language: his ability to create an infinite number of grammatical sentences and his knowledge about sentences (which elements are constituents of a given noun phrase, which sentences are synonymous, etc.). The transformationalist feels that his grammar should predict all possible sentences in the language, whether they have been previously created or not. In working with a language for which there are no living speakers, we must accept goals that are more modest. A person studying negation in Modern English, for example, can ask a native speaker whether sentences 4.95-4.96 are grammatical and whether they mean the same thing:

> 4.95   The man wouldn't say anything.
>
> 4.96   The man would say nothing.

The student of Old English can observe that certain sentences are recorded:

> 4.84   For ðy hit is nauht. "Because it is nothing."
>
> 4.85   Næfre siðan Romane ne ricsodon on Bretone. "Never since Romans ruled in Britain."
>
> 4.91   Ængum ne mæg se cræft losian. "The skill may not desert anyone."

He may speculate about whether variants of these sentences would be grammatical:

> 4.84a   For ðy hit nis nauht.
>
> 4.85a   Næfre siðan Romane ricsodon in Bretone.
>
> 4.91a   Nænigum ne mæg se cræft losian.

A person would be foolish to try to answer that these three variants definitely are or are not grammatical. Considering the current state of our knowledge about Old English and linguistics in general, we can expect our rules to account for little more than the attested sentences.

Neg copying and deletion remained through the Middle English period, but *neg* copying was probably no longer optional. In Chaucer's *Troilus and Criseyde* we find three of the four Old English negative types. First there are sentences without quantifiers, in which the negative particle remains before the verb containing tense:

> 4.97   But why he nolde don so fel a dede

That shal I seyn. (V, 50-1)

"But why he did not wish to do so wicked a deed, that shall I say."

4.98   For I, that God of Loves servantz serve,

Ne dar to Love. (I, 15-16)

"For I, who serve the servants of the god of love, do not dare to love."

4.99   A thousand Troyes whoso that me yave,

Ech after other, God so wys me save,

Ne myghte me so gladen. (II, 977-9)

"May God so wise save me, if someone gave me a thousand Troys one after the other, it could not gladden me so."

Next there are those in which *neg* has been copied before each of the quantifiers. The optional *neg* deletion rule has not been applied:

4.100   That I ne may it nevere more diserve. (III, 387)

"That I may not ever deserve it more."

4.101   But how this town com to destruccion

Ne falleth naught to purpos me to telle. (I, 141-2)

"It does not suit my purpose to tell how this town came to destruction."

4.102   Have here another way, if it so be

That al this thyng ne may yow nat suffise. (IV, 1366-7)

"Have here another way if all these things cannot satisfy you."

Sentences of this type are much less common than they were in Old English. In the third group of sentences *neg* has been copied before each of the quantifiers and deleted before the verb:

4.103   Ther is na more to seye. (I, 574)

"There is no more to say."

4.104   Al my labour shal nat ben on ydel. (V, 94)

"All my work shall not be in vain."

4.105   Now loke thanne, if they be nought to blame. (III, 316)

"Now look then, if they are not to blame."

This is the usual pattern for sentences containing quantifiers.

The negative quantifiers *nat, nought,* "not at all," at first gave emphasis to the idea of negation. A sentence such as 4.106a would have expressed negation more forcefully than one like 4.106b without *nat*:

4.106a But that nis nat the worste.
    b But that nis the worste.

By Chaucer's time, *nat*, "not," had become so common in negative sentences
that its emphatic meaning was lost, and a sentence such as *That nis nat the
worste* was not emphatically negative but merely redundant. In some dialects
neg deletion came to be used for all sentences as a means of avoiding redundancy.
In these dialects succeeding generations during the fifteenth and sixteenth centuries developed *neg* copying and deletion as obligatory rules. Rather than
4.106a or 4.106b, the usual surface structure was 4.106c:

4.106c But that is nat the worste. (I, 341)
        "But that is not the worst."

As long as children learning English heard sentences such as 4.106a as well as
those like 4.106c, they developed grammars similar to those of their parents.
After deletion of *neg* before the verb became obligatory, children heard only
sentences such as 4.106c, *But that is nat the worste,* and none like 4.106a, *But
that nis nat the worste.* As a result, they did not have sufficient data to derive
surface structures the way previous generations had done. To derive 4.106c,
earlier generations followed this sequence of transformations:

Intermediate: but that neg is quant the worste
Neg copying: but that neg is neg quant the worste
Neg deletion: but that is neg quant the worste
Phonological: But that is nat the worste.

Succeeding generations followed something like the following process:

Intermediate: but that neg is the worste
Neg placement: but that is neg the worste
Phonological: But that is nat the worste.

That is, their deep structure would not have a quantifier underlying *nat*, and the
rule which gives *neg* a phonetic shape would make it *nat* (later *not*), rather than
ne.
    By 1600 the following rules were needed by most speakers of English:

Neg copying: Copy *neg* before one quantifier.
Neg deletion: If *neg* copying has been applied, delete *neg* before tense.

The rules are no longer optional, and *neg* is copied before only one quantifier.

As a result of the application of these rules, we find the following sentences:

4.107   He never killed any of his friends. (*Henry the Fifth,* IV, vii, 39)
4.108   And let those that play your clowns speak no more than is set down for them. (*Hamlet,* III, ii, 38)
4.109   And nothing grieves me heartily indeed. (*Titus Andronicus,* V, i, 143)

In each of these sentences *neg* has been copied before a quantifier and deleted before the verb. Phonological rules have provided the surface forms of the negative quantifiers: *never, no, nothing.*

In discussing questions, we mentioned the *do* insertion rule which was added to the grammar by this time:

Do insertion: If there are no auxiliary verbs, add *do* after tense. (Optional)

Hence, *The winds did sing* and *The winds sang* were possible as synonymous sentences.

Also the negative placement transformation mentioned earlier was in the grammar by 1600:

Neg placement: If *neg* appears before tense, move it after the verb to which tense is attached.

This rule will be inapplicable in sentences such as 4.107–4.109 since *neg* will have been deleted before tense. For sentences without quantifiers, however, *neg* will be moved after the verb to which tense is attached. This may be an auxiliary verb:

4.110   All have not offended. (*Timon of Athens,* V, iv, 35)
4.111   You shall not write my praise. (*Othello,* II, i, 116)
4.112   Old lord, I cannot blame thee. (*The Tempest,* III, iii, 4)

Or it may be the main verb, whether it is *be* or some other verb:

4.113   I am not altogether an ass. (*The Merry Wives of Windsor,* I, i, 155)
4.114   I know not such, my lord. (*Timon of Athens,* V, i, 97)
4.115   Let not my jealousies be your dishonours. (*Macbeth,* IV, iii, 29)

If *do* insertion has been applied, *do* will be the verb to which tense is attached:

4.116   I do not doubt thy faith. (*Pericles*, I, ii, 111)

4.117   I do not misdoubt my wife. (*The Merry Wives of Windsor*, II, i, 166) 166)

4.118   I do not desire he should answer for me. (*Henry the Fifth*, IV, i, 187)

These are the regular ways of forming surface negative structures in Shakespeare's English, with four rules instead of the two needed for Chaucer.

Today there is variation among dialects as to whether *neg* copying and deletion are optional or not. For some dialects *neg* copying is optional, and if it is not applied, sentences like the following result:

4.119a   He wasn't doing anything.

4.120a   We haven't seen anyone.

The negative *not* remains with the auxiliary verb which contains tense, and the quantifiers are not made negative. For these dialects if *neg* copying is applied, then *neg* deletion is obligatory:

4.119b   He was doing nothing.

4.120b   We have seen no one.

In these dialects only one negative element is permitted in surface structures: with the verb or with one quantifier.

There are other dialects of Modern English for which *neg* deletion is optional. If this rule is applied, sentences such as 4.119b–4.120b result. If, on the other hand, it is not applied, the following structures result:

4.119c   He wasn't doing nothing.

4.120c   We haven't seen no one.

People speaking dialects which produce sentences such as 4.119c and 4.120c have essentially the same rules as do those who speak the other dialects, and they have the same deep structures. Many of the sentences they produce are the same, and those that are not differ in negation only in whether *neg* deletion is optional or obligatory.

For all dialects of Modern English, *neg* placement has been modified:

Neg placement: If *neg* appears before tense, move it after the auxiliary verb or form of *be* to which tense is attached; if there is no auxiliary verb or form of *be*, move *neg* after tense.

With the application of *neg* placement and a phonological rule which rewrites *neg* as *not*, the following derivations occur:

> 4.121   Intermediate: they neg could open the door
>   *Neg* placement: they could neg open the door
>   Phonological: They could not open the door.
> 4.122   Intermediate: they neg are here
>   *Neg* placement: they are neg here
>   Phonological: They are not here.

The *do* insertion rule was revised, as we said when discussing questions:

> *Do* insertion: If tense precedes a structure to which it cannot be attached, add *do* after tense.

Neg placement may provide a structure such as the following:

> 4.123   Intermediate: they neg past go
>   *Neg* placement: they past neg go

Do insertion is now applicable, since *past* cannot be attached to *neg*. Tense can be attached only to verbs.

> *Do* insertion: they past do neg go
> Phonological: They did not go.

Conclusion

In this chapter we have been examining several changes in the syntactic rules of English. The process of linguistic change begins with an alteration of already developed grammars. With our present state of knowledge, it seems that the only kind of change an adult can make in his grammar is the addition of a few rules. Whatever the rule may be—pronoun case assignment, *do* insertion, negative placement—certain speakers will add the rule to their grammars. Succeeding generations of speakers will not develop grammars exactly like those of their parents, but rather grammars based on the sentences they encounter. In this way every language that is in use is constantly changing, yet people are usually not aware of syntactic changes. Finally, it should be emphasized that syntactic change means alterations in the rules of the grammar and not just changes in individual surface structures.

Suggested Reading

Carlton, Charles R. "Word Order of Noun Modifiers in Old English Prose." *Journal of English and Germanic Philology* 62 (1963): 778–83. Reprinted in Scott and Erickson, 1968.

Fries, Charles C. "On the Development of the Structural Use of Word-Order in Modern English." *Language* 16 (1940): 199–208. Reprinted in Scott and Erickson, 1968.

Hoenigswald, Henry M. *Language Change and Linguistic Reconstruction.* Chicago: University of Chicago Press, 1960.

Jespersen, Otto. *A Modern English Grammar on Historical Principles.* Vol. 5. Copenhagen: Ejnar Munksgaard, 1940.

_____. *Negation in English and Other Languages.* 2nd ed. Copenhagen: Ejnar Munksgaard, 1966.

King, Robert D. *Historical Linguistics and Generative Grammar.* Englewood Cliffs, N.J.: Prentice-Hall, 1969.

Klima, Edward S. "Relatedness Between Grammatical Systems." *Language* 40 (1964): 1–20. Reprinted in Reibel and Schane, 1969.

Lehmann, Winfred P. "A Definition of Proto-Germanic: A Study in the Chronological Delimitation of Languages." *Language* 37 (1961): 67–74. Reprinted in Scott and Erickson, 1968.

_____. *Historical Linguistics: An Introduction.* New York: Holt, Rinehart and Winston, 1962.

Sapir, Edward. *Language.* New York: Harcourt Brace Jovanovich, 1921. Chapter 7: "Language as a Historical Product: Drift."

Traugott, Elizabeth Closs. "Diachronic Syntax and Generative Grammar." *Language* 41 (1965): 402–15. Reprinted in Scott and Erickson, 1968.

Weinreich, Uriel; Labov, William; and Herzog, Marvin I. "Empirical Foundations for a Theory of Language Change" in Lehmann and Malkiel, 1968.

CHAPTER FIVE

Morphemes and Morphemic Change

There are two possible approaches a person can take in studying grammar. He can start with the sentence as a whole and work down progressively to the smallest units, or he can start with the smallest units and work up to the whole sentence. Most traditional grammarians followed the second approach, frequently using a threefold division: (1) **phonology** (the study of sounds), (2) **inflections** (or *accidence*) and **word formation**, and (3) **syntax**. Some idea of the amount of space normally given to each of these divisions can be derived from Joseph Wright's *Grammar of the Gothic Language* (Oxford: Clarendon Press, 1910, 1954), in which 80 pages are devoted to phonology, 98 to inflections and word formation, and 12 to syntax. Most grammars of English omitted phonology. Typical school grammars began by classifying words as to parts of speech and within each part of speech according to such categories as gender, case, tense, and transitivity. Then they discussed phrases and clauses: units composed of words. Structuralists also worked in this direction, starting with **phonology**, the study of sounds and phonemes; proceeding to **morphology**, the study of morphemes, which are made up of phonemes; and ending with **syntax**, the study of larger units that are made up of morphemes.

Transformationalists have not followed this direction. Instead, they usually begin with syntax and move from there to smaller units, since their concept of phonology involves operations which depend upon syntactic information. Neither approach is entirely satisfactory, since all parts of a grammar are interrelated into one system. It is obvious that people speaking and understanding sentences do not keep the various components distinct. There are, however, advantages to the scholar or to the student focusing his attention on only one restricted section at a time. In the last three chapters we studied syntactic structures. Let us now look at a smaller unit, the **morpheme**.

During the 1940s and 1950s, linguists were fairly well agreed that a morpheme was "the smallest meaningful element in a language." They broke the word *unsuccessfully* into the four morphemes *un-, success, -ful,* and *-ly*. Each of these units has meaning, and none can be subdivided into smaller meaningful units; if *un-* is divided into *u* and *n*, neither of these units has meaning. The morpheme is not to be confused with the syllable, although in many cases the two have the same dividing point. One morpheme may consist of one syllable or of several: *cat, success, Mississippi*. Also, more than one morpheme may be found within a single syllable. *Boys'* consists of *boy, plural,* and *possessive.*

Looking more closely at the definition of the morpheme, some linguists noticed that several of the units they had been calling morphemes actually had no meaning at all: (1) *to* in *He wants to go,* (2) *that* in *I know that you are busy,* (3) *do* in *He didn't answer,* and several others. Some transformationalists restricted their use of the term *morpheme* to units in deep structures and called those in surface structures **formatives**. Others have continued to use *morpheme* for both deep and surface structures but have redefined the term. We are following this practice: **A morpheme is a minimal syntactic unit**. It is the smallest unit that can be added or deleted by a syntactic transformation.

This does not mean that we are disregarding meaning. Most morphemes do have meaning which is fairly consistent regardless of how the morpheme is used, as can be seen for *corrupt* in the following words: *corruption, corruptible, uncorruptible, corruptness, corrupter, corruptibility, corruptionist, corruptive*. The identity of the morpheme is not dependent upon its spelling. The suffix *-or* in *actor* is the same as the *-er* in *player* in spite of the differences in spelling. Both *-or* and *-er* mean the same thing, are added to the same class of words, and produce the same results. On the other hand, there are four separate morphemes spelled *-en* in *oxen* (plural), *eaten* (past participle), *woolen*, "made of," and *fasten*, "to make." Similarly, *cape*, "a sleeveless outer garment," and *cape*, "a point of land projecting into the water," are different morphemes which happen to have the same pronunciation and spelling.

Classification of Morphemes

Some morphemes such as *apple, house, cow, happy,* and *drink* have a great deal of semantic content, whereas others such as *the, with, plural,* and *past* have little meaning of their own but rather tell something about the morphemes in the first group. Those in the first group are called **lexical morphemes** (or **full morphemes**); those in the second are called **grammatical** (or **empty**) **morphemes**. Those in the second group usually express grammatical concepts, such as definiteness, case, tense, or plurality.

One way of illustrating these two classes is to use a sentence in which normal grammatical morphemes are used but in which all lexical morphemes are replaced by nonsense words:

5.1a   *The* woop*ous* climpuck*s* *were* clonk*ing at a* floos.

The sentence has no semantic content. Yet because of the grammatical morphemes *the, -ous, -s, were, -ing, at,* and *a* we see a great deal of the syntactic structure. Now let us reverse the procedure, keeping recognizable lexical morphemes but replacing the grammatical morphemes with nonsense forms:

5.1b   Glap *nerv*shast *dog*wip fleesk *bark*am prauk spid *car*.

Here we recognize the morphemes *nerve, dog, bark,* and *car,* all of which have a great deal of meaning; yet the sentence as a whole is meaningless because we are not able to recognize the syntactic structure. With both kinds of morphemes in recognizable forms, of course, the sentence is meaningful:

5.1c   The nervous dogs were barking at a car.

Although exaggerated claims have sometimes been made for what the use of nonsense words actually reveals, it does illustrate the difference between lexical and grammatical morphemes.

Like so many other units whose existence precedes their description and classification, morphemes do not always fit into neat, clearly delineated lexical and grammatical classes. Most prepositions of location have a great deal more semantic content than do the instrumental *with* and the agentive *by*, yet they have less content than most nouns and verbs. The conjunctions *and, or, nor, but, yet, for* must have some semantic content or they would all mean the same thing; yet this content is small in comparison to that of *giggle* or *acrobat*. Although the distinctions between lexical and grammatical morphemes are not always clear cut, it is usually true that prepositions, conjunctions, and articles are grammatical morphemes.

Another way in which morphemes may be grouped is into affixes and bases. The central core of a word without prefixes and suffixes is known as the **base** (or **root**). We can see the base *person* in the words *personal, personality, personalize,* and *impersonate*. An **affix** may come before a base, in which case we call it a **prefix** (*rebuild*); or it may come after the base and be a **suffix** (*manly, childish*). Some languages have **infixes**, affixes inserted within the base. Bloomfield (1933: 218) cites Tagalog, a language of the Philippines, for infixes: [súːlat] "a writing," [sumúːlat] "one who writes," [sinúːlat] "that which is written." English does not have infixes. *Unselfish* consists of three morphemes: the base *self*, the prefix *un-*, and the suffix *-ish*. A base may have more than one affix added to it. To *person* we can add *-al* and *-ity* to form *personality*. Compared to bases, affixes are limited in number and are slow to be added to the language. There are many more bases than affixes, and they are added to the language freely.

Affixes may be **inflectional** or **derivational**. Inflectional affixes express such features as plurality, case, tense, and aspect. English surface structures contain the following inflectional suffixes:

1. plurality: dog*s*   5. progressive: go*ing*
2. possession: man*'s*   6. perfective: eat*en*
3. past tense: drag*ged*   7. comparative degree: sweet*er*
4. third person singular: sing*s*   8. superlative degree: sweet*est*

Although Modern English has no inflectional prefixes, some languages do. Also, some languages have a great many more inflectional affixes than English. The addition of an inflectional affix does not produce a new word. For example, we think of singular and plural forms such as *dog* and *dogs* as different forms of the same word, not as different words. A derivational affix, on the other hand, is used to derive one word from another: *happy, happiness; fame, famous*. Many derivational affixes change the part of speech of the word:

Original word	Derived word
fame (noun)	fam*ous* (adjective)
prison (noun)	*im*prison (verb)
simple (adjective)	simp*lify* (verb)
sad (adjective)	sad*ness* (noun)
sad (adjective)	sad*ly* (adverb)
devote (verb)	devo*tion* (noun)

Other derivational affixes do not alter the part of speech:

Original word	Derived word
host (noun)	host*ess* (noun)
gang (noun)	gang*ster* (noun)
popular (adjective)	*un*popular (adjective)

English has both derivational prefixes and suffixes, but the suffixes outnumber the prefixes. With the exception of the combination *plural* and *possessive*, no more than one inflectional affix may occur with a word in Modern English. This restriction is not extended to derivational affixes: *polyunsaturated, unimportant* (two prefixes); *faithfulness, personally* (two suffixes). In surface forms, inflectional suffixes always follow derivational suffixes: *actors, personalized*.

Finally, morphemes may be classified as free or bound. A **free morpheme** is one that can stand by itself as a word: *go, friend, sad*. A **bound morpheme** is never found alone as a word, but is always joined with other morphemes: *un-*, *-ness, plural*. All affixes are bound. Bases may be free (*teacher, agreeable, vitality*) or bound (*conceive, transmit, impose*).

These classifications of morphemes are in many ways superficial in that they are formed solely in terms of surface structures. Yet the terms occur frequently enough in linguistic literature that some acquaintance with them is useful. Also we will have occasion to refer to some of them in the chapters that follow.

Morphemes in the Grammars of Individuals

Students in linguistics classes can be taught to recognize and classify morphemes, just as children in the fifth grade can be taught to recognize prefixes and suffixes. We could well ask whether morphemes have any real existence in the internalized grammar of an individual, or whether they are merely something linguists have invented. This is a question worth asking about any linguistic concept, since our purpose is to discover the individual's internalized grammar, not to invent systems, regardless of how clever our inventions may be. The fact that we can learn to recognize morphemes is not proof of their existence in a grammar. We can also learn to alphabetize words, and we know that this skill is completely outside of the internalized grammar. Learning how to alphabetize words depends solely upon the knowledge of a written alphabet and the ordering of the letters within it. Linguistic inquiry can be said to reveal aspects of an internalized grammar only if it causes a person to make explicit the knowledge that he already possesses. Our implicit knowledge of pronominalization, for example, is in no way dependent upon our knowledge of formal grammar or of a writing system. We can read the following sentences to an intelligent speaker of English:

5.2   *She* thanked the man who helped the old woman.

5.3   The old woman thanked the man who helped *her*.

5.4   Because *he* had lost his money, Tom couldn't go with us.

5.5   *He* couldn't go with us because Tom had lost his money.

Whether this person can read or not, he is able to give us the probable referent of each of the pronouns. Because his answers will agree with those made by other speakers of English, we know that there must be some kind of rule for pronominalization in the internalized grammar. Unlike the knowledge of pronoun referents, that of alphabetization must be taught. Furthermore, the latter skill is not even dependent upon one's knowledge of a language. With knowledge of the letters and their order in an alphabet, a person can easily alphabetize words from any language that uses the alphabet; knowledge of the language is not essential. Is our ability to recognize morphemes like our ability to recognize pronoun referents, or is it like our ability to alphabetize words?

First of all, we should see whether our knowledge of a given language is essential for recognition of morphemes. Earlier in this chapter we learned what a morpheme is; if it has no real existence in the grammar, we should be able to recognize morphemes in any language, not just in those for which we know the grammar:

German	English
Berechnung	estimation
Enttäuschung	disappointment
unangenehm	unpleasant
Fernsprecher	telephone

Obviously a person must know German to recognize the morphemes in the first column and English to recognize those in the second. Some kind of knowledge about what is a possible syntactic unit in a given language is always essential for identifying the morphemes in that language.

Further support for the existence of the morpheme can be found in the language of preschool age children. Such pairs as the following could be learned as separate forms: *help, helped; mow, mowed; thank, thanked; open, opened; close, closed.* That is, from his use of these words alone we cannot be sure that the child has learned to recognize *helped, mowed, thanked, opened,* and *closed* as a combination of base and past-tense morpheme. There is the possibility that he has learned these words from hearing them spoken and has added them to his lexicon as indivisible units. However, most children create past-tense forms which they have not heard anyone else use: *grow, growed; know, knowed; see, seed.* These creations show that they have learned to form past tenses by adding a *d* sound to the end of the verb. Such a process requires some kind of awareness of morphemes.

If derivational morphemes did not have some kind of existence in the grammar of the individual, the creation of new words with them would not be possible. If the agentive suffix *-er* (also spelled *-or*) were not recognized as a morpheme in *actor, player, teacher,* and *bouncer,* these words would have to be learned separately from *act, play, teach,* and *bounce.* Furthermore, it would be unlikely that anyone would invent *laugher, non-bather, cougher,* or *sneezer*; and if someone did, no one would know what the words meant. Yet people frequently do create such words, and other people understand them.

Like other parts of the individual's grammar, morphemic identification results from conclusions the person has drawn from the data available to him. Linguistic universals are possibly part of his innate competence, but the knowledge of what are the morphemes of a language must be learned from contact with the language itself. Such contact will provide sufficient evidence for recognizing the inflectional suffixes and such derivational affixes as *-ment* and *-ness* as morphemes of the language. It will also provide a basis for recognizing the bases in *jumped, hitting, retirement,* and *meanness* as morphemes. On the other hand, there will not be enough information to justify recognizing *daisy* as a combination of the morphemes *day, possessive,* and *eye* (*day's eye*). Although Chaucer was able to recognize this derivation, the speaker of English today is not able to do so without the aid of a dictionary or other information from earlier English. Nor is he likely to recognize *house* as the first morpheme in *husband* and *hussy,* or *wife* as the second morpheme in the latter. Even some more obvious cases normally go unnoticed: that the first morphemes in *nostril* and *window* are *nose* and *wind,* respectively. Regardless of its origin, the morphemic composition of a word is based upon contemporary data available to the speaker. The following words, therefore, consist of one morpheme each in the grammars of native speakers today: *daisy, husband, hussy, nostril, window.*

Another potential problem with the identification of morphemes is found in words borrowed from other languages. If English has borrowed only a few words from a particular language, then they are normally analyzed by the speaker of English as consisting of one morpheme each, regardless of the number a speaker of the other language would see. For example, the speaker of English has no reason to see more than one morpheme in *sputnik.* To the speaker of Russian it consists of three: *s* ("with"), *put* ("path, way" also in this case "travel"), *nik* ("one who," like the English agentive *-er*)—"one who travels with, fellow traveler." The speaker of Russian knows other words with the prefix *s-*, and he also knows the preposition *s*, which also means "with." He knows *put* as a morpheme in nouns and in verbs. He also knows the suffix *-nik* from other uses of it. With the possible exception of *-nik,* the speaker of English has none of this information. If he adopts *sputnik* as an English word, he adds it to his lexicon as a single morpheme.

In Modern English there are a great many words whose ultimate origin is Latin or Greek: *transport, amorous, inject, admit, descend, philanthropy, photosynthesis, heterodox,* to name a few. Each of these words consisted of more than one morpheme in the original language, but is there any evidence that they do in the internalized grammars of speakers of Modern English? Many linguists believe that there is justification for dividing *transport* into the prefix *trans-* and the bound base *port,* since the speaker of English knows other words with this prefix and with this base. Along with *transport* and *transportation,* the prefix *trans-* can be seen in such words as *transatlantic, transact, transalpine, transcend, transcribe, transfer, transform, transient, transition, translate, transplant,* and a great many more. Also the base *port* is found not just in *transport,* but also in *passport, support, report, porter, deport, import,* and other words.

Because there are a number of words with the base *port* and a number of others with the prefix *trans-*, it seems reasonable to say that these are morphemes in the internalized grammars of speakers of Modern English. Chomsky and Halle (1968), furthermore, have shown that the stress patterns of such words as *permit, reserve,* and *deter* are determined by their division into prefix and base.

Features of Morphemes

One part of a transformational grammar is the **lexicon**, or dictionary, in which the morphemes of the language are listed, along with their unpredictable features. Anything that is predictable about how the morpheme will appear on the surface is to be included in syntactic and phonological rules. In this way everything that applies systematically to classes of sounds, morphemes, or structures is stated as a rule, and everything that is idiosyncratic is stated in the lexicon.

Regardless of how clearly an object or a concept is defined, there is nothing especially logical or predictable in the choice of sounds which make up the word that expresses this meaning. The phonetic forms of most lexical morphemes have to be learned individually. Knowledge of a number of morphemes in a language does not enable a person to predict the others. For example, a child who has learned *hand, arm, elbow,* and *finger* will not come to realize that the names for the corresponding parts of his lower extremities are *foot, leg, knee,* and *toe* unless he hears these words. Nor will an adult be able to name a *carburetor* or a *condenser* the first time he sees it. The particular combination of sounds which make up a word is unpredictable and must be part of each entry in the lexicon. There are, however, many features of pronunciation which are predictable. The alternation of the second vowel in *divine* and *divinity* is the same as that found in *sublime* and *sublimity* as well as in similar pairs of words and is predictable by a rule which will be discussed in Chapter Eight. Similarly, the placement of stress (or accent) in most English words is systematic, as is the alternation between the *t* and the *sh* sound in *relate, relation; celebrate, celebration.* Also, the pronunciation of the plural of a noun is usually predictable. All predictable features of pronunciation are to be expressed as phonological rules and not as part of the entry in the lexicon. The lexical entry for each morpheme is to contain only that which is unpredictable: the basic forms for *divine, sublime, celebrate,* and other words as well as exceptions to phonological rules (e.g., the plural of *foot* is *feet* rather than *foots,* as the rule would predict).

As for syntactic features, there are probably none which are always unpredictable in the sense that the basic phonological form of the morpheme is. Earlier transformational theory would have assigned the part of speech of each

lexical entry as a syntactic feature, but recent research has questioned the existence of most of the traditional parts-of-speech categories in deep structures. It
seems quite likely that a classification of words into nouns, verbs, adjectives,
adverbs, and other classes is more meaningful for surface than for deep structures.
This idea still needs much investigation, and in the discussion which follows we
will speak of nouns and verbs as being marked in the lexicon as to part of speech.
Some idea of probable lexical entries can be gained from the following examples:

5.6   The door is *open.* (lexical entry *open*)
5.7   I will *open* the door. (lexical entry *open*)
5.8   He is a *friend.* (lexical entry *friend*)
5.9   He is *friendly.* (lexical entry *friend*)
5.10   He *denied* the evidence. (lexical entry *deny*)
5.11   His *denial* of the evidence was surprising. (lexical entry *deny*)
5.12   He is *happy.* (lexical entry *happy*)
5.13   His *happiness* is refreshing. (lexical entry *happy*)
5.14   He did it *happily.* (lexical entry *happy*)

We can compare the basic lexical entry to a syntactic deep structure and the
surface form to a syntactic surface structure; the lexical entry is converted into
the surface form by transformations or some similar process. Part of the lexical
entry will be a statement of which syntactic functions a morpheme may fill and
any idiosyncratic changes in form it undergoes for each of these. Also, for some
morphemes the lexical entries will state that they are exceptions, either not permitting certain transformations or else behaving erratically in their application.

In addition to phonological and syntactic features, there are those which per-
tain to semantics. Until we learn more about how the semantic component of a
grammar functions and interacts with the syntactic component, we cannot be
sure about how meanings should be entered in the lexicon. We do know, however, that some syntactic transformations depend upon such semantic information as whether the morpheme refers to a human or not (e.g., for the choice of
who or *which* in relative clauses), or whether the human is male or female (e.g.,
for the choice of *he* or *she* in pronominalization). Also information of this
nature is essential for deciding which morphemes may be deep structure agents,
instruments, etc. It is customary to make the following semantic classifications.
Some nouns are classified as **count nouns**: *man, chair, duck.* When these nouns
appear in the plural, they designate a collection of separate elements that may
be counted: *two chairs, three chairs, four chairs, five chairs.* Other nouns are
classified as **noncount nouns**: *water, air, sand.* These nouns do not have plural
forms and, therefore, cannot be counted; they usually designate a mass rather
than a collection of individual elements, although some such as *furniture* do not

name masses. Most noncount nouns can at times be made count, and vice versa.
For example, we may speak of the *waters of the world* or we may *eat duck*.
Count nouns may refer to something living and capable of moving (*girl, farmer,
cat, fish*), in which case we say it is **animate**; all others, such as *plant, water, rock,*
are **inanimate**. Anything animate may be **human** (*boy, nurse, Sam*) or **animal**
(*cow, horse, pig*). Humans and animals are either **male** (*Tom, man, rooster*) or
female (*Ann, heiress, hen*). Some animate nouns are not classified for sex, but
rather serve as general terms for either or both sexes: *child, teacher, animal, dog,
bird*. These classifications are illustrated in Figure 5.1.

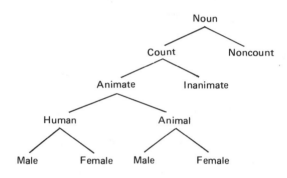

Figure 5.1

Features of verbs were introduced in Chapter Two as case structures. Such
information as the following is to be included as part of the lexical entry for each
verb: [*crack*: P (I) (A)]. That is, *crack* must be accompanied by patient, and it
may have instrument or agent or both. Each case is restricted as to the kind of
nouns that may fill the position; for example, agent nouns must be animate and
instrument nouns must be inanimate. Some verbs have additional restrictions.
Write, for example, requires a human agent, not just animate, and it does not
permit just any inanimate noun as instrument: **He wrote with a window.* All
of the features which are unpredictable are to be listed as part of the lexical
entry for each verb.

In addition to features which are inherent in each morpheme, there are those
which vary from sentence to sentence. *Car* is inherently count and inanimate,
and it retains these features in all sentences unless special conditions apply to
change the feature, such as metaphoric extension to make it human: *The car
laughed at me*. On the other hand, it is not inherently singular or plural; this is
a choice which is made for each sentence by the overall semantic content. The
lexical entry for a count noun will not classify it as singular or plural, since this
is information which must be provided by the semantic structure.

Another feature provided for nouns by the semantic structure is that of **definiteness**. Both count and noncount nouns are specified as **definite** or **non-definite**:

5.15   *The car* backfired. (definite)
5.16   *A car* backfired. (nondefinite)

In 5.15 we are referring to a specific car known to speaker and listener; in 5.16 we are not designating any specific car, because the information is unknown or else unimportant. As with plurality, there is nothing inherently definite or nondefinite about *car*. The semantic structure designates each noun as to definiteness, and a rule (possibly in the phonological component) indicates how the concept is to be expressed. On the surface there are several possibilities:

                        Definite
5.17   *The man* laughed. (count singular)
5.18   *The men* laughed. (count plural)
5.19   *The water* is boiling. (noncount)
                        Nondefinite
5.20   *A man* laughed. (count singular)
5.21   *Men* laughed. (count plural)
5.22   *Some men* laughed. (count plural)
5.23   He drank *water*. (noncount)
5.24   He drank *some water*. (noncount)

Also such determiners as *this, that, these,* and *those* denote definiteness, but they also indicate whether the object named is near or far from the speaker, and they have the additional effect of pointing out or being demonstrative.

Let us see how these features should appear in a deep structure. Omitting inherent features and adding prepositions, we draw the tree for the deep structure of *The boys laughed* like this:

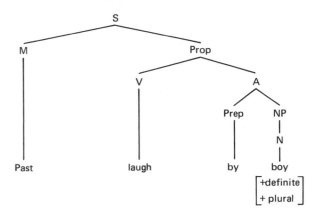

A rule will realize [+definite] as *the* unless demonstrativeness is also indicated, in which case it will be *these* or *those*. The idea of plurality will also be realized by a morpheme spelled *s*. (A more thorough explanation will be given in Chapter Seven.) After *the* and *s* have been added, the surface noun phrase will be

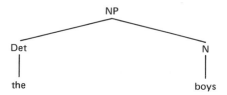

Transformations can add morphemes, but only if their meaning is given by the semantic structure and if their final forms are predictable. In the noun phrase *the boys*, the base morpheme *boy* is unpredictable and must be obtained from the lexicon. Neither *the* nor the *-s* plural is listed in the lexicon; they can be inserted by rule since their final forms are predictable from the meanings *definite* and *plural*.

In a similar way the tense of the verb is given a final form by a phonological rule (to be discussed in Chapter Seven). Verbs have other features whose final forms are predictable, namely those of **aspect**, which specify the action of the verb as beginning, ending, being repeated, etc. The **progressive aspect** denotes continuing action:

5.25   The car *is* stopp*ing*. (cf. The car stops.)
5.26   They *were* laugh*ing*. (cf. They laughed.)

In surface structures the progressive is indicated by a form of *be* and the suffix *-ing*. Depending upon the subject, the forms of *be* are (1) *am, is, are* (present tense), (2) *was, were* (past tense), (3) *be, been, being* (without tense). The deep structure for *The horses were running* looks like this:

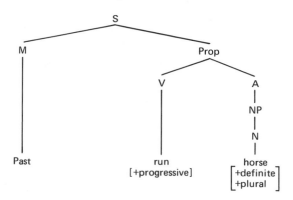

Transformations convert this into the following surface structure:

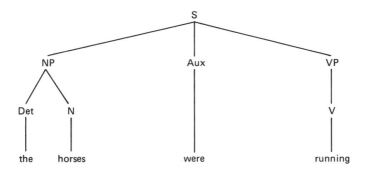

Like the final forms of *plural* and *past*, that of *progressive* is predictable and is, therefore, given by rule.

Another predictable surface form of the verb is that which is known as the **perfect**:

5.27   He *has* see*n* you. (cf. He sees you.)
5.28   They *have* eat*en*. (cf. They eat.)
5.29   We *had* help*ed* him. (cf. We helped him.)

On the surface the perfect form is *have* (*has* or *have* for present, *had* for past) and the past participial form of the verb. We encountered the past participle earlier in Chapter Two with passive structures. The verb in the deep structure of 5.27 will be given as follows:

see
[+perfect]

It is also possible to have a deep structure representation such as this:

listen
$$\begin{bmatrix} +\text{perfect} \\ +\text{progressive} \end{bmatrix}$$

Transformational rules convert this into *had been listening, has been listening,* or *have been listening*, depending upon the tense and subject.

An alternate means of treating the deep structures of progressives and perfects is the same as that for sentence 5.30:

5.30   He seemed to be honest.

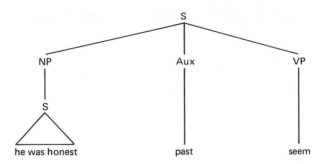

The structure underlying *He was laughing* would be something like this:

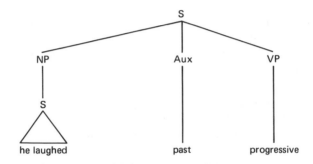

Transformational rules such as subject raising and the progressive would eventually give the surface structure *He was laughing*. We will not examine the relative merits of the two approaches, since our sole purpose here is to illustrate that certain surface forms of the verb are predictable from the semantic structure.

Noun Plurals

The features we have been considering are the most important for English, but they represent only a part of those found in the languages of the world. These features may be expressed on the surface by affixes (*buttons, jumped*), in which case we call them **inflections**. Or they may be expressed by separate words (*the book, have eaten*). In deep structures they are probably all expressed in the same way. We will now consider some of the features in more detail and account for some of their irregularities in Modern English.

Number is almost always expressed in English nouns, whether the feature is really significant or not. There is no neutral form of the noun which does not commit itself to being singular or plural. Also, present-tense verbs show agreement with third-person subjects:

5.31   The building seems tall.
5.32   The buildings seem tall.

The verb *be* shows agreement in both present and past tense with third-person subjects:

5.33   This pencil *is* sharp.
5.34   These pencils *are* sharp.
5.35   That pencil *was* sharp.
5.36   Those pencils *were* sharp.

In addition, certain other words are restricted by the number of the noun: *a, this, that (singular); many, several, these, those, etc. (plural)*. Even noncount nouns must be given number, and that is usually singular.

5.37   Patience *is* a virtue.
5.38   *These* scissors *are* dull.

As 5.38 shows, a noncount noun may be plural. In each case the noun is the morpheme which is initially given the feature singular or plural, and the other morphemes are made to agree with it.

All dialects of Modern English do not agree in their use of singular or plural nouns in certain positions. In Old English the genitive plural form of the noun was used after numbers: *six fota*, "six feet" (literally, "six of feet"). By the end of the Middle English period, all final unstressed vowels were lost, and the regular development was *six foot, seven mile, eight tooth*, etc. In some dialects this convention has been preserved, especially in nouns of measurement:

5.39a   I am six *foot* tall.
5.40a   He lives seven *mile* from here.

Other dialects have extended the use of plural forms to give

5.39b   I am six *feet* tall.
5.40b   He lives seven *miles* from here.

All dialects continue to use the earlier form for modifiers: *a six-foot pole, a seven-mile hike*.

Also, certain peculiarities in Modern English plural formations can be traced to the situation in Old English. As was true for Latin and Greek, each noun in

Old English belonged to one of several possible declensions. The declension to which a noun belonged determined the phonetic shape of its inflectional suffixes. In Chapter Four we illustrated one of these declensions with such sentences as *Se blaca hund arn*, "The black dog ran." These endings are found only in the nouns of this one declension. Each declension had its own endings. As an illustration of the various possibilities, we can look at the following declensions in Old English:

	masculine *a*	neuter *a*	*ō*	*n*	athematic
		Singular			
	"hound"	"word"	"gift"	"ox"	"foot"
Nominative	hund	word	giefu	oxa	fot
Genitive	hundes	wordes	giefe	oxan	fotes
Dative	hunde	worde	giefe	oxan	fet
Accusative	hund	word	giefe	oxan	fot
		Plural			
Nominative	hundas	word	giefa	oxan	fet
Genitive	hunda	worda	giefa	oxena	fota
Dative	hundum	wordum	giefum	oxum	fotum
Accusative	hundas	word	giefa	oxan	fet

Although there were other declensions as well, these are the most important for later developments.

The classifications such as *a* and *athematic* refer to the Indo-European system of inflectional formation, wherein each noun consisted of a base, a theme vowel or consonant, and a case ending. We can see this system preserved in classical Greek in the declension of *logos*, "word":

	Singular	Plural
Nominative	logos	logoi
Genitive	logou	logōn
Dative	logō	logois
Accusative	logon	logous

The base is *log*, the theme vowel is *o*, and the letters following *o* are the ending which designates case and number. The inflectional endings are the regular Greek developments from Indo-European. In Old English nouns, such bases as *hund, word, gief, ox,* and *fot* are easily seen, but the theme vowel or consonant and the inflectional endings have merged. In the Old English examples, the terms

a declension, ō declension, and *n declension* designate the Old English developments of the Indo-European theme vowels and consonants. Indo-European may
have had as many as ten or twelve different declensions. In one of these the
inflectional endings were added directly to the base without a theme vowel or
consonant; these are called **athematic nouns.**

Eventually only the nominative and the genitive survived in the singular and
only the nominative in the plural. For example, in Modern English we have the
following forms:

5.41   The *dog* barked. (corresponding to OE nominative singular)
5.42   The *dog's* tail wagged. (genitive singular in OE)
5.43   He threw the *dog* a bone. (dative singular in OE)
5.44   He kicked the *dog.* (accusative singular in OE)
5.45   The *dogs* barked. (nominative plural in OE)
5.46   The *dogs'* tails wagged. (genitive plural in OE)
5.47   He threw the *dogs* some bones. (dative plural in OE)
5.48   He kicked the *dogs.* (accusative plural in OE)

All the singular forms are alike except for the genitive. In pronunciation all the
plural forms are alike, although we add an apostrophe in writing the genitive.

Let us consider the developments of the various declensions, restricting ourselves to the nominative case, singular and plural.

Masculine *a* Declension

Old English		Modern English	
Singular	Plural	Singular	Plural
hund	hundas	hound	hounds
catt	cattas	cat	cats
cyning	cyningas	king	kings
stan	stanas	stone	stones

In each case the Modern English plural form is the regular development of
the Old English plural. Such changes as occurred to the vowels and consonants in the plural ending were governed by regular phonological rules. The
number of nouns in this declension was quite large in Old English times, and
the system it used for forming plurals eventually became the only regular
one.

Neuter *a* Declension

Old English		Modern English	
Singular	Plural	Singular	Plural
sceap	sceap	sheep	*sheep*
deor	deor	deer	*deer*
folc	folc	folk	folk(s)
land	land	land	lands
scip	scipu	ship	ships
lim	limu	limb	limbs

As the last four examples show, most nouns belonging to this declension now form their plurals according to the rules for nouns of the masculine *a* declension. If this change had not occurred, these nouns and a number of others would show no difference in form between singular and plural. Such constructions as *those land are* and *those ship are* would be as natural today as is *those sheep are*. *Sheep* and *deer* have not made the change but retain the Old English system for plurals of nouns in this declension.

$\bar{o}$ Declension

Old English		Modern English	
Singular	Plural	Singular	Plural
glof	glofa	glove	gloves
talu	tala	tale	tales
giefu	giefa	gift	gifts
andswaru	andswara	answer	answers

Since all unstressed vowels in final position were lost by the end of the Middle English period, the regular development of nouns in this declension would be without ending for the plural. The regular forms, then, would be six *glove*, five *tale*, four *gift*, three *answer*. All of the nouns in this declension now form their plurals according to the rules for the masculine *a* declension.

n Declension

Old English		Modern English	
Singular	Plural	Singular	Plural
oxa	oxan	ox	*oxen*
nama	naman	name	names

tunge	tungan	tongue	tongues
heorte	heortan	heart	hearts
eage	eagan	eye	eyes
eare	earan	ear	ears

The regular development of the plurals of these nouns would have been *oxen, namen, tonguen, hearten, eyen,* and *earen.* Except for *oxen,* all the nouns in this declension now form their plurals according to the rules for the masculine *a* declension. *Brethren* and *children* now have the *–en* plural, but in Old English they belonged to other declensions; the *–en* is a later addition.

Athematic Nouns

| Old English | | Modern English | |
Singular	Plural	Singular	Plural
fot	fet	foot	*feet*
toð	teð	tooth	*teeth*
gos	ges	goose	*geese*
boc	bec	book	books
gat	get	goat	goats
man	men	man	*men*
wifman	wifmen	woman	*women*
lus	lys	louse	*lice*
mus	mys	mouse	*mice*
cu	cy	cow	cows

Only seven nouns in this declension continue to form their plurals according to the Old English system, the others now using the system for the masculine *a* declension. If this change had not occurred, the plurals for *book, goat,* and *cow* would now be something like *beek, geet,* and *ky.*

Part of the lexical entry for each noun in Old English was the declension to which it belonged. The native speaker had to learn this information as one of the unpredictable features of each noun so that he would know which endings to use. During the course of the Middle English period, all nouns lost their declensional classifications in the lexicon, and most of them began forming their plurals according to the rules governing the masculine *a* declension (*hound, hounds*). A few nouns resisted this change and maintained their original plural formations; these are italicized in the above listing. To give some idea of the Old English lexical entries for nouns as compared to those of today, we can make a listing, ignoring all parts of each entry except those relating to inflection:

	Old English		Modern English	
hund	masculine *a*		*hound*	
catt	masculine *a*		*cat*	
sceap	neuter *a*		*sheep*	pl. *sheep*
land	neuter *a*		*land*	
glof	*ō*		*glove*	
oxa	*n*		*ox*	pl. *oxen*
nama	*n*		*name*	
fot	athematic		*foot*	pl. *feet*
toð	athematic		*tooth*	pl. *teeth*
gat	athematic		*goat*	

In addition, in the grammar of Old English there were rules for forming the surface case forms, singular and plural, for nouns in each declension. In Modern
English there is one set of rules for forming noun plurals in general; no noun is
labeled for declension. The only nouns that have special labels in the Modern
English lexicon are those which do not follow the rules. Although such plurals
as *oxen, sheep,* and *feet* are survivals of formations that were perfectly regular
in Old English, today they are exceptions.

Some nouns retained their exceptional plurals longer than others. *Kind* and
folk, for example, have only recently started taking the plurals *kinds* and *folks*
in some dialects; in others the plurals *kind* and *folk* are still in use. Also, some
nouns have acquired exceptional plurals since Old English times. In Old English,
fisc, "fish," belonged to the masculine *a* declension, for which *fishes* is the regular plural development. It has since then acquired the plural *fish* as well. In
addition, most types of fish now have exceptional plurals, so that we may speak
of catching six *bass, trout, perch,* or *carp*. According to most dictionaries, the
regular plurals *basses, trouts, perches,* and *carps* are also still in existence.

A number of exceptional plurals in Modern English are derived from other
languages. When such Latin nouns as *alumna, formula, fungus, stimulus, adden-
dum, bacterium, basis,* and *crisis* were first introduced into English, most of the
people who used them knew Latin and felt it only natural to borrow the plural
form along with the singular: *alumnae, formulae, fungi, stimuli, addenda, bac-
teria, bases, crises*. Also such Greek plurals as *criteria, phenomena,* and *stigmata*
were borrowed with their singulars *criterion, phenomenon,* and *stigma*. Although
each of these plurals was formed regularly and predictably by rule in the original
language, in English they are all exceptional. Most of these words retain their
original plurals so long as they are used primarily as technical terms by a limited
number of scholars. Those which pass into the general vocabulary, however,
often lose their exceptional status and begin forming their plurals by the rules
for English. Earlier *hippopotami, campi, stadia,* and *gymnasia* have become

hippopotamuses, campuses, stadiums, and *gymnasiums* for most people. Others have two plurals, depending upon the sense in which they are used: *formulae* for mathematicians but *formulas* for babies; communications *media* but *mediums* of the occult. Some nouns have undergone further changes. Originally *datum* was a singular noun with the plural *data*, as it still is for many people. Other people do not have *datum* in their lexicons, but rather treat *data* as a noncount noun like *information.*

When a noun loses its exceptional plural and begins following the rules for English plural formation, there is a change in the lexicon, as we can see from the following abbreviated entries:

Earlier Lexicon		Later Lexicon	
cat		cat	
dog		dog	
fish		fish	pl. fish
sheep	pl. sheep	sheep	pl. sheep
land	pl. land	land	
folk	pl. folk	folk	
ox	pl. oxen	ox	pl. oxen
name	pl. namen	name	
foot	pl. feet	foot	pl. feet
goat	pl. geet	goat	
alumnus	pl. alumni	alumnus	pl. alumni
campus	pl. campi	campus	

The change that occurs is a loss of part of the lexical entry. All count nouns that are not given an exceptional marking in the lexicon form their plurals by rules which we will discuss in Chapter Seven.

Another kind of change occurs when speakers make a faulty identification of morphemes. Since speakers of English form all regular plurals by rules, they are immediately able to give the plural of any new noun they learn even if they have heard only the singular. Similarly, if it is the plural that they hear first (*cosmonauts, sputniks*), they are able to change it to the singular (*cosmonaut, sputnik*). The flower *gladiolus* has the plural *gladioli*, a regular Latin formation like *alumnus, alumni*. To many people the *s* on the end of *gladiolus* sounded like a plural of a form *gladiola*, so they began saying *these gladiolus are*, rather than *this gladiolus is, these gladioli are*. The next step was to create a new singular: *gladiola*. This kind of creation from a mistaken morphemic analysis is known as a **back formation**. In the case of *gladiolus*, not one morpheme was seen but two: *gladiola* and *plural*. Another example of back formation can be seen in *peas*, originally a noncount noun like *spinach, cheese,* and *milk*. Because

of the last sound in the word, people misinterpreted it as a plural and changed
from *the peas is* (cf. *the cheese is*) to *the peas are*. Next, the new singular *pea*
was created by back formation. The process has not been applied to *cheese* to
give *one chee*, but the principle would be the same if it were. Here are some
other examples of sounds mistaken for plurals:

Original singular	Singular by back formation
eaves	eave
cherise	cherry
assets	asset
Chinese	Chinee
Portuguese	Portugee

A person developing a lexicon and grammar has no way of distinguishing back
formations such as *asset, cherry, eave,* and *pea* from such words as *knee, bee,*
and *berry*, all of which are treated as singulars whose plurals are formed regularly.
The individual's lexicon, therefore, will not be in accordance with historical facts.

Verb Inflections

    Just as the noun in Modern English has a regular system for plural formation,
so the verb has a system for forming past tenses and past participles. Like nouns,
all verbs do not conform to the system. Modern English verbs which are inflected
by rule show no difference in form between the past tense and the past participle, both of which end in the suffix spelled *d* or *ed* (a more precise description
will be given in Chapter Seven): *jump, jumped, jumped.* There are other verbs
whose past-tense and past-participial forms are produced by a change of the
vowel in the base rather than by the addition of a suffix: *ring, rang, rung.* Following the practice of the nineteenth-century philologist and collector of children's
stories, Jacob Grimm, we refer to verbs which are inflected by the addition of a
suffix (*jumped*) as **weak** and to those which change the vowel (*rang*) as **strong**.
Because of various changes not related to inflection, some verbs such as *buy* have
both vocalic change and a suffix. A form such as *bought* is classified as a weak
formation because of the *–t* suffix. The same is true for *sell, bring, catch, seek,
tell, teach, think, say, keep, deal, leap, sweep, sleep, creep,* and a few others. In
each case it is the suffix that produces the past-tense or past-participial inflection; the change in vowel is brought about for other reasons.
    In Indo-European the regular inflectional form was the strong verb, like *ring.*
At one time certain features of the verb were seemingly expressed on the surface
by the stress pattern (accent). For one feature the main stress fell on the base,

for another on the theme vowel, for another on the suffix. Vowels are frequently not pronounced the same way when they are unstressed as they are when stressed. Although Modern English spelling does not reveal this process, the first vowel in *grámmar* is not pronounced the same as the first one in *grammárian*. Other differences can be heard in the first vowels of *cóntract* (noun), *contráct* (verb); *repéat, repetítion; ácid, acídity*; and many more words. This vocalic change caused by the presence or absence of stress is called **gradation** or **ablaut**. In the Indo-European verb, the vocalic changes were predictable by rule. In the Germanic languages several changes occurred which obscured the regularity of the Indo-European system. Nevertheless, it is possible to set up rules to account for most of the vocalic changes in the Old English strong verbs, although a great many more rules are needed than were for Indo-European.

In addition to the strong verb, a new type of formation emerged in the Germanic languages: the weak formation which added a suffix, as in Modern English *drop, dropped*. During historical times there has been a steady trend of strong verbs giving way to the weak. Except for a handful of exceptions, all verbs added to the language from the early Old English period through the present have been added as weak verbs: *escalate, bulldog, tackle, rope, elbow*. Today with not more than fifty strong verbs in widespread use, it is probable that they are listed as exceptions in the lexicons of speakers of English. Like plurals such as *deer* and *oxen*, past-tense forms like *sang, ate,* and *rode* were once perfectly regular; now they are not.

Many of the Old English strong verbs have been lost from the language: *stigan*, "to go," *weorpan*, "to cast," *hatan*, "to command," *teon*, "to blame," to name a few. Others have lost their exceptional marking in the lexicon and now follow the rules for the weak formation: *bow, glide, help, melt, yield, yell, climb*. In some dialects the original strong forms *holp* and *clumb* have survived; and the past participle *molten* has survived, but only as an adjective: *molten lead*, but *The lead has melted*.

Some verbs now have both weak and strong formations: *awake, thrive, light, prove* (past participle only). There are others with alternate formations which have different meanings:

5.49   He *shined* his shoes.
5.50   The sun *shone*.
5.51   They *hanged* him until he was dead.
5.52   They *hung* the picture.

A number of verbs have remained strong but have followed the principle set by the weak verbs of not distinguishing between past-tense and past-participial forms. The past tense of *cling* was originally *clang*, but this is decidedly archaic now; *clung* is both past tense and past participle. The same change has occurred or is occurring in several other verbs: *shrink, stink, slink, swing, string, wring, sting, fling, sling, spin, spring.* For some speakers additional verbs no longer differ in their past-tense and past-participial forms: *drink (he drank it; he has drank it); sink (the boat sank; the boat has sank* or *the boat sunk; the boat has sunk); swim (he swam; he has swam)*, to name a few. In Early Modern English it seemed that all strong verbs were reducing the number of principal parts. Such forms as *have spoke, had rode, was wove,* and *have swam* are fairly common in the works of Shakespeare, Milton, and their contemporaries.

The lexical entries for most verbs do not include inflectional information; only those verbs whose inflected forms are not produced by rules have this information given. Hence, *jump, knock, drag,* and most other verbs do not have their past-tense or past-participial forms listed in the lexicon; but verbs like *see, drink,* and *eat* do. In addition, a few older past participles whose use is now restricted to an adjectival function have their own listings distinct from those of the verbs to which they are etymologically related: *drunken, shrunken, cloven, trodden.* When a verb such as *glide, climb, abide,* or *thrive* becomes weak, there is little change in the grammar; the lexical entry for the affected verb loses its exceptional marking, and it then meets the requirements of the rules for verb inflections.

Derivational Affixes

The purpose of the lexicon in the grammar we are describing is to give the morphemes of the language and their unpredictable features. All predictable features which are shared by classes of morphemes should be expressed in terms of rules and placed in the transformational or phonological component of the grammar. In this way all significant generalizations about the language will be expressed.

Probably no one would consider giving *slip, slips, slipped,* and *slipping* four separate entries in a lexicon. Although the four forms have slightly different meanings, these differences are predictable by the endings *-s, -ed,* and *-ing.* There is a basic meaning common to all four forms, a meaning which we recognize in the base *slip.* Some of the suffixes are predictable by information in the deep structure, such as [+progressive] for *is slipping* or [+perfect] for *has slipped.* Others result from such transformations as *for-to (for him to slip)* and *poss-ing (his slipping).* Still others can be predicted by a preceding present-tense *(slip, slips)* or past-tense morpheme *(slipped).* Rather than set up four separate lexical entries for *slip, slips, slipped,* and *slipping,* we give only the basic form *slip* and state rules for determining the final surface forms.

To be of any value, a rule must make a generalization about an entire class of structures, not just about one. If the statement for deriving the four surface forms of *slip* were applicable only to this one word, they would not be rules, but merely a listing of idiosyncratic features. As it is, they are applicable to all English verbs. It is true that some verbs such as *see* and *bring* differ from *slip* in the ways their past-tense and past-participial forms are realized on the surface, but they are alike in where the forms are used.

Also, it is not enough that a rule be applicable to a class of structures rather than to just one; the rule must express a generalization that is significant in revealing how some aspect of the language operates. The significance of a generalization is relative to the goals a person is trying to attain. We can make the following analyses:

$$
\begin{array}{cccc}
A_1 & A_2 & B_1 & B_2
\end{array}
$$

$$
\begin{array}{c}
\text{slip} \\
\text{slips} \\
\text{slipping} \\
\text{slipped}
\end{array}
=
\text{slip} +
\left\{
\begin{array}{c}
s \\
\text{ing} \\
\text{ed}
\end{array}
\right\}
\qquad
\begin{array}{c}
\text{slipping} \\
\text{flipping} \\
\text{clipping} \\
\text{tripping}
\end{array}
=
\left\{
\begin{array}{c}
\text{slip} \\
\text{flip} \\
\text{clip} \\
\text{trip}
\end{array}
\right\}
+ \text{ing}
$$

In A_2 we are saying that all the words in A_1 have the morpheme *slip* in common. In B_2 we are saying that all the words in B_1 have the morpheme *ing* in common. If the only reason for our analysis is to find like elements in a class of words, it seems that the following should also be possible:

$$
\begin{array}{cc}
C_1 & C_2
\end{array}
$$

$$
\begin{array}{c}
\text{slip} \\
\text{flip} \\
\text{clip} \\
\text{trip}
\end{array}
=
\left\{
\begin{array}{c}
\text{sl} \\
\text{fl} \\
\text{cl} \\
\text{tr}
\end{array}
\right\}
+ \text{ip}
$$

We would be saying that there is a class of words that have *-ip* in common. If the purpose of our investigation is to prepare a dictionary of rhymes or to determine which sounds may occur at the beginning of an English word, the results might be of interest; as a proposed generalization for syntax they are worthless. *Ing* is predictable because of the preceding progressive auxiliary *be* or because of the application of the *poss-ing* transformation. It also conveys the same meaning in all verbs to which it is joined. *Ip*, on the other hand, is not predictable. Our "generalization" does not lend itself to rules which will tell us why we find *slip* in some sentences but *slide* in others. *Ing* is a morpheme, but *ip* is not. Syntactic operations affect morphemes, not just sounds.

It is obvious, then, that a lexicon should contain only one entry for *slip, slips, slipped,* and *slipping* as well as for other verbs, all endings being introduced by rules (except for a few exceptions, such as *caught*). In this way the four forms can be shown to be related as can the corresponding inflected forms in other verbs: *slipping, dropping, knocking,* etc. This is the way different inflections are treated now in dictionaries, and no major approach to the study of language has suggested a different arrangement. The traditional treatment of words with derivational affixes has not been the same. For example, several affixes can be added to *respect*:

respect	*dis*respect
respect*able*	*dis*respect*able*
respect*ability*	*dis*respect*ful*
respect*ableness*	*dis*respect*fully*
respect*ably*	*dis*respect*fulness*

Many dictionaries indicate the relatedness of some of these words by making cross references or by listing some of them without definition at the end of an entry. A question arises as to whether this kind of treatment is adequate. There are several reasons for suspecting that it is not. (1) The central meaning of *respect,* which is found in all ten of the above words, could no doubt be better shown by giving just one entry (*respect*). General rules for derivation could then be listed separately, enabling a person to form all of the derived words even though they would not be found in the lexicon. (2) Entries such as those under *A* would reveal similarities in derived forms that would not be indicated by entries such as those under *B*:

A	B	
agree	agree	predict
laugh	agreeable	predictable
manage	laugh	rely
predict	laughable	reliable
rely	manage	regret
regret	manageable	regrettable
Rule for forming		
adjectives with *–able*		

That is, a rule stating how to form derived words would express a generalization which is only implied by a system such as *B*, which merely lists all words, whether derived or not. (3) A system which provides for derived words by rule accounts for the creation and understanding of new words, whereas the system which gives nothing more than a listing does not. The native speaker of English has not learned all derived and nonderived words separately, or the following sentences would not be intelligible:

5.53   This meat is *unfryable.*
5.54   These chairs are not *paintable.*
5.55   This fabric is *drycleanable.*

These sentences are understandable in spite of the new words they contain because the speaker of English knows the meaning of the suffix *-able*, and he knows that it can be added to verbs to produce adjectives with the meaning "capable of being____ed."

A great many derived words appear as parts of units which function as noun phrases. The following sentences provide examples:

5.56   *For Mike to accept the money* was a surprise.
5.57   *Mike's accepting the money* was a surprise.
5.58   *Mike's acceptance of the money* was a surprise.

Each of the italicized structures is derived from the structure underlying the sentence *Mike accepted the money.* A noun phrase which is derived from an underlying sentence is called a **nominalization**. In Chapter Three we saw how 5.56–5.57 are derived by the *for-to* and the *poss-ing* transformations. All three sentences share the same relationship between *Mike* and *accept* and between *accept* and *the money*. These same relationships are found in the sentence *Mike accepted the money.* In the sentence the verb contains tense but neither complementizer nor affix, whereas in the nominalizations the verb contains a complementizer or an affix but not tense. It seems, then, that we should include in our grammar a *poss-ance* transformation to accompany *for-to* and *poss-ing.*

If all verbs behaved under nominalization like *accept*, such a suggestion might be attractive. For example, we could start with the structures which underlie the following sentences:

5.59a   Ann allowed for error.
5.60a   They attended the meeting.
5.61a   Mike rejected the money.
5.62a   We achieved the goal.
5.63a   He arrived at six o'clock.
5.64a   Mark complained about the food.
5.65a   Maxine recovered from the flu.
5.66a   I departed for Atlanta.

The proposed *poss-ance* transformation would produce

5.59b	Ann's allowance for error
5.60b	their attendance at the meeting
5.61b	*Mike's rejectance of the money
5.62b	*our achievance of the goal
5.63b	*his arrivance at six o'clock
5.64b	*Mark's complainance about the food
5.65b	*Maxine's recoverance from the flu
5.66b	*my departance for Atlanta

Unlike *-ing*, which can be attached to almost all verbs, *-ance* is highly restricted, occurring with *accept, allow,* and *attend* but not with *reject, achieve,* and *arrive*. The *poss-ing* transformation is uniform for all of the above sentences:

5.59c	Ann's allowing for error
5.60c	their attending the meeting
5.61c	Mike's rejecting the money
5.62c	our achieving the goal
5.63c	his arriving at six o'clock
5.64c	Mark's complaining about the food
5.65c	Maxine's recovering from the flu
5.66c	my departing for Atlanta

However, different suffixes are required for the derived nominalizations:

5.61d	Mike's rejec*tion* of the money
5.62d	our achieve*ment* of the goal
5.63d	his arriv*al* at six o'clock
5.64d	Mark's complain*t* about the food
5.65d	Maxine's recover*y* from the flu
5.66d	my depart*ure* for Atlanta

The speaker of English has to know which suffix each verb permits, and a transformational lexicon will have to indicate this information as an unpredictable feature of each verb. A *poss-ance* transformation, then, is out of the question, but perhaps it is possible to have a more general nominalization transformation which utilizes information from the lexicon about which suffixes are possible for each verb.

Probably no linguist would suggest listing *arrival, betrayal, refusal,* and *denial* as separate lexical entries unrelated to *arrive, betray, refuse,* and *deny*, but they are far from agreeing about how the relationships should be indicated. Our suggestion of a nominalization transformation which utilizes lexical information about the suffixes permitted by each verb is not accepted by everyone. Like all other parts of the grammar, this proposed transformation may have to be changed after future research provides us with more information.

Compounding

Instead of adding affixes to a base to form a new word, we may add two or more bases together to produce a **compound**. If we add *side* and *walk* together, we form *sidewalk*. English spelling is inconsistent in its treatment of compounds. For example, *bedbug* is written solid, but *sow bug* is written open. In the discussion of compounding in *Webster's Seventh New Collegiate Dictionary*, *prizefighter* is used as an example of a word which may appear solid (*prizefighter*), open (*prize fighter*), or hyphenated (*prize-fighter*). Dictionaries vary greatly in their spelling of some compounds. The hyphenated representation *half-cocked* is given in *Webster's Seventh New Collegiate Dictionary* and in *The Random House Dictionary of the English Language*. The open *half cocked* is given in *Webster's New World Dictionary of the American Language*. And the solid *halfcocked* is given in *Funk and Wagnalls Standard College Dictionary* and in *The American Heritage Dictionary of the English Language*.

Because many compounds in English are frequently written open, it is easy to underestimate their frequency. If such formations as *life insurance company* and *football player* were written solid as *lifeinsurancecompany* and *footballplayer* as they are in German (*Lebensversicherungsgesellschaft, Fussballspieler*), their number would be more evident. The new words section of recent issues of the *Britannica Yearbook* show that around 60 percent of the words added each year are compounds. This process of word formation has been especially popular throughout the Old English and Modern English periods.

Since spelling is an unreliable guide to the identification of compounds, how can a person distinguish between a noun phrase containing an adjective and a noun such as *a blue book* ("a book that is blue") and a compound noun such as *a blue book* ("an examination booklet")? In the noun phrase the noun has a heavier stress than the adjective, whereas in the compound the first element has the heavier stress. Using the marks ′(primary), ^(secondary), and ‵(tertiary) for descending degrees of stress, we can mark the noun phrase as *a blûe boók* and the compound as *a blúe boòk*. The following words provide additional examples:

Noun phrase	Compound	Noun phrase	Compound
a greên hoúse	a greénhoùse	a roûgh néck	a roúghnèck
a hîgh chaír	a híghchaìr	a hôt dóg	a hót dòg
a hîgh báll	a híghbàll	a tîght wàd	a tíghtwàd

Although the stress pattern is usually a reliable guide to compounds, there are exceptions: *Long Island, New York, left fielder, openhearted,* etc.

Usually a compound has a more specialized meaning than the corresponding noun phrase. A *bláckbìrd* is not just any bird that is black, *a blâck bírd,* but a specific kind. Similarly, a *hígh chaìr* is a special kind of *hîgh chaír.* Similar specialized meanings can be seen in *badlands, moving van, Good Book, White House, tightrope, cold cream.*

After a compound has gained widespread use, speakers of the language may lose track of its origin as two or more morphemes and think of it as an indivisible unit. It is doubtful that many people think of *sidewalk* or *windshield* as more than one morpheme. It is possible to eat a cold *hot dog,* to write on a green *blackboard,* to take an exam in a pink *blue book,* or to celebrate July 4 as a *holiday.* Also, compounds are especially susceptible to metaphoric extension: *a goose egg, an eagle eye, a horse laugh, a cat nap, rabbit ears, a cow lick, a wolf whistle, to hog tie, a sheepskin, a pigskin, a bear hug, leapfrog.* With loss of stress on the second element or with other changes in pronunciation, the two elements in the compound may become especially obscure: *breakfast, cupboard, holiday* (from *holy day*), *hussy* (from *house wife*), *window* (from *wind eye*), *sheriff* (from *shire reeve*), *garlic* (from *gar leek*), *Sinclair* (from *St. Clair*), *Townsend* (from *town's end*), *Charleston* (from *Charles' town*).

Compounds are not restricted to structures of adjective plus noun like *blackbird* and *highball.* Here are some other possibilities:

Noun + Noun:	grass stain, doormat, cell block, grammar school, soapsuds, ropedance
Adverb + Noun:	downstroke, upstairs, off-color, onlooker
Verb + Noun:	scarecrow, watchman, daredevil
Adverb + Verb:	undertake, withstand, overtake
Adjective + Participle:	heavy-set, long-winded, short-sighted
Adjective + Adjective:	bittersweet, dead wrong, blue-black
Noun + Adjective	dirt cheap, stone cold, sky blue

The most abundant types are those consisting of noun plus noun and adjective plus noun.

Except for the comments on the parts of speech that make up a compound, our observations have all been concerned with surface manifestations. Is everything about compounds clear on the surface, or is there a need for some kind of different underlying representation which is related transformationally to surface forms? Adjectives in noun phrases such as *a dârk roóm* are derived from underlying embedded relative clauses. Could compounds perhaps be derived the same way, with underlying relatives for *a darkroom, a soft spot, a hard hat,* and others? One problem with this approach involves meaning. As we saw earlier, a compound often does not mean exactly the same thing as the corresponding noun phrase. Sentences 5.67 and 5.68 mean the same thing, but 5.69 is different:

5.67   He worked in a dârk roóm.
5.68   He worked in a room that was dark.
5.69   He worked in a dárkroòm.

In addition, there is much variation in the syntactic relationships between the parts of a compound. A *houseboat* is a boat that serves as a house, but a *house cat* is a cat that lives in a house. A wide range of relationships can be seen in the following list:

housebreaker	householder	housemother	house shoe
house cat	housekeeper	house number	house top
housecoat	houselights	house painter	house trailer
housefly	housemaid	house party	housewife
house guest	houseman	house rent	housework

One difficulty with providing underlying forms for compounds such as these is that in most cases the native speaker's understanding of the relationships is based not so much on his knowledge of the language as it is on his other knowledge, such as what a cat, a fly, a guest, or a painter normally does in regard to a house. No adequate suggestion has yet been made as to how to handle this kind of knowledge. In fact, many linguists feel that nonlinguistic knowledge such as this has no place in linguistic analysis. Yet speakers of English can create new compounds almost as readily as they can new sentences, and other people can understand them. Perhaps grammars of the future will be able to account for this ability better than we can now.

Conclusion

In this chapter we have examined the classification and features of morphemes and have considered some of the characteristics of inflectional endings, derivational affixes, and compounds. Although no aspect of language has been described completely, both syntax and phonology have progressed more rapidly in recent years than morphology. Linguists have barely begun to investigate the deeper properties of the morpheme that are not obvious on the surface.

Suggested Reading

Bloomfield, Leonard. *Language*. New York: Holt, Rinehart and Winston, 1933. Chapters 13-16, 22-23.

Chomsky, Noam. "Remarks on Nominalization" in Jacobs and Rosenbaum, 1970.

Francis, W. Nelson. *The Structure of American English*. New York: Ronald Press Company, 1958. Chapter 4.

Fraser, Bruce. "Some Remarks on the Action Nominalization in English" in Jacobs and Rosenbaum, 1970.

Gleason, H. A., Jr. *An Introduction to Descriptive Linguistics*. New York: Holt, Rinehart and Winston, 1955, 1961. Chapters 5-9.

Hockett, Charles F. *A Course in Modern Linguistics*. New York: Macmillan Co., 1958. Chapters 14-15.

Lees, Robert B. *The Grammar of English Nominalizations*. Bloomington: Indiana University Research Center in Anthropology, Folklore, and Linguistics, 1963.

Marchand, H. *The Categories and Types of Present-Day English Word-Formation*. University, Ala.: University of Alabama Press, 1966.

Nida, Eugene A. *Morphology*. Ann Arbor: University of Michigan Press, 1946, 1949.

Stageberg, Norman C. *An Introductory English Grammar*. New York: Holt, Rinehart and Winston, 1965, 1971. Chapters 8-10.

CHAPTER SIX

The Sounds of English

A grammar links meaning with sound. It is the competence a person has in a language which permits him to produce sound waves in a systematic way so that someone else with a similar grammar can interpret the sound and gain an idea which is more or less that which the speaker intended. We have no way of directly observing this internalized grammar. To study it, we rely upon the sentences produced by the grammar and the speaker's comments about his language.

The chief concern of our linguistic investigation is to learn how this grammar or some part of it functions and to re-create it on paper. It is customary to refer to the results of a linguistic investigation also by the term *grammar*. As scholars in any field learn more about their discipline, they often have to reevaluate their earlier beliefs. Linguists are no exception. Not only are there major differences between the forms of grammars prepared by traditionalists, structuralists, straticationalists, transformationalists, and others, but scholars within any one of these groups are by no means in agreement as to the best form of a grammar. Since 1957 the model of a transformational grammar has undergone several revisions.

According to the model used in this book, a transformational grammar is bounded by meaning at one end and sound at the other. Neither meaning nor sound is part of the grammar, but what lies in between is. It has been customary to draw models of the grammar in the direction from top to bottom:

or from left to right following conventions derived from writing practices in the Western world.

173

Such directions are merely arbitrary and have no real significance to the grammar. A model moving in the direction from lower right diagonally across the page to upper left would not affect the content of the grammar.

The grammar begins with a **semantic structure**. Since there is still much we do not know about semantics, the term **deep structure** is used in this book. This semantic, or deep, structure is processed through a series of **transformations**, the final outcome of which is known as a **syntactic surface structure**. At some stage in the derivation—probably at the level of the semantic structure or of the first transformations—**morphemes** are inserted from a **lexicon**. Primarily these will be morphemes with lexical meaning, such as *chair, ox, jump, happy*. Other morphemes, such as *for* and *to*, are added by later transformational rules. A syntactic surface structure is not a phonetic realization since it does not tell us how any of the morphemes will be eventually pronounced or what effect they will have upon one another. **Phonological rules** are needed to produce a **phonetic surface structure**. Here the grammar ends. Perhaps linguists in the future will show us how phonetic structures are subjected to **performance features** to produce actual sentences. We can illustrate these various parts of the grammar by means of a diagram, as seen in Figure 6.1.

Just as we started our study of syntax with surface rather than deep structures, we will begin the study of phonology with surface phonetic forms. In each case we start with the more familiar, easily observed structures and work back to the more abstract. We can approach the study of sounds from three different standpoints: (1) how they are received by the listener, (2) how they are transmitted through the air, and (3) how they are produced by the speaker. Any of these three approaches provides valuable information, and if we are to obtain a complete description we need all three. However, there are problems involved with the first two approaches: They require special laboratory equipment. In this book we will restrict ourselves to the third approach since no special equipment is needed for it.

All of the organs used in producing speech are used for other purposes as well. The lungs and the muscles that control them draw in air to provide the body with oxygen and then exhale the air containing carbon dioxide. At times we block the flow of air from leaving the body by closing the **vocal cords**, two bands of cartilage in the **larynx** (popularly called the *Adam's apple*). For normal breathing the vocal cords are wide apart in a V shape. If they are brought tightly together, air is trapped in the chest cavity, thereby providing pressure when we want to lift weight or we strain for any other purpose. When we breathe normally, we can inhale and exhale either through the nose or through the mouth.

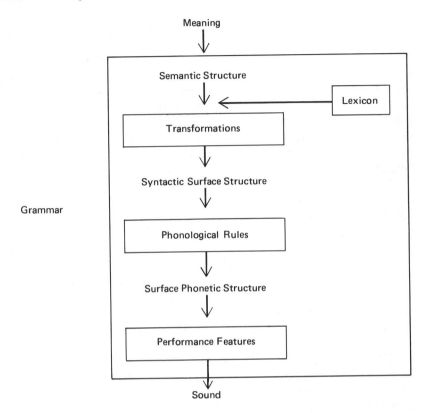

Figure 6.1

When breathing through the mouth, we may raise the **velum**, or soft palate, which is the back half of the roof of the mouth and ends in the **uvula**, a soft, fleshy appendage that hangs downward. It is also possible to breathe through the mouth while leaving the velum lowered, but when breathing through the nose, we must lower the velum. When we lower the velum, we provide a passage from the nasal cavity to the lungs; when it is raised, the nasal passage is closed. We can easily watch in a mirror this raising and lowering of the velum. Other organs are used primarily for eating: the teeth for chewing and the tongue for directing food between the teeth. All of these organs, then, are used for breathing and eating as well as for speaking. We could argue that breathing and eating are more important for basic survival than is speaking. Man can survive without speaking; he cannot without breathing or eating. Yet man is not just another animal whose chief interests are basic survival. The activities he performs by means of his language are extremely important to him.

In this book we are concerned only with the sound producing function. Also, we are interested solely in speech sounds, those sounds which may combine with others to produce words, rather than gasps, clicks, grunts, and similar sounds. In English all speech sounds are formed by acting on the air flow as it is leaving the lungs and passing from the body. We do make a few gasps and clicking sounds by acting on air being inhaled, but these are not *speech* sounds. In a few language families, such as Hottentot and Bushman (spoken in southern Africa), various clicks are speech sounds, just as the English vowels and consonants are. Languages that have clicks as speech sounds are rare in the world, and English does not happen to be one of them.

The Production of Speech Sounds

If the flow of air leaving the lungs is unimpeded, it is nothing more than quiet breathing. To produce sound, we must alter the air flow in some way, usually at several points simultaneously. The first point at which we can modify the flow of air is at the vocal cords. Instead of leaving them wide open as we do for normal breathing or closing them completely as for straining, we may bring them close enough together that air can still pass through but only by setting them in motion and causing a vibrating or buzzing sound. This is the same principle by which a reed musical instrument works or by which we make the "Bronx cheer" by holding the tongue between the lips and forcing air through the narrow opening. Sounds that are produced with vibration of the vocal cords are said to be **voiced**. Another way of stating this is to say that they have the feature of voice, which we write [+voice]. Sounds that are produced without vibration of the vocal cords are said to be **voiceless**, or to lack the feature of voice: [-voice]. It is impossible for a person to see his vocal cords with just a mirror; but he can feel their motion by holding his hand over his throat while he pronounces a prolonged [z], the initial sound in *zip*. The sound [z] has the feature [+voice]. This should be contrasted with an [s], the first sound in *sip*, which has the feature [-voice].

The next major point at which the air flow can be modified is at the velum. If the velum is lowered, the air flows through the nasal cavity, and the sound is said to be a **nasal**. We represent this feature as [+nasal]. The initial sounds of *map* and *nap*, [m] and [n] respectively, are nasal sounds. While holding either of these sounds, if the speaker pinches his nose to, the sound stops; on the other hand, he can hold his hand firmly over his mouth, and not stop the sound. Sounds produced with the flow of air coming through the mouth are called **oral** or **non-nasal sounds**: [-nasal]. If a person holds an [s] or [z] sound and pinches his nose to, the sound continues, whereas if he holds his hand firmly over his mouth it stops. In some languages there are sounds produced by the air being released through the mouth and nose simultaneously. These sounds are said to be nasalized. They serve no distinctive function in English.

In the mouth there are several points at which the air flow may be obstructed. In each case obstruction is produced by bringing a lower organ—the tongue or lower lip—against an upper surface—the roof of the mouth, the upper teeth, or the upper lip. Along these upper surfaces there are many possible points of contact, especially along the roof of the mouth. However, there is a definite limit as to the number of these the human ear can distinguish. For most languages of the world, including English, there are only four significant points of contact.

First, the lower lip may come in contact with the upper lip or upper teeth, as in the production of [m] as in *moon*, or of [v], the first sound in *vat*. These are often called **labial** sounds. We could distinguish between *bilabials* (sounds such as [m] in which the two lips are brought together) and *labiodentals* (sounds such as [v] in which the lower lip comes in contact with the upper teeth). However, because there are apparently no languages in which this is the only distinguishing feature between two sounds, we will use the term *labial* for both bilabials and labiodentals.

Second, the tongue tip may come in contact with the teeth (**dental** sounds), as in the first sound of *those*, [ð̆]; or the upper gum ridge, or **alveolum** (**alveolar** sounds), as in the production of the English [t], the first sound in *town*. In many languages, such as French, German, and Russian, this sound is dental rather than alveolar. Since there are apparently no languages in which the only difference between two sounds is in whether they are dental or alveolar, we will not distinguish them here.

Next, the body of the tongue may come in contact with the hard **palate** (**palatal** sounds), as for the sound spelled *sh* in *ship*: [š]. The tongue approaches but does not touch the roof of the mouth slightly back of the alveolum for this sound, as contrasted with the alveolum for [s]. Because the tongue is so close to the alveolum in the production of [š], some linguists call it an **alveolo-palatal** sound. We will refer to it merely as *palatal*.

Fourth, the body of the tongue may come in contact with the **soft palate**, or **velum** (**velar** sounds), as in the production of [k], the initial sound of *keep* and *caught*.

Some linguists have made no further classification of these points of contact, calling sounds *labial, dental, palatal,* or *velar*. Others have noticed that under certain circumstances the palatal and the velar sounds behave similarly, as opposed to the dentals and labials. Other similarities have been seen between the labial and velar sounds, as opposed to the palatals and dentals. For these reasons, terms showing these combinations have been formed. The most recent of these terms are found in *The Sound Pattern of English* by Noam Chomsky and Morris Halle (New York: Harper & Row, 1968). Sounds produced with an obstruction at the alveolum or farther forward (i.e., alveolars, dentals, and labials) such as

[m, ð, s, t] are known as **anterior** sounds: [+anterior]. Sounds produced with
an obstruction farther back than the alveolum—palatals and velars such as [š, k] —
as well as sounds produced without an obstruction (to be discussed later in this
chapter) are [–anterior]. The term used to distinguish dentals and palatals from
labials and velars is **coronal**. If the blade of the tongue (that part which in a re-
laxed position lies opposite the alveolum) is raised above the rest position to
produce an obstruction as it is for [t, s, š], the sound is [+coronal]; this includes
dentals, alveolars, and palatals. Sounds produced without raising the blade of
the tongue are [–coronal]. These include the labials and velars. In the production of the velars, the body of the tongue is raised, but the blade is not; they are,
therefore, [-coronal]. Sounds produced without an obstruction are, of course,
[-coronal].

In addition to the place at which an obstruction occurs, the manner in which
it is formed is also important. The obstruction may cause the flow of air to stop
altogether, as it does for [p, t, k]; or it may allow the air to flow through the
oral cavity without stopping but still be modified, as it does for [v, ð, s]. Sounds
produced with a continuous air flow through the oral cavity are [+continuant].
Those produced with the air blocked and later released (such as [p, t, k]) and
those in which the air passes through the nasal cavity (such as [m, n]) are
[–continuant].

By a combination of actions, we can form sounds that are recognizable as
speech sounds. For example, if we allow the vocal cords to vibrate, raise the
velum, form an obstruction at the labial region, and stop the flow of air before
releasing it, we produce a sound which we symbolize as [b], the first sound in
back. We can describe this sound with features as follows:

$$\begin{bmatrix} +\text{anterior} \\ -\text{coronal} \\ -\text{nasal} \\ +\text{voice} \\ -\text{continuant} \end{bmatrix}$$

We abbreviate a combination of features such as this by means of a symbol
in brackets, such as [b]. All of these symbols together are called a **phonetic
alphabet**. The symbols used in this text and in most other discussions of phonology differ in some ways from those found in the International Phonetic Alphabet. They are also different from the pronunciation symbols used in most
dictionaries.

The production of speech sounds is a complex process, involving the interaction of several organs at once. The following examples reveal the features
involved in the production of sixteen English sounds with the abbreviation for
each combination of features written in brackets. A word in which the sound is
found is given after each symbol.

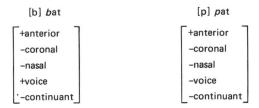

[b] *b*at

$$\begin{bmatrix} \text{+anterior} \\ \text{--coronal} \\ \text{--nasal} \\ \text{+voice} \\ \text{--continuant} \end{bmatrix}$$

[p] *p*at

$$\begin{bmatrix} \text{+anterior} \\ \text{--coronal} \\ \text{--nasal} \\ \text{--voice} \\ \text{--continuant} \end{bmatrix}$$

These sounds are produced with an obstruction at the alveolum or farther forward, [+anterior], and with the blade of the tongue not raised, [--coronal]; this defines the labial region. [b] and [p] are formed with the velum raised, [--nasal], and with the flow of air blocked before it is released, [--continuant]. They differ from each other in that for [b] the vocal cords are vibrating, [+voice], and for [p] they are not, [--voice].

[d] *d*o

$$\begin{bmatrix} \text{+anterior} \\ \text{+coronal} \\ \text{--nasal} \\ \text{+voice} \\ \text{--continuant} \end{bmatrix}$$

[t] *t*o

$$\begin{bmatrix} \text{+anterior} \\ \text{+coronal} \\ \text{--nasal} \\ \text{--voice} \\ \text{--continuant} \end{bmatrix}$$

These sounds are produced with an obstruction at the alveolum or farther forward, [+anterior], and with the blade of the tongue raised, [+coronal]; hence, they are dentals or alveolars. They are formed with the velum raised, [--nasal], and with the flow of air blocked before it is released, [--continuant]. They differ from each other in that [d] has the feature [+voice] and [t] has [--voice]. The features also show how these sounds differ from [b] and [p]. The sounds [b, p] are [--coronal], whereas [d, t] are [+coronal].

[ǰ] *j*udge

$$\begin{bmatrix} \text{--anterior} \\ \text{+coronal} \\ \text{--nasal} \\ \text{+voice} \\ \text{--continuant} \end{bmatrix}$$

[č] *ch*urch

$$\begin{bmatrix} \text{--anterior} \\ \text{+coronal} \\ \text{--nasal} \\ \text{--voice} \\ \text{--continuant} \end{bmatrix}$$

Like the preceding sounds, these are produced with the velum raised and with the flow of air interrupted momentarily. They differ from each other in that one is voiced and the other voiceless. In some languages these are not considered as single sounds but rather as combinations, [č] being [tš] and [ǰ] being [dž]. [ž] is the consonant sound in the middle of *measure*. Some linguists refer to [č]

and [ǰ] as **affricates**. There are only two in English, but some languages have
others, such as [c], which in English is a combination of the two sounds [ts] as
in *wits*. Except for the point of contact and the feature of stridency, which will
be introduced below, the sounds [č, ǰ] in English do not function differently
from [b, p, d, t] ; they are, therefore, described by means of the features given
on the preceding page.

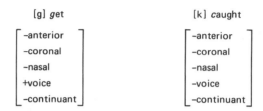

[g] *g*et

⎡ −anterior ⎤
| −coronal |
| −nasal |
| +voice |
⎣ −continuant ⎦

[k] *c*aught

⎡ −anterior ⎤
| −coronal |
| −nasal |
| −voice |
⎣ −continuant ⎦

The features [−anterior] and [−coronal] classify these sounds as velars. Like the
preceding sounds, they are [−nasal] and [−continuant]. They differ from each
other in that [g] has the feature [+voice] and [k] has [−voice]. We are speaking solely of sounds, not spelling. It does not matter whether it is spelled *c* or *k*;
the first sound in *kit* and *caught* is [k].

If we begin at the labial region and move backward to the velum, we can
group these eight [−continuant] sounds according to their place of obstruction:

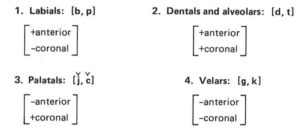

1. Labials: [b, p]

⎡ +anterior ⎤
⎣ −coronal ⎦

2. Dentals and alveolars: [d, t]

⎡ +anterior ⎤
⎣ +coronal ⎦

3. Palatals: [ǰ, č]

⎡ −anterior ⎤
⎣ +coronal ⎦

4. Velars: [g, k]

⎡ −anterior ⎤
⎣ −coronal ⎦

There is one other noncontinuant sound, known as the **glottal stop**, in which the
air is blocked briefly in the larynx and then released. This sound is heard in
certain noises we make for "yes" and "no": *unh huh* and *unh unh*. It often precedes a vowel at the beginning of a word, especially when the speaker is emphasizing the word. For some speakers it is found instead of [t] in such words as
battle and *bottle*. It is represented as [ʔ]. Since it is not used in English to distinguish one morpheme from another, we will have no more to say about it.

We can also use features to describe continuant sounds. The eight sounds
that follow are produced by forming an obstruction with the lower lip or tongue
against an upper surface. Instead of blocking the flow of air completely, the
speaker leaves a narrow passage through which the air is forced.

1. Labials

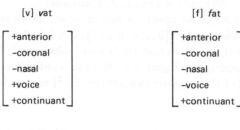

[v] *v*at

$$\begin{bmatrix} +\text{anterior} \\ -\text{coronal} \\ -\text{nasal} \\ +\text{voice} \\ +\text{continuant} \end{bmatrix}$$

[f] *f*at

$$\begin{bmatrix} +\text{anterior} \\ -\text{coronal} \\ -\text{nasal} \\ -\text{voice} \\ +\text{continuant} \end{bmatrix}$$

2. Dentals and Alveolars

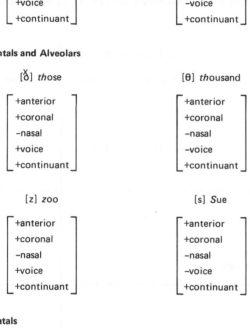

[ð̌] *th*ose

$$\begin{bmatrix} +\text{anterior} \\ +\text{coronal} \\ -\text{nasal} \\ +\text{voice} \\ +\text{continuant} \end{bmatrix}$$

[θ] *th*ousand

$$\begin{bmatrix} +\text{anterior} \\ +\text{coronal} \\ -\text{nasal} \\ -\text{voice} \\ +\text{continuant} \end{bmatrix}$$

[z] *z*oo

$$\begin{bmatrix} +\text{anterior} \\ +\text{coronal} \\ -\text{nasal} \\ +\text{voice} \\ +\text{continuant} \end{bmatrix}$$

[s] *S*ue

$$\begin{bmatrix} +\text{anterior} \\ +\text{coronal} \\ -\text{nasal} \\ -\text{voice} \\ +\text{continuant} \end{bmatrix}$$

3. Palatals

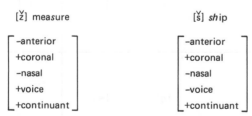

[ž] mea*s*ure

$$\begin{bmatrix} -\text{anterior} \\ +\text{coronal} \\ -\text{nasal} \\ +\text{voice} \\ +\text{continuant} \end{bmatrix}$$

[š] *sh*ip

$$\begin{bmatrix} -\text{anterior} \\ +\text{coronal} \\ -\text{nasal} \\ -\text{voice} \\ +\text{continuant} \end{bmatrix}$$

There are languages such as German and Russian which have velar continuant consonants, but most dialects of English do not.

With only the features we have given, [ð̌] and [z] are shown as the same sound, as are [θ] and [s], yet any speaker of English recognizes a difference between *think* and *sink*, two words which differ only in the initial sounds. To show the differences in these sounds, as well as to show certain generalizations that will be needed in the next chapter, we introduce the feature **[+strident]**,

which indicates a noisiness in production. The following sounds are [+strident]:
[v, f, z, s, ž, š, ǰ, č]. All others in English are [−strident].

The sixteen sounds that we have discussed so far are known as **obstruents** and
have the feature [+obstruent]: [b, p, d, t, ǰ, č, g, k, v, f, ð̆, θ, z, s, ž, š]. All
other consonants and the vowels have the feature [−obstruent]. The obstruents
for English are summarized in Figure 6.2. All of the continuants except [ð̆, θ]
are [+strident]; all of the noncontinuants except [ǰ, č] are [−strident].

	[−continuant]		[+continuant]	
	[+voice]	[−voice]	[+voice]	[−voice]
⎡+anterior⎤ ⎣−coronal⎦ (labials)	[b]	[p]	[v]	[f]
⎡+anterior⎤ ⎣+coronal⎦ (dentals and alveolars)	[d]	[t]	[ð̆] [z]	[θ] [s]
⎡−anterior⎤ ⎣+coronal⎦ (palatals)	[ǰ]	[č]	[ž]	[š]
⎡−anterior⎤ ⎣−coronal⎦ (velars)	[g]	[k]		

Figure 6.2

Turning next to the nasal sounds in English, we find the following:

[m] *m*oon	[n] *n*ow	[ŋ] si*ng*
−obstruent	−obstruent	−obstruent
+anterior	+anterior	−anterior
−coronal	+coronal	−coronal
+nasal	+nasal	+nasal
−continuant	−continuant	−continuant
+voice	+voice	+voice
−strident	−strident	−strident

In the production of these sounds, the velum is lowered and the air passes through the nasal cavity. They are voiced, nonstrident, and nonobstruent. Since the flow of air is blocked at the mouth, they are [−continuant]. The fact that the flow of air continues through the nasal cavity is irrelevant to this feature. These sounds differ in the point at which the air is blocked in the mouth: the lips, the alveolum, or the velum. This point of contact affects the shape of the oral cavity and, therefore, gives each nasal its individual quality. Although English has only these three nasals, there are languages which have others. Both Italian and Spanish, for example, have a palatal nasal: [ɲ], as in Spanish *señor, huraño* and Italian *signore, regno*. In addition, some languages have nasalized vowels, as in the French words *prince, un, France*. Since these sounds are not used in English to distinguish one morpheme from another, they are not discussed further in this book. We will be concerned solely with [m, n, ŋ]. Because of the spelling, some people have trouble at first recognizing [ŋ]. The spelling of *sing* looks as though the word ends in [ng]. This can be shown to be false, since the blade of the tongue does not touch the alveolum in the production of this sound; rather, the body of the tongue touches the velum. A word such as *sink* ends in [ŋ k], the presence or absence of [k] being the only distinguishing feature between *sink* and *sing*. The word *singer* has only [ŋ] as the central consonant, whereas *finger* has [ŋg].

The obstruents and nasals constitute a class of sounds which we call the true **consonants**. A consonant is defined as a sound whose production requires a major obstruction. This obstruction can be complete closure, as with the non-continuant obstruents and the nasals; or it may be less severe, as with the continuant obstruents. In either case there is a major obstruction: two parts of the mouth either blocking the flow of air or coming so close together as to modify it severely. These sounds have the feature [+cons], **cons** being an abbreviation for **consonantal**.

The opposite of consonantal is **vocalic**: [+voc]. These sounds are produced without any obstruction, but rather with varying positions of the jaw and tongue which alter the shape of the oral cavity. A sound is said to be vocalic if the jaw is no higher than it is for [iy] or [uw], the vowel sounds in *he* and *who* respectively. For these sounds the jaw is quite high, especially if we contrast them with the [a] sound in *father*, yet there is no obstruction as there is with [v, z, ð].

It would seem logical that all sounds should fall neatly and exclusively into one of the categories [+voc] or [+cons]. For most sounds this is true, but for five it is not. The sounds heard initially in *yet, wet,* and *hot* — [y, w, h] —are formed with a constriction narrower than that for [iy] and [uw]; yet there is no obstruction. They are, therefore, [−cons] and [−voc]. Two others, the initial sounds in *red* and *let* — [r, l] —have a major obstruction and are, therefore, [+cons]. For technical reasons beyond the scope of this book they are also classified as [+voc]. We, therefore, have four groups of sounds according to the consonantal and vocalic features:

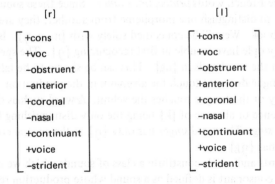

+cons	−cons	+cons	−cons
−voc	+voc	+voc	−voc
obstruents	vowels	[r, l]	[y, w, h]
and nasals			

The two sounds [r] and [l] are often referred to as **liquids**. In English they have the following features:

[r]	[l]
+cons	+cons
+voc	+voc
−obstruent	−obstruent
−anterior	+anterior
+coronal	+coronal
−nasal	−nasal
+continuant	+continuant
+voice	+voice
−strident	−strident

There are many variations of the [r] sound. For most speakers of American English, the sound at the beginning of a word, such as *red*, is formed with the tip of the tongue raised and turned backward behind the alveolum and not actually touching the palate. Some linguists refer to this position as **retroflex**. This is actually the only variety of [r] that is described by the features listed above. For many speakers there is no raising of the tongue tip in the [r] that occurs before consonants, as in *beard* and *barn*, the body of the tongue rising toward the palate to form the obstruction; for others there is no noticeable [r] sound in *beard* or *barn*. Other variations of the [r] include the rapid "flap" of the tongue tip against the alveolum or upper teeth as in the pronunciation of *very* in some British dialects as well as in Spanish in such words as *caro* and *pero*. There is also a variant formed by trilling the tongue tip, as found in Spanish *carro, perro* and Russian *raznyj, rama*. Another variant is formed by trilling the uvula, a form of [r] found in many dialects of French and German. The [l] sound is often called a **lateral** since the tongue tip rests on the alveolum while the air passes freely on both sides of the tongue. Although there are certain other modifications that may be made in the production of this sound, such as raising the body of the tongue, the features for [l] present no real problems.

Since vowels are produced with no obstruction, they are necessarily [-anterior] and [-coronal]. Whereas these two features classify a consonant as velar, they are unrevealing for vowels. They are predictable from the feature [-cons]. Similarly, English vowels have the features [-obstruent, -nasal, +continuant, +voice, -strident]. Since these features are predictable for English vowels, they are relatively uninteresting. Of more consequence are the positions of the tongue and the jaw, since it is these positions that alter the shape of the oral cavity and give each vowel its characteristic quality.

For English we specify three jaw heights:[†] one that we call **high**, one that we call **low**, and a third in between that is neither high nor low. The point of reference for these relative heights is the position of the jaw for the production of [ey], the vowel sound in *cake*. Vowels produced with the jaw higher, as for [iy], the vowel in *be*, are [+high] and [-low]. Those that are produced with the jaw lower, such as [a], the first vowel sound in *father*, are [+low] and [-high]. Below are examples of vowels in each of the three positions with a key word following each symbol:

$$\begin{bmatrix} +high \\ -low \end{bmatrix} \qquad \begin{matrix} [iy] & beet \\ [i] & bit \end{matrix}$$

$$\begin{bmatrix} -high \\ -low \end{bmatrix} \qquad \begin{matrix} [ey] & bait \\ [e] & bet \end{matrix}$$

$$\begin{bmatrix} -high \\ +low \end{bmatrix} \qquad \begin{matrix} [æ] & bat \end{matrix}$$

In addition to jaw height, the position of the tongue in relation to the front and back of the mouth is important in the production of vowels. If the tongue is no farther back than it is for the production of [ey], the sound is [**-back**]; if it is farther back, as for [uw] and [ow], the vowel sounds in *boot* and *boat*, it is [**+back**]. Following is a chart containing the significant vowels for English:

[†]The usual classification is in terms of tongue height, which is the same as that of the jaw. Since the position of the jaw is more readily observed than that of the tongue, it has been used as the position of reference.

	[-back]	[+back]
$\begin{bmatrix} +\text{high} \\ -\text{low} \end{bmatrix}$	[iy] beet [i] bit	[uw] boot [u] put
$\begin{bmatrix} -\text{high} \\ -\text{low} \end{bmatrix}$	[ey] bait [e] bet	[ow] boat [ʌ] but
$\begin{bmatrix} -\text{high} \\ +\text{low} \end{bmatrix}$	[æ] bat	[ɔw] bought [a] pot

By reading the chart downward first with the [-back] vowels and then with those that are [+back], a person can readily observe the changing jaw positions. By reading across (*beet, boot*), he can observe the tongue position.

The system used in this book for transcribing vowels shows two groups: those which are transcribed with one symbol, such as [i], and those which have two symbols, such as [iy]. Those transcribed with two symbols are formed with more tension in the articulatory organs than are the others. Sounds such as [iy] and [uw], then, are said to be **tense vowels** and to have the feature [+tense]. The others are **lax vowels** and have the feature [-tense].

The three sounds which are [-voc] and [-cons], that is, [w, y, h] are described by some of the same features we use for vowels. [y] is [+high], [-back], and [+voice]. [w] is [+high], [+back], and [+voice]. [h] is [+low], [+back], and [-voice]. These sounds are often called **glides**. When they occur before vowels as in [hat], [wet], [yet], they function as consonants; when they combine with a vowel as in [meyt] or [mown], they function as vowels. They are, therefore, sometimes called **semivowels**.

Two vowels or a vowel and a following glide that are combined as one indivisible unit within a single syllable constitute a **diphthong**. Hence, the tense vowels [iy, ey, uw, ow, ɔw] are all diphthongs. It is still not clear whether this is the best way to treat these vocalic segments or not. Many linguists have different opinions and consequently use a different set of symbols for the vowels than are presented here. There are three sounds, however, which are almost uniformly accepted as diphthongs, although the representations of them are not the same in all books:

[ay]   as in *my, night, bike*
[aw]   as in *house, pout, round*
[oy]   as in *boy, coy*

Two other vowels will be introduced in the next chapter: [ə], the unstressed vowel in *sofa, feather, palace*; and [ɨ], the unstressed vowel in *careless, bracelet, padded* (for some dialects). Some speakers have [ə] for all of these words and may not have [ɨ] at all.

Redundancy and Distinctive Features

The features we have given in this chapter describe the various movements of the vocal apparatus in producing speech sounds. In forming [z], we cause the vocal cords to vibrate, raise the velum, form an obstruction with the blade of the tongue at the alveolum, and allow the flow of air to pass through the obstruction without stopping but with a noisy sound. For this complex of features, [+cons, -voc, -nasal, +voice, +ant, +cor, +cont, +strident], we write the abbreviation [z]. This configuration of pluses and minuses uniquely defines this sound as distinct from all others in English.

Using the thirteen features we have presented, we could have 8,192 possible combinations of features or distinct sounds, but the number that actually exists in any language is much smaller than this. Some of the combinations are physically impossible to produce. Because of its shape, the human jaw cannot be high and low at the same time; hence, the combination [+high, +low] never exists. We can always predict that a sound which is [+high] is [-low] and one that is [+low] is [-high]. Because of the absence of obstruction in the production of [+vocalic] segments, there is no possibility for the friction which is named by the feature [+strident]. There are, then, no strident vowels, and a strident nasal is also impossible, even for a person with swollen adenoids. In addition, the definitions of the features make at least some of them mutually exclusive. Since the anterior and coronal features are defined in terms of the position of obstruction in the oral cavity, sounds that are [-cons] are necessarily nonanterior and noncoronal. In addition to the restrictions imposed by the physical characteristics of the speech apparatus, perception plays a strong role in limiting the number of speech sounds utilized by any language. Because of the continuous nature of some of the articulatory dimensions, it is theoretically possible to have an infinite number of sounds. The tongue can touch the roof of the mouth anywhere between the teeth and the uvula, not in just four places. Also, the jaw can be raised or lowered by infinitesimal degrees; it does not have just three positions of height. No language makes use of all these different contrasts in sounds, because most of them are below the threshold of perception, especially in normal discourse. Although no one has yet determined the maximum number of sounds a person can distinguish with the precision needed by human languages, the number must be far short of a hundred; most languages make use of fewer than fifty.

No language uses all of the speech sounds that can be produced, and probably none use the maximum number that could be perceived in effective communication. Each language selects a certain number of sounds. Of these, some sounds such as [p, t, k] occur in almost all languages; others, such as voiceless vowels, are rare. As we noted in the first part of this chapter, English has selected thirty-eight, counting diphthongs.

As a result of universal physical restrictions and selections by individual languages, some features are predictable by the presence of others. If we know that a sound is [-cons], we also know other features:

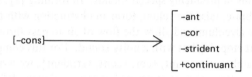

In English we also know that a sound which is [-cons] is [+voice] and [-nasal]. Or if a sound in English is [+nasal], we can predict certain other features:

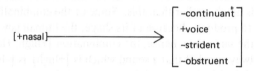

We call any feature **redundant** if it is predictable from other features. A feature which is not predictable is **distinctive**. Another way of expressing this is to say that a distinctive feature is essential for distinguishing one morpheme from another and that morphemes can be distinguished without the use of redundant features.

In English there are only three sounds which have the feature [+nasal]: [m, n, ŋ]. The feature [+nasal] is distinctive, then, in setting these sounds off from all others in English. We need to see now which features are distinctive in distinguishing them from one another. Both [m] and [n] are [+anterior], and [ŋ] is [-anterior]. Since only one sound in English shares the features [+nasal] and [-anterior], only these two are distinctive in describing [ŋ]. Other features such as [+voice] and [-strident] are still in existence, but they are predictable, or redundant. The feature [+anterior] distinguishes [m] and [n] from [ŋ]. We use the feature coronal to distinguish [m] from [n]. The distinctive features for [m], then, are [+nasal, +anterior, -coronal], and those for [n] are [+nasal, +anterior, +coronal].

The features we have discussed so far may be distinctive or redundant. All of them can be distinctive under certain conditions. There are other features, however, which may be distinctive in some languages but which are always redundant in English. The English vowels that are [+back] and [+tense] are always formed with the lips rounded and, therefore, have the feature [+round]. Except for [u], all other vowels are [-round]. There are no two vowels in English which have the same features except for rounding. In addition to vowels, a consonant which precedes a rounded vowel also has the feature [+round]. This feature is called **labialized** in some texts. Rounded consonants can be illustrated with examples such as the following:

[+round]	[-round]
*m*oon	*m*ean
*b*oat	*b*ait
*f*ull	*f*ill
caught	cot

The features [+round] and [-round] are never distinctive in English, but for some languages such as French and German there are front vowels which differ only in whether they are rounded or not.

There is a puff of air as part of the articulation of some English sounds. This can be readily observed by holding the hand in front of the mouth and saying *pit*. The [p] in this word is said to be **aspirated** and to have the feature [+aspirate]. The [p] in this word can be contrasted with the [p] in *spit*, which is **unaspirated**. Aspiration is usually predictable in English. It occurs with [p, t, k] when these sounds occur initially before a stressed vowel (*pot, top, kit*) or within a word if they begin a stressed syllable (*appoint, attack, accost*). At the end of a word they may or may not be aspirated, depending on performance factors. In all other positions they are unaspirated: *spot, stop, skit, apple, attic, accent*. Except for final position, aspiration is always predictable in English and is, therefore, never used to distinguish two morphemes.

Another feature which is predictable because of position is the duration of time expended in the production of nonobstruents. We say that a sound which is held for a relatively long period of time has the feature [+long]. This feature can be observed in the vowels in the following words:

[+long]	[-long]
bead	beat
his	hiss
leave	leaf
laid	late
lag	lack

The vowels that have the feature [+long] are all followed by voiced obstruents;

those that are [-long] are followed by voiceless obstruents. This patterning of [+long] and [-long] is found in all nonobstruents, not just vowels:

	[+long]	[-long]
[n]	sins	since
[m]	limber	limper
[r]	heard	hurt
[l]	willed	wilt

Just because length is not a distinctive feature in English today does not mean that it never was. In both Old English and Middle English, some morphemes were distinguished solely by the presence of a long vowel in one and a short vowel in the other, as can be seen in the following Old English examples. The colon indicates length.

[+long]		[-long]	
[ni:θ]	"strife"	[niθ]	"abyss"
[he:lan]	"to calumniate"	[helan]	"to conceal"
[læ:t]	"he led"	[læt]	"late"
[mæ:y]	"male kinsman"	[mæy]	"he is able"
[du:n]	"down"	[dun]	"dunn"
[fo:r]	"journey"	[for]	"before"
[ma:ga]	"son"	[maga]	"stomach"

Since Middle English times the system has changed so that no two morphemes are distinguished by vocalic length alone.

As we can see from the feature of length, it is often not adequate to use just plus and minus values. For some purposes numbers on a scale are more satisfactory. For example, a vowel is longer before a voiced noncontinuant obstruent than before a voiceless one, but it is still longer before a voiced continuant, as seen in *beet, bead, bees*. In addition, aspiration and especially length are affected by such factors as emphasis, anger, and sarcasm. If a person wishes to reinforce the clarity of his speech, he may increase the length of the nonobstruents, just as he may increase the aspiration on [p] to distinguish *pat* from *bat*.

Distinctive features are used to distinguish morphemes, as voicing does in *his* and *hiss*. Features that are redundant do not distinguish morphemes.

Natural Classes

Because of their feature combinations, some sounds are very much alike. The consonants [f] and [v] , for example, share all the same features except for voice. On the other hand, [t] and [w] are not similar sounds since they differ in many features. For certain groups of similar sounds it is possible to state one or more features which they share but which exclude all other sounds in the language. The feature [+nasal] is shared by [m, n, ŋ] ; this feature also excludes all other sounds in English. If a feature or a combination of features specifies a group of sounds and excludes all others, we call this group a **natural class**. The sounds [m, n, ŋ] , then, constitute a natural class, since the feature [+nasal] is shared by all of them and it excludes all other sounds.

We can see other natural classes in the following groups:

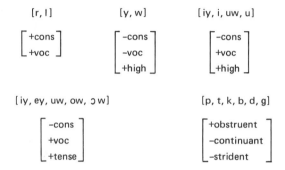

In each case it requires fewer features to specify a natural class than it does any member of the class. For example, it takes three features to specify either [r] or [l] , but only two to specify the natural class [r, l] .

Often it is possible to add a feature and subdivide a natural class into smaller classes. For example, [+obstruent] specifies the natural class with the following members:

$$[p, b, t, d, č, ǰ, k, g, f, v, θ, ð, s, z, š, ž]$$

If we add the feature [–continuant] , we have a smaller class:

$$\begin{bmatrix} +obstruent \\ -continuant \end{bmatrix}$$
$$[p, b, t, d, č, ǰ, k, g]$$

The class can be made even smaller by including voice:

$$\begin{bmatrix} +obstruent \\ -continuant \\ -voice \end{bmatrix}$$
$$[p, t, č, k]$$

The feature [+anterior] can be added:

$$\begin{bmatrix} \text{+obstruent} \\ \text{--continuant} \\ \text{--voice} \\ \text{+anterior} \end{bmatrix}$$
[p, t]

Finally, if we specify [+coronal], we no longer have a class of sounds but one specific sound:

$$\begin{bmatrix} \text{+obstruent} \\ \text{--continuant} \\ \text{--voice} \\ \text{+anterior} \\ \text{+coronal} \end{bmatrix}$$
[t]

The features in each case show which properties the members of the class share.

At times we speak of one configuration of features as being more **general** than another. In one sense of this term we can say that [+obstruent, --continuant] defines a more general class of sounds than does [+obstruent, --continuant, --voice]. In this sense of the term, a rule will be more *general* than another if it applies to a larger natural class than the other rule. The term *general* is also used to distinguish a natural class from a group of sounds which do not constitute a natural class. In this sense, a rule which applies to [r, l] is more general than one which applies to [r, l, k], since the first group is a natural class but the second group is not. We can illustrate the two meanings as follows:

More general	Less general
A [b, p, d, t, g, k]	[b, d, g]
B [b, d, g]	[b, d, g, i, u, w]

If both groups constitute natural classes, as in A, the more general rule is the one which applies to the larger natural class. But if one group constitutes a natural class, whereas the other does not, the rule involving the natural class is the more general. A person should be careful to keep the two meanings separate and not confuse generality with the number of sounds involved. In B it is the smaller group of sounds that is the more general. The real test of generality is the number of features required to define the group. The fewer features required, the more general the group.

Natural classes group similar sounds together. Phonological rules apply to natural classes rather than to random groups of unrelated sounds. By the use of features we can reveal natural classes in a way that would be impossible if we used alphabetic symbols instead. With nothing more than alphabetic symbols, [r] and [l] look no more similar than do [r] and [d]; yet with features, we can show that [r, l] constitute a natural class, whereas [r, d] do not.

Sequential Constraints

We have seen that from all possible sounds each language selects only certain ones. English has [θ] and [ð], although many other languages do not. Also, Modern English does not have [x], the consonant sound spelled *ch* in German *acht*, although this sound did exist in earlier stages of English. In addition to restrictions resulting from the selection of sounds, there are those on the order in which the sounds of the language may occur. A native speaker of English recognizes the following as possible morphemes, although he has not heard them before: [plæf], [frowt], [spruwk], [eyf]. These potential words contain only the sounds of English and do not violate any constraints of ordering. The following, however, are not possible English morphemes, not because they contain non-English sounds but because they violate ordering constraints: [žuwk], [ŋat], [bdik], [kpra].

Any consonant of English may occur at the beginning of a word except [ž] and [ŋ]. There is nothing inherently difficult about pronouncing words beginning with either sound; it is just a peculiarity of English that prohibits [ž] and [ŋ] in initial position. All of the consonantal segments occur freely at the ends of words. All vocalic segments except [u] may occur at the beginning of a word, but most of the lax vowels do not occur at the end.

There are also constraints on which sequences of sounds may occur together. At the beginning of an English word, only three combinations of two obstruents are possible: [sp, st, sk]. That is, in any two-obstruent cluster at the beginning of a word, the first sound is [s] and the second is a member of the natural class [p, t, k]. Also the combination [s] plus anterior nasal is possible: [sm] and [sn]. Although other clusters occur in a few words, such as [sf] in *sphere*, these are exceptions. If we had treated [č] and [ǰ] as the clusters [tš] and [dž] instead of as single units, there would be two other possible clusters. Most linguists today treat these affricates as single units, and we will continue to do so as well. In English there are no clusters of more than two pure consonants (i.e., [+cons, –voc]) at the beginning of a word. There are, however, other clusters with the liquids [r, l] and the high glides [w, y] as the second element: [br, bl, fr, fl, kr, kl] etc. Also there are three-unit clusters with liquids and glides as the third unit: [skw, spl, spr] etc.

Because of these sequential constraints a number of features are predictable in addition to those we discussed under Redundancy and Distinctive Features. If we know that an English word begins with a nasal, we know that the sound has the feature [+anterior], since [ŋ] is not permitted in this position. We can illustrate distinctive and redundant features by first giving a word with all features specified and then with only the distinctive features given. See Figure 6.3.

	[s	p	e	n	d]	[s	p	e	n	d]
Vocalic	−	−	+	−	−	−	−	+	−	−
Consonantal	+	+	−	+	+	+	+	−	+	+
High	−	−	−	−	−			−		
Back	−	−	−	−	−			−		
Low	−	−	−	−	−			−		
Anterior	+	+	−	+	+		+		+	+
Coronal	+	−	−	+	+		−		+	+
Tense	−	−	−	−	−			−		
Voice	−	−	+	+	+					+
Continuant	+	−	+	−	−					−
Nasal	−	−	−	+	−		−		+	
Strident	+	−	−	−	−					
Round	−	−	−	−	−					
Long	−	−	+	+	−					
Aspirate	−	−	−	−	−					

Figure 6.3

Morphemes will be entered in the lexicon in the form of matrices in which the rows are features and the columns are the individual segments. Only the distinctive features will be given. The lexicon will also contain a set of redundancy rules which will supply all predictable features before any phonological rules are applied.

If there were no sequential constraints, with an inventory of 35 phonemes there would be potentially 35 words one phoneme in length, 1,225 words two phonemes in length, and 42,875 words three phonemes in length. But English does have constraints. First of all, each word must contain a vowel, thereby eliminating such "words" as [k], [b], [zd], [rd], [mvk], and [flb]. Second,

English does not permit two occurrences of the same sound in succession within one syllable, eliminating [iib], [dda], and [eee]. The number of possible words is further reduced by excluding combinations prohibited universally or specifically in English: [dki], [wgæ], [upw], etc.

One way of accounting for all the sequences of sounds in English would be to make an enormous list of the words that exist, such as is attempted by a good unabridged dictionary. Probably all linguists would find this proposal unsatisfactory since it expresses no generalizations about the language and recognizes no system. Such a listing would show [fruwt] to be a word of English but not [fruwk] or [fnuwt]. No distinction would be made between the last two words; they would merely be excluded. A more satisfactory proposal would be to devise a group of rules which describe which sequences of sounds are permitted in English. Such rules would permit both [fruwt] and [fruwk] but not [fnuwt]. Just as syntactic rules would predict sentences not yet created, rules for sequential constraints would specify all possible morphemes, both those previously recorded and those not yet created. Such rules would approximate the knowledge possessed by a fluent speaker of English which permits him to say that [fruwk] is a possible English morpheme but [fnuwt] is not.

One result of sequential constraints is a phenomenon known as **neutralization**. A feature may usually be distinctive in specifying separate morphemes, such as tenseness in [iy] and [i], as evidenced in *week* vs. *wick, peel* vs. *pill, neat* vs. *knit,* and other pairs. Before [r] there is no contrast between [iy] and [i]; in fact, for many speakers it is not possible to tell which of the vowels they are using in such words as *fear, beer,* and *dear.* The vowel is obviously [+high] and [-back], but the feature of tenseness has been neutralized. Features may be neutralized in some dialects but not in others. Such neutralizations have resulted in *caught* and *cot* sounding alike for some speakers, *horse* and *hoarse* or *merry* and *marry* for others, and *pen* and *pin* for still others. For most speakers of English the feature [tense] is neutralized in vowels before the nasal [ŋ].

Phonetic Transcription as a Record of Physical Reality

At one time many linguists felt that if they included enough details, such as voicing, aspiration, and lip rounding, they would be able to transcribe an act of speech with objective precision. It has since been shown that even the most detailed transcriptions by the most proficient phoneticians are not records of any physical reality, but rather the transcriber's conception of what was said. Because of factors such as the imperfection of the human speech apparatus and matters of performance, it is probably impossible for a person to say a word twice in exactly the same way. When a person forms a [t], unless the tongue is radically distant from the alveolum, the listener hears it as [t], even though a dozen repetitions may all be slightly different. If we were to indicate all of the variations by means of separate symbols, we would need an infinite number. Instead of indicating the infinite number of sounds a person can produce, the transcriber differentiates only those that are *heard* as different. Some transcription systems can indicate several hundred different sounds; none indicate the infinite number that a person can make.

In any act of speech, sounds affect one another. We see this in English in consonant rounding before a round vowel and in vocalic lengthening before a voiced consonant. Vowels especially are affected by preceding or following segments, especially by the liquids and nasals. A person needs little training in phonetics to hear differences in the vowel [ow] in the following words: *coat, code, coal, core, cone, comb, cosy.* These differences are predictable in each case from the segment following the vowel, and neither our feature system nor the alphabetic abbreviations for this configuration of features, [ow], indicates them. If we were to concern ourselves with such predictable features, we would have to add many more features to our inventory and expand the alphabetic abbreviations to at least several hundred symbols. A vowel is pronounced differently before each of the segments that follow it. Also, position in a sentence affects pronunciation, as can be seen with *core* in *The core was rotten* and *It was rotten to the core.*

In addition, recordings of words and sentences made in laboratories show that the so-called sounds of speech are not even discrete units, but rather they merge with one another in a continuum. So it is in a sense inaccurate to speak of the *sounds* of speech. When we speak of the individual units of which a morpheme is composed, we are talking in terms of our concept of these units, not of anything that is really present in the physical world.

Exercises

I. The production of Speech Sounds
   A. All sounds that an English speaking person makes are not speech sounds: smacking the lips, gargling, imitating a train, making various clicking sounds to show disapproval. Try to classify several of these sounds according to the feature system.
   B. List the features which are different for the following pairs of sounds:

   1. [g, k]   6. [iy, uw]
   2. [t, k]   7. [ey, e]
   3. [s, t]   8. [uw, ow]
   4. [w, y]   9. [r, l]
   5. [v, b]   10. [m, n]

C. Why is it difficult to say a tongue twister such as "She sells sea shells down by the seashore" or "Peter Piper picked a peck of pickle peppers"? Is it just the repetition of [s] or [p]?

D. Write the following words in phonetic notation:

1. patch	6. gosh	11. dale	16. beige
2. rung	7. join	12. heel	17. south
3. bought	8. knife	13. wit	18. writhe
4. those	9. cook	14. vast	19. wreath
5. thumb	10. kook	15. yes	20. tongue

E. People who speak over radio and television have sometimes been cautioned not to include too many s-like sounds in the same sentence. Why?

F. Why are most continuant obstruents strident? Why is it possible for affricates to be strident but not other noncontinuant obstruents?

G. Discuss the validity of this statement: "English has five vowels: *a, e, i, o,* and *u.*"

II. Distinctive Features, Natural Classes, and Sequential Constraints

A. Some of the following feature combinations are possible, but others are not. If the combination is impossible, explain why. If it is possible, tell whether it actually occurs in English.

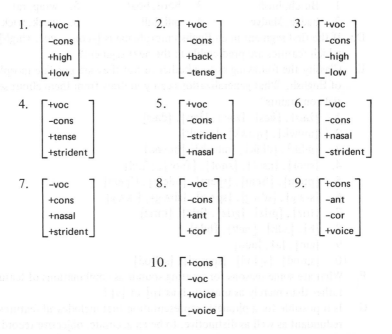

B. Give the natural class of sounds designated by each of the following feature combinations:

1. $\begin{bmatrix} -\text{cons} \\ -\text{voc} \end{bmatrix}$
2. $\begin{bmatrix} -\text{cons} \\ -\text{voc} \\ +\text{voice} \end{bmatrix}$
3. $[+\text{nasal}]$

4. $\begin{bmatrix} +\text{nasal} \\ -\text{anterior} \end{bmatrix}$
5. $\begin{bmatrix} +\text{cons} \\ -\text{voc} \\ -\text{nasal} \\ +\text{anterior} \end{bmatrix}$
6. $\begin{bmatrix} +\text{cons} \\ -\text{voc} \\ -\text{nasal} \\ +\text{anterior} \\ +\text{voice} \end{bmatrix}$

7. $\begin{bmatrix} +\text{cons} \\ -\text{voc} \\ -\text{ant} \\ -\text{cor} \end{bmatrix}$
8. $\begin{bmatrix} -\text{cons} \\ +\text{voc} \\ -\text{back} \end{bmatrix}$
9. $\begin{bmatrix} -\text{cons} \\ +\text{voc} \\ +\text{high} \\ +\text{tense} \end{bmatrix}$

C. Features express the characteristics of sounds which distinguish one morpheme from another. The feature which distinguishes *sip* from *zip* is voicing in the first segment. Each of the following pairs of morphemes differs only by one distinctive feature in one segment. Name it.

1. Butch, bush
2. badge, Madge
3. boot, boat
4. pill, bill
5. wrap, rat
6. week, wick

D. If the first segment in an English morpheme is [−cons, −voc, +high], which features are predictable in the next segment?

E. Classify the following as to whether or not they are possible morphemes of English. What generalizations can you draw from them about sequential constraints?

1. [ǯæs], [šæs], [zæs], [ǰæs], [dæs]
2. [muwk], [ŋuwk], [nuwk]
3. [ndik], [dhik], [mbæk], [bmæk]
4. [snol], [nsol], [znol], [fnol], [šnol]
5. [ptem], [fsem], [spem], [bdem], [fpem]
6. [stʌg], [sdʌg], [spʌg], [sbʌg], [skʌg]
7. [triz], [priz], [griz], [lriz], [mriz]
8. [b], [zdk], [zæk], [bdg]
9. [aio], [a], [ado]
10. [sprod], [splod], [spmod], [spbod]

F. What are some reasons for treating sounds as combinations of features rather than merely as units such as [p] or [a]?

G. Is it possible for a phonetic representation that includes all features, redundant as well as distinctive, to be an accurate, objective record of an act of speech? Explain.

Suggested Reading

Chomsky, Noam, and Halle, Morris. *The Sound Pattern of English*. New York: Harper & Row, 1968.

Francis, W. Nelson. *The Structure of American English*. New York: Ronald Press, 1958. Chapter 2: "The Sounds of Speech: Phonetics."

Halle, Morris. "On the Bases of Phonology," *Il Nuovo Cimento* 13, Series X (supplement, 1958): 494-517. Reprinted in Fodor and Katz, 1964.

Heffner, R-M. S. *General Phonetics*. Madison: University of Wisconsin Press, 1960.

Hockett, Charles F. *A Manual of Phonology*. Baltimore: Waverly Press, 1955.

Jakobson, Roman. *Child Language, Aphasia, and Phonological Universals*. Translated by Allan R. Keiler. The Hague: Mouton, 1968.

Jones, Daniel. *The Pronunciation of English*. Cambridge: Cambridge University Press, 1956.

Joos, Martin. *Acoustic Phonetics*. Baltimore: Linguistic Society of America, 1948.

Ladefoged, Peter. *Elements of Acoustic Phonetics*. Chicago: University of Chicago Press, 1962.

Malmberg, Bertil. *Phonetics*. New York: Dover Publications, 1963.

Pike, Kenneth L. *Phonetics*. Ann Arbor: University of Michigan Press, 1943.

Stanley, Richard. "Redundancy Rules in Phonology." *Language* 43 (1967): 393-436.

Trager, George L., and Smith, Henry Lee, Jr. *An Outline of English Structure*. Washington, D.C.: American Council of Learned Societies, 1957.

Trubetzkoy, N. S. *Principles of Phonology*. Translated by Christiane A. M. Baltaxe. Berkeley: University of California Press, 1969.

CHAPTER SEVEN

Phonological Rules

Each speaker of a language has an internalized grammar which enables him to produce and to understand the sentences of that language. If a person possesses a grammar of English, he is able to express his thoughts with a system of sound combinations which another person can understand if he also possesses a grammar of English. The purpose of linguistic study as we are treating it in this book is to acquire an understanding of this internalized grammar.

There are two different kinds of features that a person uses in producing and understanding the sentences of a language: unpredictable and predictable. We refer to one eating utensil as a *spoon*: [spuwn]. The use of this particular sequence of sounds is arbitrary, and a person learning English must learn to associate the sequence [spuwn] with a particular eating implement that has a handle and a bowl. He has no way of predicting that the sound sequence will be [spuwn], rather than [spiyn] or [spuwm]. There are, however, certain features which are predictable. If the first two segments are obstruents in an English word, the first must be [s] and the second [p], [t], or [k]. The third segment cannot be an obstruent. These features are predictable because of a system of sequential constraints found in English. Other features are also predictable in [spuwn]. Since the second segment, [p], is an obstruent and it follows [s], the feature of voicing is predetermined, but the features coronal and anterior are not. The [p] is predictably unaspirated since it follows [s]. Similarly, the [uw] is predictably long since it precedes the voiced [n].

Inflectional Suffixes

Continuing with the notion of predictable and unpredictable representations, we are unable to predict whether a count noun will be singular or plural; only the meaning underlying each sentence can tell us that. Once we know that a noun is plural, we can usually predict the phonetic form of the plural morpheme. Of course, a few nouns such as *mouse, ox,* and *deer* do not conform to the pattern for English plural formations; the person learning English has to learn the plurals of these words along with their singulars. But for most English nouns the phonetic forms of the plural morpheme are predictable, as we can see from the following potential words: [wuwp], [wuwb], [wuws]. Any fluent speaker of English who is introduced to these words does not have to be told how their plurals are pronounced. He knows that they are [wuwps], [wuwbz], and [wuwsiz] (or [wuwsəz] in some dialects).

It is not surprising that there is a system for plural formation. If each noun had its own idiosyncratic plural, the process of vocabulary acquisition would be doubled. Each time we learned the name of a new object, we would have to learn two forms—the singular and the plural—rather than just one. According to this method, each noun would have its own individual plural, and *books* and *rugs* would be as unique as *oxen* and *geese* are. The lexicon would have to list the plural for each noun. This method would account for the plurals of most nouns, but it would not tell us anything about those not listed, such as words that had been accidentally omitted or new words coined after the lexicon was formed.

There are several more attractive systems for plural formation. (1) All plurals could be pronounced alike. The plurals for [wuwp], [wuwb], and [wuws] show that this is not the system for English. In fact, there are three different phonetic forms. (2) The meaning of the noun could determine the form of the plural. For example, nouns designating humans might have one ending, those designating animals another, and those designating inanimate objects a third. Again, this cannot be the system for English, since we are able to give the plurals for words whose meanings we do not know, such as our three potential words. Furthermore, any system based on meaning can be shown false for English by pointing out *actor, bear,* and *rug,* all of which have a plural pronounced [z]. (3) A third possibility is that the function of the noun in the sentence determines the form of the plural. For some languages such as Russian, Latin, and Old English, this suggestion would be worth investigating. For Modern English, however, it is not the system. We can give the plural of a noun isolated from a sentence, and we can illustrate a noun in several functions in different sentences:

7.1   The *girls* ran.
7.2   He chased the *girls.*
7.3   He gave the *girls* a present.

The plural of *girl* is the same for all sentences, regardless of how it is used either in the deep structure or on the surface. (4) Another possibility is that the sound of some part of the word determines how it is pronounced. Since [wuwp], [wuwb], and [wuws] differ only in their last segments, it must be [p], [b], or [s] that determines the form of the plural morpheme.

We can list several words ending in [p] and show that they all have [s] as the plural: *cup, cap, top, wrap, cantaloupe, antelope, parsnip.* We can follow this procedure for other sounds:

Plural in [s]

[p]	cup, cap, top, wrap, cantaloupe, antelope, parsnip
[t]	bat, boat, seat, mate, ballot, braggart
[k]	cake, week, lock, relic, Cadillac
[f]	oaf, cuff, belief, photograph
[θ]	oath, death, labyrinth, breath, booth

Plural in [z]

[b]	tub, knob, astrolabe
[d]	weed, centipede, escapade, grenade
[g]	flag, drug, bag, egg
[v]	cave, laxative, preserve, relative
[ð]	lathe
[m]	room, reform, perfume
[n]	sun, commission, delegation, persimmon
[ŋ]	rung, inning, reopening
[r]	fear, hair, murder, composer
[l]	pill, proposal, moral, official, molecule
[iy]	bee, hostility, university, personality
[uw]	shoe, flue, stew
[ey]	way, day, Chevrolet
[ow]	doe, buffalo, albino
[aw]	bough, sow, cow
[ay]	sigh, lie, guy
[oy]	boy, toy, joy

Plural in [iz] or [əz]

[s]	pass, kiss, reference, conveyance
[z]	fizz, phase, maze
[š]	wish, lush, push
[ž]	garage, loge, mirage
[č]	church, match, witch
[ǰ]	judge, hedge, cage

Such a listing as this will correctly give the plural of each noun unless it is an exception such as *sheep* or *foot*. But we want our explanation to do more than give the same forms produced by the speaker's internalized grammar. We want to account for these final forms in a way that is as close as possible to that in which the speaker of the language produces them. Since there are only 28 final sounds heard with any frequency in English, it is possible that each person has learned individually the ending that goes with each one. Such a process would be similar to learning whether each of 28 people drinks coffee, tea, or milk for breakfast. If this is the way a speaker of English determines which form of the plural to use with each word, then a list such as the one we have given is the most satisfactory way to represent the facts.

On the other hand, there may be some shorter and easier means for determining the form of the plural than memorizing a list of 28 items. This is the same as our example of drinking various beverages for breakfast. If we discovered that all of the coffee drinkers were brunets, all the tea drinkers were blonds, and all the milk drinkers were redheads, we would surely use this generalization based on hair coloring to keep the beverages apart. It is easier to remember three items than 28. The same principle is true with language, although the generalizations here are usually more significant than hair coloring. If there is a possible generalization which reduces the inventory of elements to be learned, it will be selected rather than a more lengthy listing. Starting with the sounds which precede a plural in [iz] or [əz] (depending on the dialect), we see that they are all [+strident], but they are not all of the strident sounds since [f] and [v] are not in the group. They do constitute the natural class of [+strident, +coronal] sounds. Instead of listing the six sounds [s, z, š, ž, č, ǰ], we can give the two features that define the natural class and thereby reduce the number of items to be learned from six to two. After disposing of the sounds that are [+strident, +coronal], we can easily describe the other groups: [s] follows all other segments that have [−voice]; [z] follows all others that have [+voice]. Such a description of the system is much easier to learn than is one that lists the sounds of English and pairs them with the appropriate endings.

We have given several possible ways of accounting for noun plurals:

1. All plurals are idiosyncratic; there is no system.
2. All plurals are pronounced alike.
3. The meaning of the noun determines the form of the plural.
4. The function of the noun in the sentence determines the form of the plural.
5. The pronunciation of some segment in the word determines the form of the plural.

The first four were shown to be inaccurate, and the fifth proposal was shown as the means by which regular plurals are formed in English. Following the fifth proposal, we listed the segments with which an English morpheme may end and gave the plural form for each. We then saw that these lists can be grouped into natural classes.

This account can be stated more precisely than we have given it:

Rule 7.1   Rewrite *Pl* as [z].

Rule 7.2   Insert [i] (or [ə] in some dialects) if this [z] follows a segment that is [+strident, +coronal].

Rule 7.3   Rewrite [z] as [s] if it follows a voiceless segment; i.e., change [+voice] to [-voice] if it follows a segment with the feature [-voice].

We can illustrate these rules as follows:

	/kæb/ + Pl	/kæp/ + Pl	/pæs/ + Pl
Rule 7.1	kæbz	kæpz	pæsz
Rule 7.2			pæsiz
Rule 7.3		kæps	
Surface	[kæbz]	[kæps]	[pæsiz]
Spelling	cabs	caps	passes

This is the means by which we will account for noun plurals in our grammar.

Actually, rules 7.2 and 7.3 apply to more structures than just noun plurals. Possessives of nouns follow the same patterns as plurals:

[iz]		[s]		[z]	
[s]	Bess's	[p]	ape's	[b]	cub's
[z]	Liz's	[t]	rat's	[d]	stud's
[š]	lush's	[k]	crook's	[g]	nag's
[ž]	garage's	[f]	Ralph's	[r]	actor's
[č]	Butch's	[θ]	Seth's	[l]	girl's
[ǰ]	Madge's			[m]	Sam's
					etc.

The apostrophe is a spelling device only and not part of the phonetic representation. Furthermore, endings on present-tense verbs whose subjects are third person and singular are pronounced the same way:

[iz]		[s]		[z]	
[s]	he passes	[p]	he sleeps	[b]	he rubs
[z]	he chooses	[t]	he sits	[d]	he bleeds
[š]	he wishes	[k]	he talks	[g]	he hugs
[ž]	he massages	[f]	he laughs	[m]	he dreams
[č]	he watches			[ŋ]	he sings
[ǰ]	he budges			[ey]	he obeys
					etc.

Rules 7.2 and 7.3 even apply to such contracted forms as *he's* from *he is* and
Bess's from *Bess is* (that is, if the latter contraction is possible):

<table>
<tr><td align="center">[iz]</td><td></td><td align="center">[s]</td><td></td></tr>
<tr><td>[s]</td><td>Bess's here.</td><td>[p]</td><td>Your lip's cut.</td></tr>
<tr><td>[z]</td><td>The maze's empty.</td><td>[t]</td><td>The hat's gone.</td></tr>
<tr><td>[š]</td><td>The lush's here.</td><td>[k]</td><td>The cake's good.</td></tr>
<tr><td>[ž]</td><td>The loge's full.</td><td>[f]</td><td>This stuff's hot.</td></tr>
<tr><td>[č]</td><td>Your watch's fast.</td><td>[θ]</td><td>The path's narrow.</td></tr>
<tr><td>[ǰ]</td><td>The judge's late.</td><td></td><td></td></tr>
</table>

[z]

[b]	The stub's no good.
[d]	The road's crooked.
[m]	The ham's burned.
[v]	The cave's dark.
[iy]	A bee's in the room.
[uw]	This shoe's black.
	etc.

By 7.2 and 7.3 we can derive all of these surface forms:

	Plural /ræt z/	Possessive /keyt z/	Third singular /strʌ t z/	is /hæt z/
Rule 7.2				
Rule 7.3	ræts	keyts	strʌ ts	hæts
Surface	[ræts]	[keyts]	[strʌ ts]	[hæts]
Spelling	rats	Kate's	struts	hat's

	/bæǰ z/	/mæǰ z/	/bʌ ǰ z/	/ǰʌ ǰ z/
Rule 7.2	bæǰiz	mæǰiz	bʌ ǰiz	ǰʌ ǰiz
Rule 7.3				
Surface	[bæǰiz]	[mæǰiz]	[bʌ ǰiz]	[ǰʌ ǰiz]
Spelling	badges	Madge's	budges	judge's

In 7.2 and 7.3 we have discovered rules which are applicable to several different
structures. This lends confidence to the belief that these rules make a significant
generalization about English.

Next let us look at the formation of past-tense forms of verbs. Following the possibilities we used for plurals, we could suggest that all past forms are idiosyncratic and that a person has to learn two forms, past and present, each time he learns a new verb. If this is so, a native speaker will have no idea what the past-tense forms of the potential words [riys], [riyz], and [riyt] might be. Yet most speakers of English will agree that they should be [riyst], [riyzd], and [riytid]. There must be a system, then, and it must be based on the features of the last segment in the word. As we add other words ending with these segments, we see that this is what determines the form the past tense will take:

Past in [t]:   miss, lease, sass, curse, boss—all with [s]
Past in [d]:   please, pose, refuse, raise—all with [z]
Past in [id]:   cite, rest, roost, roast, bait—all with [t]

Next we will consider other final segments, although the fact that [s] and [z] differ only in voicing makes us suspect that the feature *voice* determines the form:

Past in [t]		Past in [d]		Past in [id] or [əd]	
[s]	miss	[z]	please	[t]	state
[f]	stuff	[v]	shove	[d]	head
[š]	wish	[ð̌]	clothe		
[p]	snap	[ž]	garage		
[k]	bake	[b]	stub		
[č̌]	munch	[g]	shrug		
		[ǰ]	budge		
		[uw]	sue		
		[iy]	tee		
		[ow]	mow		
		[ey]	pay		
		[ay]	sigh		
		[aw]	plow		
		[oy]	enjoy		
		[m]	slam		
		[n]	sun		
		[ŋ]	bang		
		[r]	fear		
		[l]	peel		

As with the plurals, a listing such as this would produce the correct forms after we had eliminated such verbs as *sing, sleep,* and *catch.* The sounds also constitute

natural classes, and we can give the following rules for a more economical statement of the facts:

Rule 7.4   Rewrite *past + Verb* as *Verb + [d]* .
Rule 7.5   Insert [i] ([ə] in some dialects) before this [d] if it follows
            [t] or [d].
Rule 7.6   Rewrite [d] as [t] if it follows a voiceless segment.

These rules can be illustrated as follows:

	Past + /snæp/	Past + /pliyz/	Past + /steyt/
Rule 7.4	snæpd	pliyzd	steytd
Rule 7.5			steytid
Rule 7.6	snæpt		
Surface	[snæpt]	[pliyzd]	[steytid]

It should be noted that these three rules are similar to those for plural formation. Rules 7.1 and 7.4 add a segment: [d] or [z]. Rules 7.2 and 7.5 insert [i]
if this segment is similar to the one it precedes. Rules 7.3 and 7.6 devoice this
segment if the preceding segment is voiceless. A complete grammar would combine 7.3 and 7.6 into one rule which would insure that any cluster of obstruents
in English contains only segments which agree in voicing.

It is important that these rules be applied in the order given. Obviously rule
7.4 must come first, but it may not be so obvious why 7.5 should precede 7.6.
Let us try applying the rules in the reverse order.

	Past + /snæp/	Past + /steyt/
Rule 7.4	snæpd	steytd
Rule 7.6	snæpt	steytt
Rule 7.5		steytit
Surface	[snæpt]	[steytit]

For verbs ending in /t/ this would incorrectly change the past-tense ending [d]
to [t]. If rule 7.5 precedes 7.6, the presence of the voiced [i] will prevent this.

Nouns and verbs which do not follow these rules for plural or past-tense formation will have a direction in the lexicon which will block the application of
the rule. The plural or past-tense form will be given as an exception:

deer + plural ⟶ deer	Past + see ⟶ saw
mouse + plural ⟶ mice	Past + catch ⟶ caught
ox + plural ⟶ oxen	Past + set ⟶ set

The lexical entry for each word will include all unpredictable features of the word: syntactic, semantic, and phonological. Most words will not have lexical entries for their plurals or past-tense forms, since these will be formed by phonological rules. In essence this practice is the one already followed by most dictionaries.

These rules for the representation of the plural and past-tense morphemes are called **phonological rules**, and they are different from **redundancy rules**. Redundancy rules fill in predictable features, as in the following representation of *pass*:

	/p/	/æ/	/s/		/p/	/æ/	/s/
vocalic	−	+	−		−	+	−
consonantal	+	−	+		+	−	+
high					−	−	−
back		−			−	−	−
low		+			−	+	−
anterior	+	+			+	−	+
coronal	−	+			−	−	+
tense					+	−	−
voice	−				−	+	−
continuant	−	+			−	+	+
nasal					−	−	−
strident		+			−	−	+
round					−	−	−
long					−	−	−
aspirate					+	−	−

Phonological rules do not fill in redundant features; rather, they change features from plus to minus or vice versa, rearrange segments, add segments, or delete segments. Rule 7.3 above is an example of a phonological rule that changes a feature value: [+voice] to [−voice]. Rule 7.2 adds a segment: [i]. An example of deletion is a rule that removes the second vowel of /difərənt/ to produce [difrənt]. Rearrangement can be seen in a rule in some dialects which changes [eyprən] to [eypərn]; the sequence [rə] has been rearranged to [ər].

Phonological rules are parallel to the transformational rules in syntax. We have seen that they perform the same four kinds of functions and that they are performed in a prescribed order. Just as transformational rules convert deep structures to surface syntactic structures, phonological rules convert **underlying phonological forms** to **surface phonetic forms**. We will follow the practice of enclosing underlying phonological forms in **virgules**—/kæpz/—and surface phonetic forms in **square brackets**—[kæps] .[†] At times we will refer to underlying phonological forms as **systematic phonemic representations** and to surface phonetic forms as **systematic phonetic representations** or merely as **phonemic** and **phonetic** representations. Since all linguists do not use the terms *phonemic* and *phonetic* to refer to the same ideas, a person is always advised to determine as early as possible just what the speaker or author means by the terms.

Stress Placement with Simple Words[††]

For each English word of two or more syllables, one syllable is pronounced with more force, or stress, than the others. Stress is often marked with an acute accent mark: *contríte, élephant, constítuent*. Most dictionaries assume that stress is unpredictable and, therefore, an idiosyncratic property of each word. Whereas they do not give the plural for each noun or the past tense for each verb, they do give the stress pattern for every word of two or more syllables. Some linguists feel that this approach to stress placement is inadequate, that for most words the stress pattern is predictable. Although much research still remains to be performed on English stress patterns, there have already been enough results to show much of the system.

Let us examine the words in column A to see if they contain some property not found in those in column B:

A	B
decíde	consíder
consóle	abándon
amúse	astónish
surpríse	cáncel
sincére	cértain
remóte	líttle
compléte	sólid
machíne	wínter
careér	peóple
políce	cústom

[†]The use of these symbols causes problems at times, especially when we need to speak of levels of representation between the phonemic and the phonetic. Also, it is customary to use brackets rather than virgules for phonemic representations of derived words and for phrases and sentences, as we will see later in this chapter. There is a definite need for a revision of the symbols used to denote the various levels of representation.

[††]For a fuller discussion of phonological rules, especially those for stress placement, see Noam Chomsky and Morris Halle, *The Sound Pattern of English* (New York: Harper & Row, 1968). The material presented in this chapter is greatly influenced by this work.

All of the words in column A have stress on the last vowel; none of those in column B do. If there is a pattern, it does not involve the number of syllables in the word, for most of the words in both columns are two syllables in length. It cannot be the English system that stress always falls on the vowel in a prescribed syllable such as the first, last, or next to last. Nor is the part of speech of the word important; both columns contain nouns, adjectives, and verbs. The final segment must not be the determining factor, as it is for plurals, since final [n] is found in both columns (*machine, abándon*), as are [r] (*sincére, consíder*) and [d] (*decíde, sólid*). However, if we look at the last vowel, we do see a pattern. In column A, the last vowel in each word is tense. All diphthongs are considered tense. In column B, the last vowel is not tense in any of the words. We can form a tentative rule:

Rule 7.7   Place stress on the last tense vowel of a word.

Next we need to add more words with a tense vowel in the final syllable to see whether our rule is accurate: *condóne, reláte, survíve, maroón, balloón, maríne, brigáde*.

Having determined the rule for words with a tense vowel in the final syllable, we next turn to those with a lax vowel to see where stress falls in them. As the following lists show, lax vowels may be stressed:

A	B
eléct	consíder
suggést	cóvet
colléct	abándon
depénd	astónish
collápse	detérmine
abrúpt	cértain
exáct	ópen
corréct	sólid
absúrd	hándsome
overt	sílver

For reasons which will be made clear shortly, only verbs and adjectives have been included. The difference between the words in the two columns cannot be the number of syllables or the part of speech, nor can it be the final segment. And both columns contain words with lax vowels in their final syllables. The difference is that the words in column A all end with a cluster of two or more consonants, whereas those in column B end in not more than one consonant. Stress placement is performed before inflectional endings such as past and plural are given a phonetic shape. Otherwise the consonant cluster resulting from the addition of [d] would give such incorrent results as [əbændənd], *abandóned*. We have begun to state rules for assigning stress to verbs and adjectives:

Rule 7.7   Place stress on the last tense vowel of a word.

Rule 7.8   Place stress on the last vowel of a verb or adjective if it is followed by a cluster of two or more consonants.

Rule 7.9   Place stress on next to the last vowel of a verb or adjective if neither of the above conditions is met.

Nouns with a tense vowel in the final syllable follow Rule 7.7, as do verbs and adjectives. Those with final lax vowels do not follow 7.8 and 7.9: *ásterisk, fórest, lábyrinth, móment.* Since these words end in two-consonant clusters, we expect the last vowel to be stressed. It is not. Let us examine some more nouns:

A	B	C
aréna	surrénder	aspáragus
amoéba	compléxion	sýllable
halitósis	lántern	élephant
sécret	cóuncil	metrópolis
ágent	tárget	cínema
únit	veránda	análysis
aróma	appéndix	vénison
horízon	uténsil	ársenal

If we disregard the last lax vowel and all consonants following it, we are left with the following **noun remnants**:

A	B	C
arén-	surrénd-	aspárag-
amoéb-	compléx-	sýllab-
halitós-	lánt-	éleph-
sécr-	cóunc-	metrópol-
ág-	tárg-	cínem-
ún-	veránd-	análys-
aróm-	appénd-	vénis-
horíz-	uténs-	ársen-

Using these remnants, we can form the following rules:

Column A: Place stress on the last tense vowel of a noun remnant.

Column B: Place stress on the last vowel of a noun remnant if it is fol-
             lowed by a cluster of two or more consonants.

Column C: Place stress on next to the last vowel of a noun remnant if
             neither of the above conditions is met.

These are practically the same rules as 7.7–7.9, and we are missing a generalization if we state them separately for noun remnants and for verbs and adjectives.
We can combine them as follows:

Rule 7.7′   Place stress on the last tense vowel of a word or a noun
             remnant.

Rule 7.8′   Place stress on the last vowel of a verb, adjective, or noun rem-
             nant if it is followed by a cluster of two or more consonants.

Rule 7.9′   Place stress on next to the last vowel of a verb, adjective, or
             noun remnant if neither of the above conditions is met.

Rule 7.10   Place stress on the only vowel of a monosyllabic word or noun
             remnant.

Rule 7.10 is needed to assign stress to words such as *rún* and *párent*.
   We can illustrate the rules for stress placement with examples:

1. *believe*: The last syllable contains a tense vowel; the part of speech is,
    therefore, not important. The tense vowel receives stress: *belíeve*.
    (Rule 7.7′)

2. *resist*: The word is a verb ending with a cluster of two consonants.
    The vowel before this consonant cluster receives stress: *resíst*. (Rule
    7.8′)

3. *deliver*: The word is a verb. The last vowel is not tense and it is not
    followed by a consonant cluster. Stress falls on next to the last vowel:
    delíver. (Rule 7.9′)

4. *horizon*: The word is a noun, and the last vowel is lax; this lax vowel
    and the consonant that follows are removed from consideration, leav-
    ing *horiz-*. Since the last vowel in the noun remnant is tense, it re-
    ceives stress: *horízon*. (Rule 7.7′)

5. *appendix*: The word is a noun, and the last vowel is lax. Since the
    word is a noun, the final consonant cluster [ks] does not affect stress
    placement. The final lax vowel and the following consonants are
    dropped from consideration: *append-*. The noun remnant ends in
    the consonant cluster [nd]. This consonant cluster determines stress
    placement on the preceding vowel: *appéndix*. (Rule 7.8′)

6. *elephant*: The word is a noun. The final lax vowel is dropped from

consideration along with all consonants that follow it: *eleph-*. In the
noun remnant the last vowel is lax, and it is not followed by a consonant cluster. The rules apply to pronunciation, [f] , not spelling, *ph*.
Stress, therefore, falls on the preceding vowel: *élephant*. (Rule 7.9′)

Stress Placement with Affixes

With the rules for stress placement we see that phonology is not independent
of the rest of the grammar. These rules as well as many others in the phonological component require syntactic information for their application. Knowledge
of part of speech is essential for correct stress placement. This dependence upon
syntactic information is especially obvious in stress placement for words that are
formed by the addition of affixes.

In some cases the derived word has a stress pattern different from that of the
original word: *ínstrument, ȋnstruméntal; áccident, âccidéntal*. The mark ^ indicates **secondary stress**, which is weaker than ′ or **primary stress**. If we use the
information that *instrumental* is an adjective derived from the noun *instrument*,
we can assign the correct stress placement without the addition of new rules.
We can show this information about *instrumental* as follows:

$$[\ [\text{instrument}]_N \ + \ \text{al} \ ]_{Adj}$$

Most affixes contain the boundary marker + to indicate their status as morphemes below the level of words. To assign stress, we start with the innermost
brackets: [instrument]$_N$. This is a noun with a final lax vowel. We disregard
this vowel and the following consonants: *instrum-*. The noun remnant ends in
a lax vowel, and it is not followed by a consonant cluster; stress, therefore, falls
on the preceding vowel: [ínstrument]$_N$. If our final word were *instrument* instead of *instrumental*, this would correctly assign stress and we would be through.
Since our word is *instrumental*, however, we have an additional step. After assigning stress to *instrument*, we erase the innermost brackets:

$$[\text{ínstrument} \ + \ \text{al}]_{Adj}$$

We are now concerned with applying the stress rules for an adjective. As we will
see shortly, adjectival suffixes containing lax vowels are disregarded just as final
lax vowels in nouns are. Of the remainder, *instrument-*, we are considering an
adjective; hence the final consonant cluster requires stress placement on the
vowel before it, giving

$$[\text{ínstruméntal}]_{Adj}$$

By a special convention, any time we add stress to a word which has already received stress (such as the first vowel in *instrument*), all previously placed stresses are reduced:

$$[\hat{\text{i}}\text{nstrum\'ental}]_{\text{Adj}}$$

We say that stress assignment rules are applied **cyclically**. Of the rules for assigning stress to verbs, adjectives, and nouns, we go down the list applying all possible rules for the element within innermost brackets, *instrument* in our example. We call this the **first cycle**. After these brackets are erased, we again run through the rules and apply all that are possible; this is the **second cycle**. If there are still brackets which can be erased, we proceed to the third cycle, the fourth, and so on until we reach the outermost brackets.

We can follow the same rules as we did for *instrumental* in deriving the stress placement for *accidental*:

$$[\ [\text{accident}]_{\text{N}} + \text{al}]_{\text{Adj}}$$

First cycle
    Rule 7.9 ′ $[\text{\'accident}]_{\text{N}}$
Second cycle $[\text{\'accident} + \text{al}]_{\text{Adj}}$
    Rule 7.8 ′ $[\text{\'accid\'ental}]_{\text{Adj}}$
    Stress reduction $[\hat{\text{a}}\text{ccid\'ental}]_{\text{Adj}}$

On the first cycle the noun *accident* receives stress on the first vowel. The last vowel is lax; of the remnant, *accid-*, the last vowel is lax and is not followed by a consonant cluster, thereby placing stress on the preceding vowel. On the second cycle the adjective *accidental* receives stress on the next to the last vowel. The suffix with the lax vowel is disregarded, and the remainder, *accident-*, ends in a consonant cluster. The previously assigned stress is reduced to secondary: *âccidéntal*. Since we are now at the outermost brackets, there are no further cycles.

Some derived words retain the stress on the same syllable as that of the original word:

$$[\ [\text{propose}]_{\text{V}} + \text{al}]_{\text{N}}$$

Starting with the first cycle, we place stress on the final tense vowel of the verb:

$$[\text{prop\'ose}]_{\text{V}}$$

Erasing innermost brackets, we now have a noun on the second cycle:

$$[\text{prop\'ose} + \text{al}]_N$$

The final lax vowel and the following consonant of the noun are disregarded. Of the remnant *propose-*, the last vowel is tense and receives stress:

$$[\text{prop\'osal}]_N$$

Stress reduction is inapplicable since the new stress is placed on the same vowel as the former.

Earlier we said that adjectival suffixes containing lax vowels are disregarded as are final syllables of nouns with lax vowels. Let us see the reason for this.

$$[\,[\text{instrument}]_N + \text{al}]_{\text{Adj}} \qquad [\,[\text{person}]_N + \text{al}]_{\text{Adj}} \qquad [\,[\text{vigil}]_N + \text{ant}]_{\text{Adj}}$$

On the first cycle the nouns receive stress placement and innermost brackets are erased:

$$[\text{\'instrument} + \text{al}]_{\text{Adj}} \qquad [\text{p\'erson} + \text{al}]_{\text{Adj}} \qquad [\text{v\'igil} + \text{ant}]_{\text{Adj}}$$

If we were to treat these like other adjectives, *instrumental* would receive the correct stress placement. The last vowel is lax, and it is not followed by a consonant cluster; stress is placed on the preceding vowel. In *personal*, however, this line of reasoning would place stress incorrectly on the second vowel: *persónal*. *Vigilant* ends in a consonant cluster, thereby incorrectly requiring stress on the last vowel: *vigilánt*. If we disregard the final lax vowel of the suffix and the consonants following it, we are able to assign stress correctly. The remnant *instrument-* ends in a consonant cluster, thereby placing stress on the preceding vowel: *instrumént-*. Each of the remnants *person-* and *vigil-* ends in a lax vowel and no consonant cluster; stress goes on the preceding vowel: *pérson-* and *vígil-*. Hence, stress placement proceeds as follows:

$$[\,[\text{person}]_N + \text{al}]_{\text{Adj}} \qquad\qquad [\,[\text{vigil}]_N + \text{ant}]_{\text{Adj}}$$

First Cycle		
Rule 7.8′	$[\text{p\'erson}]_N$	
Rule 7.10		$[\text{v\'igil}]_N$
Second Cycle	$[\text{p\'erson} + \text{al}]_{\text{Adj}}$	$[\text{v\'igil} + \text{ant}]_{\text{Adj}}$
Rule 7.9′	$[\text{p\'ersonal}]_{\text{Adj}}$	$[\text{v\'igilant}]_{\text{Adj}}$

Stress reduction is inapplicable.

Stress Placement in Phrases and Sentences

For the kinds of words we have considered, the rules place stress in a manner that agrees with the native speaker's knowledge. When words are combined to form sentences, the syllables within a word retain the same stress relationships to each other as they have when the words are pronounced in isolation:

7.4   The donkey swallowed an apple.

The first syllable of *donkey* has stronger stress than the second, whether the word is in isolation or in a sentence. The same principle holds true for *swallowed* and *apple*. But if we compare the stressed syllables of the various words in the sentence, we discover that they do not all have the same strength if we read with normal sentence intonation and do not give special emphasis to any word. The first syllable of *apple* has the strongest stress of all; *the* and *an* are not stressed. By listening carefully, we can hear that the first syllable in *donkey* is stronger than that in *swallowed*.

The pattern for placing stress in structures larger than the word will be clearer if we start with phrases and build up to sentences. The heaviest stress is on a syllable in each of the italicized words:

7.5   swallowed an *ápple* (verb phrase)
7.6   a large *élephant* (noun phrase)
7.7   slightly *górgeous* (adjective phrase)

In each case it is the last word in the phrase that takes the heaviest stress.

Let us make this a bit more precise. The syntactic surface structure provides us with a noun phrase such as the following:

$$[\text{ a } [\text{large}]_{\text{Adj}} \; [\text{elephant}]_{\text{N}} \;]_{\text{NP}}$$

On the first cycle the adjective *large* receives stress, as does the noun *elephant*:

$$[\text{lárge}]_{\text{Adj}} \; [\text{élephant}]_{\text{N}}$$

We erase innermost brackets:

$$[\text{a lárge élephant}]_{\text{NP}}$$

None of the rules we have given so far are applicable, since they apply only to nouns, verbs, adjectives, and noun remnants, and not to structures larger than the word. We need a new rule:

Rule 7.11   For structures larger than the word, place primary stress on
              the last stressed vowel.

This rule will keep the primary stress on the first vowel of *elephant*; the convention of reduction of other stresses will change that on *large* to secondary:

$$[\text{a lârge élephant}]_{NP}$$

This rule, called the **nuclear stress rule**, accounts for stress placement in structures larger than the word.
     Let us now return to our original sentence:

$$[\ [\text{the } [\text{donkey}]_N \ ]_{NP} \ [\ [\text{swallowed}]_V \ [\text{an } [\text{apple}]_N \ ]_{NP} \ ]_{VP} \ ]_S$$

Since the NP and the VP are equal, neither embedded within the other, they are
treated simultaneously. For the purpose of clarity, however, we will treat one
and then the other. Starting with the noun phrase, in cycle one primary stress
is placed on the first vowel:

$$[\text{dónkey}]_N$$

Brackets are erased, and on the second cycle we are dealing with a noun phrase:

$$[\text{the dónkey}]_{NP}$$

The nuclear stress rule applies; but since there is only one previously assigned
stress, there are none to be reduced, and the stress pattern of the phrase remains
unchanged.
     Turning to the verb phrase, we treat the most deeply embedded structures:
swallowed and *apple*:

$$[\text{swállowed}]_V \qquad [\text{ápple}]_N$$

Primary stress is assigned on the first cycle. Innermost brackets are erased, and
on the second cycle the nuclear stress rule is applied to the noun phrase:

$$[\text{an ápple}]_{NP}$$

As with *the donkey*, there are no stresses to be reduced. Brackets are again
erased:

$$[\text{swállowed an ápple}]_{VP}$$

The nuclear stress rule assigns primary stress to the first syllable of *apple*, and all other stresses are reduced:

[swâllowed an ápple]$_{VP}$

Putting the noun phrase and the verb phrase together, we have

[[the dónkey]$_{NP}$ [swâllowed an ápple]$_{VP}$]$_S$

Erasing innermost brackets and applying the nuclear stress rule, we derive

[the dônkey swàllowed an ápple]$_S$

The mark ` indicates **tertiary stress**, one degree weaker than secondary. With only one new rule, the nuclear stress rule, and the cyclic principle we are able to provide the correct stress pattern for any structure larger than a word.

Underlying and Surface Forms of Vowels

Let us now return to single words with affixes to try to account for some of the apparent irregularities that exist in certain words. The addition of affixes can shift the stress placement in a word in a systematic way which is predictable by rule. Often this shifting of stress is accompanied by a change in vowels. For example, *parent* has the phonetic representation [pǽrənt], but *parental* has [pəréntəl]. If we are to show that these words are related, differing only in the adjectival suffix *-al* in *parental*, we encounter a problem in deciding which lexical representation to use. If we use both [pǽrənt] and [pərent] in the lexicon, we are not showing that the two forms are more closely related than [pǽrənt] and [pǽtənt]. We are, in fact, suggesting that [pǽrənt] and [pərent] are as unsystematically related as *go* and *went*. Yet the vowel alternation in *parent, parental* is found in other pairs of words as well: *accident, accidental*; *experiment, experimental*; *department, departmental*; *development, developmental*, to name a few. A more attractive suggestion would be to select either /pǽrənt/ or /pərent/ as an **underlying representation** for both surface forms. In this way we would be showing that the two forms are systematically related. Yet there is a problem with this suggestion. If /pǽrənt/ is selected as the underlying form, how are we to know that the underlying /ə/ changes to [e], rather than to some other vowel in the surface form [pəréntəl]? Or, if /pərent/ is the underlying form, how can we predict that /ə/ will change to [æ] in [pǽrənt]? Clearly we need only one underlying representation, but neither /pǽrənt/ nor /pərent/ is acceptable. In syntax we were not required to use as underlying representations only those which could appear as surface manifestations; in phonology we should also be allowed to use relatively abstract underlying forms which do not appear on the surface. If we use /pærent/ as the underlying representation, both surface forms [pærənt] and [pərent] can be accounted for by systematic rules.

Let us see how this is possible. In the following words all of the unstressed vowels have something in common:

éstimàte [éstəmeẏt]
dilápidàted [dəlǽpədèytəd]
Fránkenstèin [fréyŋkənstàyn]
sàtisfáction [sæ̀təsfǽkšən]
Kánsas [kǽnzəs]

Each unstressed vowel is phonetically [ə].† The grammar needs the following rule:

Rule 7.12   Reduce all unstressed lax vowels to [ə].

For *parent* and *parental*, we have the following derivations:

Underlying form	/pærent/	/pærent + æl/
Stress rules	pǽrent	pæréntæl
Rule 7.12	pǽrənt	pəréntəl
Surface form	[pǽrənt]	[pəréntəl]

By assigning /pærent/ as the underlying representation, through the regular rules of stress placement and vowel reduction (7.12) we are able to show the systematic relationship between the surface forms [pǽrənt] and [pəréntəl].

With abstract underlying representations we are able to show how other pairs of surface forms are related:

Underlying	Surface	
/græmær/	[grǽmər]	[grəmǽriən]
/telegræf/	[téləgræ̀f]	[təlégrəfiy]
/vʌlgær/	[vʌ́lgər]	[vəlgǽrətiy]

†For many speakers of English there are two reduced vowels: [ə] and [ɨ]. The second of these sounds is sometimes called "barred *i*," and for many people it is the last vowel in *business, bracelet, careless,* and a great many other words. Since the rules which determine the selection of [ə] or [ɨ] are not yet clear, we will simplify our presentation by using only one reduced vowel: [ə]. For some speakers of English this is the only reduced vowel.

/+ æl/   [pʌ́rsənəl]   [pʌ̀rsənǽlətiy]
/nowbil/   [nówbəl]   [nòwbílətiy]
/mowment/   [mówmənt]   [mòwméntəs]
/metæl/   [métəl]   [mətǽlik]

These abstract underlying forms show the relationship among different surface
forms, such as [métəl] and [mətǽlik]. Often an underlying form is similar to
the conventional spelling of the word:

/pærent/   parent   /+ æl/   -al
/græmær/   grammar   /mowment/   moment
/vʌlgær/   vulgar   /metæl/   metal

The reason for this will become clear in Chapter Nine, where we show that English spelling is based on underlying rather than surface forms.

Let us now see how the rule for vowel reduction fits in with the stress placement rules.

Underlying	$[[sentr]_N + æl]_{Adj}$	$[[[sentr]_N + æl]_{Adj} + ətiy]_N$
First Cycle		
Stress placement	$[séntr]_N$	$[séntr]_N$
Second Cycle		
Stress placement	$[séntræl]_{Adj}$	$[séntræl]_{Adj}$
Third Cycle		
Stress placement		$[sêntrǽlətiy]_N$
Postcyclic		
Vowel reduction	$[séntrəl]$	$[sêntrǽlətiy]$

Non-low final vowels become tense before the vowel reduction rule takes place;
thus, the final [iy] of *centrality* does not reduce.

We should now see why vowel reduction is not applied cyclically, as stress
placement is, but rather only once at the end of the cycle, i.e., postcyclically.
Let us consider *centrality*:

Underlying:	$[[[sentr]_N + æl]_{Adj} + ətiy]_N$
First Cycle	
Stress placement	$[séntr]_N$
Vowel reduction	(not applicable)

Second Cycle
    Stress placement $[\text{séntræl}]_{\text{Adj}}$
    Vowel reduction $[\text{séntrəl}]_{\text{Adj}}$

Third Cycle
    Stress placement $[\text{sêntrələtiy}]_{\text{N}}$
    Vowel reduction   (not applicable)

With this derivation we obtain [ə] as the second vowel instead of [æ]. Since rules applied in succeeding cycles can shift the stress pattern, vowel reduction must not be performed until all cyclical operations are completed.

Spirantization and Palatalization

Under certain circumstances the derivation of words with affixes causes changes in addition to stress placement and vowel reduction, as shown in the [t] and [s] alternation below:

	A	B
	permit	permissive
	constant	constancy
	democrat	democracy
	president	presidency

As with the vowels in *parent* and *parental*, we reject listing /pərmit/ and /pərmis/ or any of the other pairs above as two separate forms in the lexicon. Obviously the variation of [t] and [s] is not an isolated occurrence in *permit* and *permissive*, but a regular, systematic alternation that occurs in words ending in /t/ to which certain suffixes are added. In each case the suffix begins with a high vowel or glide: /i/ or /y/. The change of /t/ to [s] before a suffix beginning with a high front vowel or glide is called **spirantization**. The words in column B above have underlying forms as follows:

$$[\ [\text{pərmit}]_{\text{V}} + \text{iv}\ ]_{\text{Adj}}$$
$$[\ [\text{kanstənt}]_{\text{Adj}} + y\ ]_{\text{N}}$$
$$[\ [\text{demakræt}]_{\text{N}} + y\ ]_{\text{N}}$$
$$[\ [\text{prezədent}]_{\text{N}} + y\ ]_{\text{N}}$$

These underlying forms show that the words in column B are related to those in column A. Spirantization converts the /t/ of the underlying representation to the [s] of the surface form.

Another change known as **palatalization** occurs when one of the alveolar obstruents /s, z, t, d/ is followed by the glide /y/ and an unstressed vowel. The word *pressure* offers an example of the process:

$$[\ [pres]_V + y \partial r]_N$$

The alveolar /s/ becomes the palatal [š] : [prešyər]. A later rule deletes the [y] to give [prešər]. Other words which undergo palatalization and glide deletion are *official, expression, confession,* and a great many more. Some words first undergo spirantization, changing /t/ to /s/; the /s/ then palatalizes to [š]:

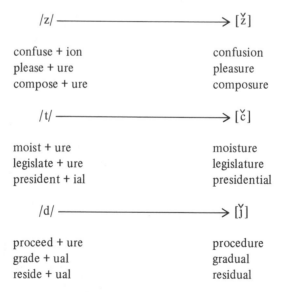

/t/ ⎯⎯⎯⎯⎯⎯→ /s/ ⎯⎯⎯⎯⎯⎯→ [š]

commit + ion	commission
act + ion	action
delegate + ion	delegation
prohibit + ion	prohibition

Other examples of palatalization are as follows:

/z/ ⎯⎯⎯⎯⎯⎯⎯⎯⎯⎯⎯⎯⎯⎯→ [ž]

confuse + ion	confusion
please + ure	pleasure
compose + ure	composure

/t/ ⎯⎯⎯⎯⎯⎯⎯⎯⎯⎯⎯⎯⎯⎯→ [č]

moist + ure	moisture
legislate + ure	legislature
president + ial	presidential

/d/ ⎯⎯⎯⎯⎯⎯⎯⎯⎯⎯⎯⎯⎯⎯→ [ǰ]

proceed + ure	procedure
grade + ual	gradual
reside + ual	residual

We can summarize these rules with the derivation of *action*:

$$[\ [\text{ækt}]_V + \text{yən}]_N$$

First Cycle
    Stress placement $[\text{ǽkt}]_V$
Second Cycle
    Stress placement $[\text{ǽktyən}]_N$

    Spirantization $[\text{ǽksyən}]_N$

    Palatalization $[\text{ǽkšyən}]_N$

    Glide deletion $[\text{ǽkšən}]_N$

Palatalization is not restricted to the word, but applies to larger structures as well:

pass you	[pǽšuw]
his youth	[hižuwθ]
can't you	[kænčuw]
would you	[wujuw]

Performance factors may block the application of palatalization, but in normal speech it is found frequently. Vowel reduction accounts for the usual pronunciation of *the* and *a* as [ðə] and [ə]. They must be given underlying forms with full vowels, however, since they may be emphasized, as in "I didn't say he's *a* major; I said he's *the* major," in which case they are pronounced [ey] and [ðiy].

Conclusion

Phonological rules convert a syntactic surface structure into a phonetic manifestation. Like syntactic transformational rules, they add, delete, rearrange, and substitute. They do not affect meaning, nor do they alter syntactic structures.

Phonological rules rely upon syntactic information for their application. For example, the rules for stress placement can function properly only if we know whether a unit is a noun, an adjective, a verb, or a structure larger than a word. Without the syntactic information that is supplied by a tree or a labeled bracketing, we are unable to predict the stress patterns for words and sentences.

A person may ask what the purpose of underlying phonological forms is, and why the lexicon does not provide surface phonetic representations to syntactic structures. Such a procedure is possible, but it would create two problems. First, the lexicon would have to be expanded considerably to give separate entries for [prés] and [présšər], for [dəpárt] and [dəpárčər]. Second, and more seriously, such an approach would fail to show the system that controls these alternations. The differences in stress, vowels, and consonants between *resident* and *residential* would be considered as idiosyncratic as that between *go* and *went, good* and *better,* or *ox* and *oxen.* Yet the same process which causes the alternation of [s] and [š] causes that of [t] and [č] in *depart* and *departure* or of [t] and [š] in *resident* and *residential,* as well as similar alternations in hundreds of other pairs of words. The change in stress pattern and in vowels between *resident* and *residential* is governed by the same principles which cause that between *grammar* and *grammarian, rigid* and *rigidity,* and hundreds of other pairs. By the use of underlying forms and phonological rules, we can show that many apparently idiosyncratic surface forms are in fact perfectly regular. This is also the purpose of underlying structures in syntax.

The goal of our grammar is to account for as much of the native speaker's knowledge of the language as is possible. Only by limiting the lexicon to truly idiosyncratic, unpredictable information and stating all generalizations as rules can we hope to approach this goal.

Exercises

A. In this chapter several possibilities for the formation of noun plurals were rejected. Were these objections valid only for English, or is it possible that they apply to other languages as well?

B. Under the discussion of noun plurals, a listing was given of the final sounds which take each of the three endings. Add one additional word after each of the sounds.

C. Use rules 7.1–7.3 to form the plurals of the following words: *strap, match, laugh, bead, ridge.* Use your internalized grammar to check the results.

D. Why is a description of plural formation such as that given in rules 7.1–7.3 preferable to a listing of the sounds which take each of the three endings?

E. Use rules 7.4–7.6 to give the past-tense forms of the following verbs: *drag, stop, pass, paste, pad.*

F. How does our grammar indicate the past-tense forms of *go, say, sing,* and *be*?

G. How does a phonological rule differ from a redundancy rule? Use original examples.

H. How do phonemic and phonetic representations differ?

I. Use the stress placement rules to explain why the following words are stressed as they are:

1. office	4. gentle	7. country
2. condone	5. elect	8. account
3. consider	6. wonder	9. abrupt

10. family	17. theater	24. collection
11. decide	18. abandon	25. amazement
12. sudden	19. suppose	26. straighten
13. legend	20. recipe	27. delightful
14. direct	21. disturbance	28. consolation
15. attend	22. awaken	29. doubtful
16. seldom	23. political	30. amusement

J. What reason is there for trying to formulate rules for stress placement rather than listening to a word as it is pronounced and marking stress according to what is heard? The second possibility would account accurately for all words and leave no exceptions, whereas with our present state of knowledge the rules are incomplete and leave a great many exceptions.

K. Use rules to account for the stress patterns in the following phrases and sentences:
1. a noble effort
2. rather friendly
3. shot a tiger
4. A man opened the door.
5. The table collapsed.

L. What is meant by a cyclic rule? By a postcyclic rule? What reasons are there for making a distinction?

M. Why must the rules for stress placement within a single word be applied before the nuclear stress rule?

N. Why does the lexicon contain abstract underlying representations rather than surface forms?

O. By using other forms of each of the following words, with or without affixes as we did for *parent* and *parental*, provide underlying forms:

1. molecular	6. general	
2. organ	7. addition	
3. production	8. prosper	
4. moral	9. confirm	
5. principal	10. competition	

P. Read the following sentences as you would use them under the following circumstances: (1) to a small child, (2) to a close friend in a normal conversation, (3) as a repetition to someone who did not understand you the first time:
1. Watch what you are doing.
2. I will miss you.
3. We fed your rabbits.
How does the situation affect palatalization, vowel reduction, and other aspects of pronunciation?

Q. Mark off the suffixes from the following words and indicate where spiran-
    tization and palatalization have occurred:

    1. communication   6. comical
    2. subversive   7. exposure
    3. corrective   8. gracious
    4. Grecian   9. painful
    5. dependency   10. culture

Suggested Reading

Chomsky, Noam, and Halle, Morris. *The Sound Pattern of English*. New York:
    Harper & Row, 1968.
Halle, Morris. "Phonology in Generative Grammar." *Word* 18 (1962): 54–72.
    Reprinted in Fodor and Katz, 1964.
_____. *The Sound Pattern of Russian*. The Hague: Mouton, 1959.
Harms, Robert T. *Introduction to Phonological Theory*. Englewood Cliffs,
    N.J.: Prentice-Hall, 1968.
Postal, Paul M. *Aspects of Phonological Theory*. New York: Harper & Row,
    1968.

CHAPTER EIGHT

Phonological Change

In the last two chapters we examined the features of English sounds and the rules that constitute the phonological component of the grammar. We considered this aspect of the grammar from a synchronic viewpoint, without attention to changes in time. We will now examine phonology from a diachronic perspective, in which we study the alterations in the grammar that occur from one period of time to another.

The most common kind of change in a language is the addition of a word to the lexicon. When *astronaut* was added, the lexicon was given one more entry with semantic, syntactic, and phonological information specified. Beyond this increase in the lexicon, the addition of the word brought no changes to the grammar. The word can function as a deep-structure case category that undergoes the already existing syntactic rules to become part of a surface structure. It can be classified as count and human. It also follows the rules for plural formation and the other rules of the phonological component. The addition of *astronaut* did not affect the grammar beyond increasing the size of the lexicon.

There are other ways in which the lexicon but no other part of the grammar can be affected. The loss of the entry *eftsoons* did not alter any rule in the grammar; it merely diminished the size of the lexicon. When some speakers altered their pronunciation of *ration* from [ræšən] to [reyšən], they changed the lexical form of this one word, but the phonological rules remained unaffected.

In addition to changes in individual lexical entries, there are those which alter the phonological rules themselves and affect the phonetic forms of whole classes of words. If a rule is added which deletes [r] whenever it follows a vowel, as in *heard, purse, far, pour*, the results are more far reaching and, therefore, more interesting than changes in individual words. In the discussion that follows we will consider three kinds of change in the rules of a grammar: addition, generalization, and loss.[†]

[†]For a more extensive discussion of these processes see Robert D. King, *Historical Linguistics and Generative Grammar* (Englewood Cliffs, N.J.: Prentice-Hall, 1969). King includes a fourth process, reordering, which we are not including in this discussion. Although this process has probably occurred a number of times, with our present state of knowledge, uncomplicated examples in English are rare.

Rule Addition

One of the most common kinds of change in phonology is the addition of a new phonological rule. One such addition was the palatalization rule, which changed the alveolar obstruents /t, d, s, z/ to the palatals [č, ǰ, š, ž] if they were followed by the glide /y/ and an unstressed vowel. Speakers of English who did not add this rule had the following underlying and surface forms. (As elsewhere, underlying forms are greatly simplified so that we may concentrate on the issue at hand without the distraction of other rules.)

	righteous	gradual	pressure	vision
Underlying:	/raytyəs/	/grædyuwəl/	/presyər/	/vizyən/
Surface:	[raytyəs]	[grædyuwəl]	[presyər]	[vizyən]

Those who added the rule also added a later one which deleted /y/ if it followed a palatal obstruent (i.e., /č, ǰ, š, ž/), and they had the following forms:

	/raytyəs/	/grædyuwəl/	/presyər/	/vizyən/
Underlying:	/raytyəs/	/grædyuwəl/	/presyər/	/vizyən/
Palatalization:	raytčyəs	græǰyuwəl	prešyər	vižyən
/y/ deletion:	raytčəs	græǰuwəl	prešər	vižən
Surface:	[raytčəs]	[græǰuwəl]	[prešər]	[vižən]

Although the surface forms of *righteous, gradual, pressure, vision,* and similar words contained the palatal obstruents [č, ǰ, š, ž] , related words such as *right, grade, press,* and *envisage* had the alveolars [t, d, s, z] . The most satisfactory way for the grammar to show the relationships between such words as *grade* and *gradual* is to give both of them an underlying form with /d/ and incorporate a palatalization rule in the grammar. In this way, the alternation of [d] and [ǰ] is shown to be not an idiosyncratic feature of these words but rather a regular alternation that occurs with a great many other pairs of words. The addition of the palatalization rule, therefore, left the underlying forms unchanged, but it altered the pronunciations of many surface forms.

As with other changes in language, the palatalization rule was not added simultaneously to the grammars of all speakers. No doubt there were periods of time in which the presence or absence of the rule said a great deal about how old the speaker was, which region of England he lived in, and which social class he belonged to. The earliest evidence that the palatalization rule was added is found in the fifteenth-century Paston letters, in which spellings such as *sesschyonys,* "sessions," and *conschens,* "conscience," are seen.[†] Later spellings which reflect

---

[†] All citations in this paragraph are from H. C. Wyld, *A History of Modern Colloquial English* (Oxford: Basil Blackwell, 1956), pp. 293–94). Additional examples can be found in E. J. Dobson, *English Pronunciation 1500–1700* (Oxford: Clarendon Press, 1957, 1968).

the presence of the rule are *ishu*, "issue," *fondashon*, "foundation," *shur*, "sure." Further evidence for the rule can be found in statements made by various people about this pronunciation, as when we are told that *ocean* is pronounced "oshan" and that *sugar* is pronounced with "sh." Eventually the rule spread to all speakers of English.

Some rules last for only a short period of time. Speakers of later generations do not incorporate them into their grammars, but rather develop different underlying forms from those of their predecessors. The palatalization rule is not of this kind. There have been enough alternations such as *confess, confession; palace, palatial; moist, moisture; confuse, confusion* for people developing grammars to continue including the palatalization rule. Further evidence for the continuation of the rule is found in the modern pronunciations [kænčuw], [wujuw], [mišuw], and [pliyžuw] for "can't you," "would you," "miss you," and "please you." These pronunciations and a great many more of this type are apparently considered the normal spoken form by most speakers of English, but the rule can be readily omitted for purposes of emphasis or clarity.

Palatalization is applicable only when the alveolar obstruent is followed by the glide /y/. Since such words as *odious, medium,* and *piteous* have underlying /i/ instead of /y/, palatalization does not occur. There are differences among dialects as to whether /y/ or /i/ is found in certain words:

	Underlying /y/	Underlying /i/
Rhodesia	[rowdiyžə]	[rowdiyziə]
immediate	[imiyjət]	[imiydiət]
nausea	[nɔwžə]	[nɔwziə]
gaseous	[gæšəs]	[gæsiəs]
idiot	[ijət]	[idiət]
Indian	[injən]	[indiən]

For some words such as *Indian*, social attitudes affect the presence of underlying /y/ or of /i/. Of the examples we have just given, there are probably very few people who have all the words with underlying /y/ or all with /i/.

Rule Generalization

Sometimes a rule that is added to the grammar undergoes later changes so that it applies to a larger, more general class of sounds than the original rule did. Palatalization may be an example of such rule generalization. Examples of the palatalization of /s/ before /y/ plus unstressed vowel are found as early as the fifteenth century, but evidence for the inclusion of /z, t, d/ is not found until the sixteenth and seventeenth centuries. However, it may well be that the rule

230   Linguistics and the English Language

applied to all four sounds from the start and that the early evidence for palatalization of /z, t, d/ is by chance no longer extant or that the change was merely not reflected in writing.

A generalization of a rule about which we have more definite information is the loss of /y/. As we saw in the preceding section, a rule was added to the grammar which deleted the glide /y/ after palatal obstruents, i.e., after those segments with the following feature combination:

$$\begin{bmatrix} +\text{cons} \\ -\text{voc} \\ +\text{coronal} \\ -\text{anterior} \\ -\text{nasal} \end{bmatrix} \qquad /\check{c}, \check{j}, \check{s}, \check{z}/$$

For many dialects of American English, the rule was generalized to apply to all palatal segments that were [+cons] and [-nasal], not just the obstruents: /č, ǰ, š, ž, r/. And it was also extended to include segments that are [+anterior] and [+continuant]: /č, ǰ, š, ž, r, l, θ, ð, s, z/. The surface forms listed under B resulted in the dialects that adopted this extension; those under A do not show it:

		A	B
righteous	[č]	[raycǒs]	[raycǒs]
gradual	[ǰ]	[græǰuwəl]	[græǰuwəl]
pressure	[š]	[prešər]	[prešər]
vision	[ž]	[vižən]	[vižən]
rude	[r]	[ryuwd]	[ruwd]
lunatic	[l]	[lyuwnətik]	[luwnətik]
enthusiasm	[θ]	[enθyuwziyæzəm]	[enθuwziyæzəm]
pursue	[s]	[pərsyuw]	[pərsuw]
resume	[z]	[rəzyuwm]	[rəzuwm]

Examples with [ð] are rare or nonexistent. Although speakers with the A forms are to be found in the United States, those with the B forms are by now much more numerous. The earlier, more restricted form of the rule, as exemplified by the forms under A, is probably still more common in British English, although within the last two decades there have been indications that the extended form of the rule has been gaining ground.

In American English an even more generalized form of the rule has emerged so that instances of /y/ after /n, t, d/ are included. This extension of the rule is illustrated on the following page:

		Without extension	With extension
news	[n]	[nyuwz]	[nuwz]
tune	[t]	[tyuwn]	[tuwn]
due	[d]	[dyuw]	[duw]

During the 1940s speakers who had or who did not have this extension of the rule could be fairly well recognized as to the section of the country in which they lived. Since that time the extension has spread to most younger speakers in all parts of the United States.

The rule for the deletion of /y/ after palatal obstruents was thus made to apply to a larger class of segments. Originally it applied to /y/ following segments which were

$$
\begin{bmatrix}
+\text{cons} \\
-\text{voc} \\
+\text{coronal} \\
-\text{anterior} \\
-\text{nasal}
\end{bmatrix}
$$

It has finally been generalized by some speakers to apply to the following larger class:

$$
\begin{bmatrix}
+\text{cons} \\
+\text{coronal}
\end{bmatrix}
$$

There is no indication that the rule is being further generalized to include segments that are [–coronal]:

[p]	[pyuwniy]	puny
[b]	[byuwtiy]	beauty
[f]	[fyuw]	few
[v]	[vyuw]	view
[m]	[myuwzik]	music
[k]	[kyuwt]	cute
[g]	[argyuw]	argue
[h]	[hyuwmən]	human

In some dialects initial [h] is lost in such words as *human, humid,* and *hue,* but the [y] remains. There is also no indication that initial [y] is being lost as in *eunuch, ewe, Yukon,* etc.

The changes to the grammar that are illustrated by /y/ deletion are first **rule addition** and second **rule generalization**.

Rule Loss

A third type of change that may occur in a grammar is **rule loss**. That is, a rule which has been part of the grammar of a language ceases to be incorporated into the grammars of speakers of succeeding generations. Early in the Old English period a phonological rule was added which changed the feature [+back] to [-back] under certain circumstances. This change is known as **umlaut**, and in its broadest application also includes changing [-back] to [+back] and even changing the plus or minus value of *high*. Umlaut was not restricted to Old English, but occurred in all of the Germanic languages except Gothic: Old Norse, Old High German, Old Saxon, Old Frisian, and Old Low Franconian.

One aspect of the umlaut rule was that a vowel in a stressed syllable was changed from [+back] to [-back] if the next syllable contained [i] or [y], that is, a segment that was [-cons, -back, +high]. Other features, such as rounding, were not affected. After the addition of the umlaut rule, the following surface forms were produced:

Underlying:	/muːs/	/muːsiz/	/ful/	/fullyan/	/toːθ/	/toːθiz/
Umlaut:		müːsiz		fúllyan		töːθiz
Surface:	[muːs]	[müːsiz]	[ful]	[fúllyan]	[toːθ]	[töːθiz]
	"mouse"	"mice"	"full"	"to fill"	"tooth"	"teeth"

As usual, the underlying forms have been simplified to avoid rules not related to the subject under discussion. The high front rounded vowel [ü] does not exist in Modern English, but it is found in such German words as *hübsch, drücken*, and *Büschel*. The non-high [ö] is found in such German words as *schön, Löffel,* and *nötig*. As a result of the umlaut rule, only one feature was changed:

$$
\begin{bmatrix} -\text{cons} \\ +\text{voc} \\ \mathbf{+back} \\ +\text{round} \\ \text{etc.} \end{bmatrix} \longrightarrow \begin{bmatrix} -\text{cons} \\ +\text{voc} \\ \mathbf{-back} \\ +\text{round} \\ \text{etc.} \end{bmatrix}
$$

Somewhat later another rule was added which changed vowels that were [-back] to [-round]. At first this rule affected just [ö] unrounding it to [e];

later the rule was generalized to include all front vowels, unrounding [ü] to [i] as well.† With the addition of this rule, the derivations were as follows:

Underlying:	/mu:s/	/mu:siz/	/ful/	/fullyan/	/to:θ/	/to:θiz/
Umlaut:		mü:siz		füllyan		tö:θiz
Unrounding:		mi:siz		fillyan		te:θiz
Surface:	[mu:s]	[mi:siz]	[ful]	[fillyan]	[to:θ]	[te:θiz]
	"mouse"	"mice"	"full"	"to fill"	"tooth"	"teeth"

For certain nouns the plural forms were different in two ways from the singulars: in the ending and in the vowel–[mu:s] but [mi:siz]. Because of this redundancy it was possible to drop one of the expressions of plurality without loss of meaning. Hence, in Old English manuscripts we do not find spellings for [mu:s] and [mi:siz], for [to:θ] and [te:θiz], but rather [mu:s] *mus* and [mi:s] *mis*, [to:θ] *top* and [te:θ] *tep*. Umlaut was applicable to only one group of nouns in Old English, those that were athematic (see Chapter Five); the others had plural endings with vowels other than /i, y/. After the loss of the ending /iz/, the feature which caused the umlaut in such surface forms as [mi:s] and [fe:t] was no longer evident to the child developing a grammar.

In addition, the /y/ was deleted in such words as /fillyan/ and /settyan/, eliminating further evidence for umlaut:

Underlying:	/fullyan/	/findan/	/do:myan/	/me:tan/
Umlaut:	füllyan		dö:myan	
/y/ deletion:	füllan		dö:man	
Unrounding:	fillan		de:man	
Surface:	[fillan]	[findan]	[de:man]	[me:tan]
	"to fill"	"to find"	"to deem"	"to meet"

The surface forms of these verbs would show no reason for treating [fillan] differently from [findan] or [de:man] from [me:tan]. Later generations would develop the underlying forms /fillan/ and /de:man/, and the rules for umlaut, deletion of /y/, and unrounding would not be incorporated into the grammar. Similarly, plurals such as [te:θ] and [mi:s] would be derived from underlying /te:θ/ and /mi:s/. By the end of the Old English period there were only a few nouns with umlaut plurals, and they were no doubt entered in the lexicon as irregular forms.

†Because of differences in dialects, the actual situation was somewhat more complex than we are presenting it here. The ending [iz] in plurals was lost before the time of the earliest extant manuscripts. [ö] was probably unrounded to [e] in all dialects well before the end of the Old English period, but [ü] survived in some dialects well into the Middle English period.

Umlaut and unrounding are examples of rules which existed in the grammars of several generations of speakers of English. The rules were then lost, not being incorporated into the grammars of later generations. We know that umlaut was no longer a rule in the grammar when the present participial *-ing* gained widespread usage during the late Middle English period but did not affect the back vowels in such words as *soothing* and *shouting*, with underlying /o:/ and /u:/. Nor did the [i] of the suffix *-ish* cause umlauting in *foolish* or *bookish*. The loss of the rule caused a change in the lexicon in underlying phonological representations of a number of words.

Some Traditional Processes

Earlier accounts of phonological change usually assumed that all changes operated briefly, altering certain morphemes currently in the lexicon. The change then ceased to function, and morphemes added later were not affected. The concept of underlying phonological forms has revised this attitude. Some additions, such as the palatalization rule, remain in the grammars of several generations of speakers. In addition to accounts of such changes as umlaut and palatalization, many earlier works discussed various processes of change: metathesis, epenthesis, syncope, assimilation, and others. Since there is still much which we find worthwhile in these earlier accounts of phonology, let us see how processes such as metathesis and assimilation fit into our model of changes in grammars by means of rule addition, loss, and generalization.

In English there has always been a tendency to transpose segments. Old English manuscripts show such variations as *hros* and *hors*, "horse"; *ðurh* and *ðruh*, "through"; *wacsan* and *wascan*, "to wash." This transposition is called **metathesis**. One of the most persistently metathesized words in Old English was *acsian, ascian,* "to ask." Even today this word undergoes metathesis by some speakers from [æsk] to [æks]. Other examples of early metathesis can be seen in Old English *beorht*, Middle English *briht*, "bright"; OE *þridda*, ME *thridde, third*, "third"; OE *urnan, rinnan,* "run"; OE *bridd,* ME *brid, bird,* "bird"; OE *cræt*, ME *cart*, "cart"; OE *græs, gærs,* "grass"; ME *drit*, NE *dirt.* The segments most frequently metathesized in English are [r] and a vowel, although we occasionally find the process elsewhere. Hence, in Modern English we hear the following variations:

	Original form	Metathesized form
apron	[eyprən]	[eypərn]
perceptive	[pərseptiv]	[prəseptiv]
perspiration	[pərspəreyšən]	[prespəreyšən]

prescription	[prəskrip̌šən]	[pərskrip̌šən]
portrayed	[portreyd]	[prətreyd]
pretty	[pritiy], [pridiy]	[pərdiy]
modern	[madərn]	[madrən]
different	[difrənt]	[difərnt]
cavalry	[kævəlriy]	[kælvəriy]
calvary	[kælvəriy]	[kævəlriy]
irrelevant	[irelǝvǝnt]	[irevǝlǝnt]
hundred	[hʌndrid]	[hʌndərd]
pronounce	[prǝnawns]	[pǝrnawns]

It is interesting that attitudes toward metathesized forms have changed since
earlier times. Many examples of metathesis in Old English have become the
standard today: *grass, cart, bird,* etc. More recent examples, such as those in
the above listing, although widespread among speakers of English, are not found
in the standard dialect. There is apparently no dialect of English today in which
metathesis operates as a regular, predictable process. Rather, it selects morphemes whimsically. There is, therefore, no metathesis rule in English grammar.
Speakers who pronounce *apron* as [eypǝrn] may have a different underlying
form for the word than do those who pronounce it [eyprǝn].

A different process can be seen in **epenthesis**, the addition of a segment not
originally present. We find OE *bremel,* NE *bramble;* OE *æmtig,* ME *empty;* OE
ganra, NE *gander;* OE *spinel,* ME *spindle;* OE *þymel,* ME *thimble;* OE *þuma,* ME
thumbe; OE *þunor,* ME *thunder.* In Modern English we regularly find epenthetic
consonants between nasals and following voiceless continuant obstruents. Hence,
we have *consume, resume, presume,* but *consumption, resumption, presumption,*
all with epenthetic [p]. In many dialects of English epenthetic consonants are
found regularly in this position, although spelling does not always indicate their
presence:

	before [s]	before [f]	before [θ]
[p] after [m]	[glimps]	[kʌmpfərt]	[sʌmpθiŋ]
			[warmpθ]
[t] after [n]	[sints] since		[pæntθǝr]
	[prints] prince		[æntθǝm]
	[wʌnts] once		

The epenthetic consonant agrees with the preceding nasal in the features coronal,
anterior, and continuant; it agrees with the following consonant in voice. Unlike
metathesis, epenthesis in this position is predictable and, therefore, is included
in the grammar as a phonological rule.

Some linguists distinguish between **epenthesis**, addition within a word, and **epithesis**, addition at the end. The following words show epithetic consonants:

ME againes	NE against
ME amonges	NE amongst
ME ancien	NE ancient
OE behæs	NE behest
ME boun	NE bound
ME len	NE lend
ME soun	NE sound

The same process can be seen in some dialects of Modern English in the pronunciations [drawnd], [varmənt], [əkrɔ wst], and [wʌ nst] for *drown, vermin, across,* and *once.* There were probably dialects of Middle English in which there was a rule which produced epithetic consonants. If so, it has since been lost. Modern English *against, ancient,* and *bound* have final /t/ or /d/ in their underlying forms.

Instead of being rearranged (metathesis) or added (epenthesis, epithesis), segments may be deleted. We saw an example of this process in the /y/ deletion rule which follows palatalization. During the Middle English period, [w] between [s] or [t] and a back vowel was lost: OE *twa, swa, andswaru* became NE *two, so, answer.* In spite of the spelling, none of these words is pronounced with a [w] today, and there has probably been no reason during modern times for [w] to appear in the underlying forms of these words. Another example of deletion occurred during the early Modern English period, when [l] was lost if a consonant followed in the same syllable. There was a time in which no [l] was pronounced in any of the following words: *calm, alms, psalm, palm, talk, walk, yolk, folk.* For many speakers the [l] in some or all of these words has been reinserted. A person's language can be influenced by what he reads (or sees spelled) as well as by what he hears. Also, a change in redundancy rules may cause loss of segments. Old English permitted initial clusters of the glide [h] and liquids [l, r] or nasal [n]; such combinations as seen in *hleapan,* "to leap," *hring,* "ring," and *hnutu,* "nut" were fairly common. Also, initial velar stop plus nasal was permitted, accounting for the [gn-] in OE *gnætt,* "gnat," and *gnagan,* "gnaw," and also for the [kn-] in *cnafa,* "knave," *cneo,* "knee," *cnawan,* "to know." In Modern English there are sequential constraints prohibiting all of these initial combinations. A similar change occurred during Middle English times to initial [hw-], reducing it to [w-] with loss of [h]. This change has not been uniformly spread across all dialects so that there is variation even today. Speakers who have made the change do not distinguish in pronunciation between the following pairs: *which, witch; what, watt; when, wen; where, wear; whale, wail.* Others distinguish them by the presence of [h] in *which, what, when, where,* and *whale*. Each of these processes is regular, and each was caused by the addition of a rule. At least one generation would have had underlying /gn-/ in *gnat* and *gnaw*, but a rule added during their lifetimes changed this to surface [n-] . Succeeding generations would have had no reason to have underlying /gn-/ or a rule changing it to surface [n-] ; their lexical representations would have had /n-/ for such words as *gnat* and *gnaw*. Each of these changes affected only a single generation. Later generations had different underlying representations than their predecessors.

Vowels can be lost as well as consonants. The loss of a vowel within a word is known as **syncope**. In many cases syncope can be looked upon as an extreme case of vowel reduction: Instead of merely reducing to [ə] , the vowel is lost altogether. Examples of syncope can be found below:

	A	B
hindrance	[hindərəns]	[hindrəns]
difference	[difərəns]	[difrəns]
interesting	[intərəsti ŋ]	[intrəsti ŋ]
secretary	[sekrəteriy]	[sekrətriy]
necessary	[nesəseriy]	[nesəsriy]
dictionary	[dikšənæriy]	[dikšənriy]
believe	[bəliyv]	[bliyv]

Also, contractions such as *didn't, can't,* and *don't* have syncopated vowels. If a vowel is lost at the end of a word, the process is known as **apocope**. Middle English *name, hope, tale, synne, pipe,* all with final [ə] , lost the final vowel by the end of the period. Although there is still a final *e* in spelling for many of these words, it is merely an orthographic device to indicate tenseness of the preceding vowel and does not represent a final vowel sound. In most instances of apocope, rules have been in the grammars of English for only one generation.[†] For some grammars, however, syncope in such words as *secretary* and *necessary* is still governed by a rule. For all grammars of English there is a rule for deriving contracted forms such as *can't*.

So far we have seen processes by which segments are rearranged, added, or deleted. We next would like to see if there are processes by which one segment is substituted for another. We have, in fact, already seen several examples of this process. The umlaut rule changes an underlying /u/ to [ü] . Actually, it is more accurate to say that the umlaut rule changes a *feature* rather than a *segment*, since it is not all of the features of underlying /u/ that are changed, but just

[†]In Noam Chomsky and Morris Halle, *The Sound Pattern of English* (New York: Harper & Row, 1968), underlying final vowels which are later deleted are given for some words.

[+back] to [-back]. The reason for umlaut is the existence of a high front /i/ or /y/ in the following syllable; the back /u/ becomes like the following /i/ or /y/ in the feature [-back]. The process by which a feature or features of one segment become like those in a neighboring segment is known as **assimilation**. In the rules for forming plurals and past tenses, the voiced /z/ and /d/ become the voiceless [s] and [t] if they are preceded by a voiceless segment. That is, they change from [+voice] to [-voice] to become like the preceding segment in voicing.

Voicing assimilation is a process which is still present in grammars of English. We see it in particular in certain words to which suffixes have been added. *Worth*, *north*, and *south* end in voiceless [θ], but after the addition of suffixes beginning with vocalic segments, a rule changes them from [-voice] to [+voice]: *worthy*, *northern, southern*. Change of this feature can be seen also in *louse, lousy*; *house, houses*. It operates in reverse direction, from [+voice] to [-voice], in *wide, width*; *broad, breadth*. Occurring more often in grammars of Americans than in those of Englishmen is a rule which changes [-voice] to [+voice] in underlying /t/ when it comes between two vowels, the first of which is stressed. For speakers with this rule, the surface forms of the following words have [d] instead of [t]: *butter, batter, Betty, letter, water, bitter, pity, at all, get it, shut up, caught us*. All of these words have underlying /t/, since a person can omit the voicing rule for emphasis or clarity.

Assimilation may also change the features coronal and anterior, thereby affecting the place of the obstruction in consonants. The third and fourth segments of *hypnotize*, [hipnǝtayz], are [-pn-]. Along with other features, these segments have the following:

    [p]   [n]
$$\begin{bmatrix} \text{+anterior} \\ \text{-coronal} \end{bmatrix}$$ $$\begin{bmatrix} \text{+anterior} \\ \text{+coronal} \end{bmatrix}$$

Some speakers change [+coronal] in the fourth segment to [-coronal] to make it like the preceding [p] in this feature:

    [p]   [m]
$$\begin{bmatrix} \text{+anterior} \\ \text{-coronal} \end{bmatrix}$$ $$\begin{bmatrix} \text{+anterior} \\ \text{-coronal} \end{bmatrix}$$

Hence, their pronunciation is [hipmǝtayz]. Nasals preceding obstruents are especially susceptible to assimilation. In fact, there is a rule in English today which says that nasals agree with immediately following obstruents in the features anterior and coronal. This rule was probably in existence as early as Old

English times and possibly even earlier. Within a morpheme before labials we find only [m], never [n] or [ŋ]: *compose, imbibe*. If the word *grandpa* loses the [d], it is pronounced [græmpɔw]. This also accounts for [græmps] instead of [grænps]. Old English *hænep* comes into Modern English as *hemp*, not *henp*, because after the [e] was lost by syncopation, the [n] changed to [m] because of the following [p]. Old French *confort* became *comfort* in Middle English because of assimilation. In like manner, dentals and alveolars are preceded by [n], not [m] or [ŋ]: *conduct, intuition, enthusiasm, encircle*. After the loss of [ə], Middle English *amet* comes into Modern English as *ant* because of the following [t]. And, as might be expected, velar obstruents are preceded by [ŋ], not [m] or [n]: *sink, rank, hunger, English, linguist*. If the second [p] is lost in *pumpkin*, the pronunciation is usually [pʌŋkin], not [pʌmkin]. Latin had a similar rule, the results of which are seen in the following prefixes which English borrowed. All of these prefixes were *com-* in earlier Latin.

[m]	[n]	[ŋ]
combine	concert	congregate
compact	condone	congress
commute	contain	congruous
complex	consonant	conquer

The words in [ŋ] also have alternate pronunciations in [n].

Assimilation may affect only one feature, so that a segment is made similar to a neighboring one but not identical with it, as in the examples we have been considering. We call this **partial assimilation**. There is also **complete assimilation**, in which all features of a segment become the same as those in a neighboring segment. The classic example of this process is the word *assimilate* itself. Earlier Latin had *ad + similare*; then a complete assimilation rule was added changing [d] to [s]. The change alters these features:

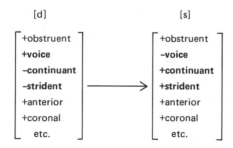

Later Latin had *assimilare*, not *adsimilare*. English has borrowed a great many words with original Latin *ad-*. Here are a few examples with the features which were changed and the Modern English word:

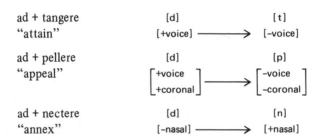

| ad + tangere | [d] | [t] |
| "attain" | [+voice] ⟶ | [-voice] |

| ad + pellere | [d] | [p] |
| "appeal" | $\begin{bmatrix} +\text{voice} \\ +\text{coronal} \end{bmatrix}$ ⟶ | $\begin{bmatrix} -\text{voice} \\ -\text{coronal} \end{bmatrix}$ |

| ad + nectere | [d] | [n] |
| "annex" | [-nasal] ⟶ | [+nasal] |

A parallel group of prefixes can be seen in *immaterial, incompetent, irrelevant,* and *illegal*, all from early Latin *in-*.

We find, then, that such rules as epenthesis and assimilation were added to English and have remained in the grammars of speakers of the language without altering underlying representations. Other changes such as metathesis and reduction of consonant clusters were in the grammars of only a single generation of speakers; for later generations different underlying forms were developed.

Evidence for Phonological Change

So long as we are concerned with the phonological system of present-day English, there is no problem in collecting material to study. If the person making the study is a native speaker of the language, he can discover quite readily whether he distinguishes in pronunciation between *horse* and *hoarse* or *ten* and *tin*. He knows whether he pronounces the glide [y] in *consume, due, few,* or not. He can gain further information by listening to the speech of others. Although there are many problems regarding underlying forms and phonological rules, collecting information about actual pronunciations is no problem.

Learning about earlier pronunciation is a different matter. Outside of science fiction there are no time machines to project people back to the sixteenth century, to the fourteenth, or to the ninth so that they can hear the speech of the time. And tape recorders, phonograph records, and other devices for preserving speech are so recent as to be of no help in telling us about earlier periods of the language. Without the information provided by a living native speaker or a mechanical recording, we can never recover all of the details of earlier English, but we can use other devices to acquire information from written records.

The first of these devices we can use to determine earlier pronunciation is **orthographical evidence**. When the Latin alphabet was introduced into England, the Latin letters were used to represent the same (or nearly the same) sounds in

Old English as they did in Latin. The letters *p, b, m, t, d, n, i, e, a, o, u* were
used to spell [p, b, m, t, d, n, i, e, a, o, u]. Our knowledge of Latin pronunciation and of the Latin alphabet gives us much information about the pronunciation of Old English. If we examine written documents from a time before spelling
was standardized, such as the early Old English period, or if we look at the writing
of an unsophisticated speller, we can often learn a great deal. The spellings *ishu*
and *shur* cited earlier in this chapter show that palatalization had occurred. When
Old English scribes stopped writing *y* in such words as *mys* and *fyllan* and began
spelling them *mis* and *fillan*, there is evidence that [ü] had unrounded to [i].
When we find *Wednesday* spelled *Wensday*, we know that the original [d] is no
longer pronounced. Today if a naive speller writes *Authur, hud, domitory* for
Arthur, heard, dormitory, he is probably not pronouncing [r] between a vowel
and a consonant. Of course, an individual spelling by itself means little: The
writer may have been distracted, or he may be a bad speller who is indicating
neither convention nor pronunciation. When several spellings follow the same
pattern, however, we are on firmer ground. We know that *gh* no longer represented a sound to the people who first wrote *nite* and *lite* for *night* and *light*. If
we also find *bite* spelled *bight*, this will give us further evidence that *gh* does not
represent a sound. A spelling like *bight* is known as an **inverse spelling**.

   Another means for determining earlier pronunciation is **orthoepic evidence**,
statements that are made by grammarians and others about pronunciation.
Richard Mulcaster in his *Elementarie* (1582) gives a list of words in which [l] is
not pronounced: *calm, balm, talk, walk, chalk, calf*. He says they are pronounced *cawm, bawm*, etc.[†] Christopher Cooper in 1685 lists words which are
pronounced alike although they have different spellings: *coming, cummin*;
coughing, coffin; *jerkin, jerking*. The final consonant in *coming, coughing,* and
jerking, then, was [n]. Since the seventeenth century, there have been many
grammars, dictionaries, spelling books, and other works in which statements are
made about English pronunciation.[††]

   A third source of information is **metrical evidence**. Often we can determine
stress patterns by the meter of a line of poetry, as in *Julius Caesar* (I, ii, 45):

   Nor construe any further my neglect

in which *construe* has primary stress on the first syllable, as indicated by the
iambic pattern of the line. In *Hamlet* (I, iii, 58–59) we find

   And these few precepts in thy memory
   Look thou character. Give thy thoughts no tongue

[†]Cited in H. C. Wyld, *A History of Modern Colloquial English* (Oxford: Basil Blackwell,
1956), p. 297.

[††]A good discussion of these sources is found in E. J. Dobson, *English Pronunciation 1500–
1700* (Oxford: Clarendon Press, 1957, 1968).

in which *character* has primary stress on the second syllable. If these were the only instances of pronunciations of *construe* and *character* with these stress patterns, we might assume that Shakespeare was merely taking poetic liberties. But each of these pronunciations is found in several other places in the plays, thereby adding to the validity of the evidence.[†] Other metrical evidence is found in **rhyme**. For many speakers of English today, none of the following pairs of lines rhyme:

> "Pussy cat, pussy cat, where have you been?"
> "I've been to London to see the queen."

> Jack and Jill went up the hill to fetch a pail of water;
> Jack fell down and broke his crown, and Jill came tumbling after.

> There was a little girl who had a little curl right in the middle of her
>   forehead.
> When she was good she was very, very good, but when she was bad
>   she was horrid.

Obviously *been* was originally pronounced with a tense vowel to rhyme with *queen* (as it still is for many Englishmen); in some dialects *after* was pronounced to rhyme with *water*; *forehead* was pronounced [farəd] (as it still is by some people). Just as we know that Byron pronounced *Don Juan* as [ǰuwən] to rhyme with *new one* and *true one*, so we know Coleridge pronounced *Geraldine* [ǰerəldayn] to rhyme with *Leoline*. Similarly, Pope rhymed *join* and *nine* (*Rape of the Lock*, III, 29-30), probably indicating a diphthong something like [ʌy] or possibly [ay] in both words, as did Keats with *vile* and *toil* (*Endymion* II, 146-47).

A less productive and often overlooked source is the **pun**, the play on words. In *Twelfth Night* (II, v, 3) we find the following:

> Nay, I'll come. If I lose a scruple of this sport, let me be boiled to
>   death with melancholy.

This play on *boil, bile* was possible because Shakespeare and his audience were accustomed to hearing them pronounced alike, at least by some speakers. In *Henry IV, Part One* (V, iii, 59) we find

> Well, if Percy be alive, I'll pierce him

[†]Helge Kökeritz, *Shakespeare's Pronunciation* (New Haven: Yale University Press, 1953) is an excellent source for this subject.

indicating that *Percy* and *pierce* could be pronounced with the same vowel: [ʌ] or possibly [a].

A fifth source of information is **comparative evidence**, in which we compare forms in different periods of a language, different dialects, or related languages. Included in this kind of evidence is the treatment of loanwords. The Middle English words *bird, clerk,* and *turn* had [ir], [er], and [ur] respectively, as can be shown by orthographic evidence and rhymes. Today for most speakers of American English they all have [ʌr]. By comparing the two periods of the language, we can show that a change has occurred. By looking at other dialects, we can gain further information; in certain dialects spoken in northern England and in Scotland, this change has not occurred, and *bird, clerk,* and *turn* are still pronounced with different vowels. We can observe a further change as evidenced by differences in British and American English in the presence of [ʌ] or [a] in *clerk, Derby, Kerr, Berkeley,* and a few other words.

Let us now examine the evidence for one change in the English vowel system. We will then try to formulate the rules which were added to the grammar to account for this change.

During the fifteenth century a group of phonological rules was added to English which affected the surface forms of all the tense vowels. From orthographic evidence we can assume the following vowels in Old English and Middle English, basing our information largely on Latin and Old French spelling practices:

OE	ME	NE	NE example
[iː]	[iː]	[ay]	bide
[eː]	[eː]	[iy]	meet
[æː]	[æː]	[iy]	sea
[a]	[aː]	[ey]	name
[uː]	[uː]	[aw]	house
[oː]	[oː]	[uw]	mood
[aː]	[ɔː]	[ow]	boat

In Latin, [i, e, a, o, u], tense or lax, were spelled *i, e, a, o, u,* and so they were in Old English. These conventions were generally continued during the period of Norman influence, except that [uː] was spelled *ou*. Evidence that a change has occurred can be found in various occasional spellings found in documents from the fifteenth century:

ME	[iː]	neynthe ("ninth"), feyre ("fire"), bleynde ("blind")
ME	[eː]	besychyn ("beseech"), myte ("meet"), dyme ("deem")
ME	[aː]	credyll ("cradle"), maid ("made"), feder ("father")

ME [u:]   abaught ("about"), faunde ("found"), hause ("house")
ME [o:]   gud ("good"), stude ("stood")[†]

The spelling *ey* in *feyre* suggests the pronunciation [ey]; this would be a very odd spelling if the pronunciation were still [i:]. Similarly, *y* in *myte* suggests [i:], not ME [e:]. The *e* in *credyll* must have been for [e:], not [a:]; the *au* in *faunde* must have been for [aw], not [u:]; and the *u* in *gud* must have been for [u:], not [o:]. There are a great many such spellings in documents from the fifteenth and sixteenth centuries, enough, in fact, to present convincing evidence of a change.

    Furthermore, the orthoepists were not silent about the tense vowels. During the sixteenth and seventeenth centuries, a number of works appeared which described English pronunciation. Because of the length of the descriptions, none are given here in detail. One comment that frequently occurred during the sixteenth century was that the English *e* was pronounced like the French *i*, that is, [i].[††]

    Metrical evidence is found in rhymes, especially of words that had [æ:] in Middle English. There was a period in some Early Modern English dialects when this vowel was raised to [e:] but not yet to [i:]. Hence, *sea, grease,* and *tea* rhymed with *way* and *say*. We find Dryden rhyming *bear* and *year* ("Song to a Fair Young Lady," lines 2, 4), *bears* and *years* (*MacFlecknoe*, lines 15-16), *break* and *weak* (*Absolom and Achitophel*, lines 287-88). We find Pope rhyming *away* and *tea* and later *obey* and *tea* ("The Rape of the Lock," I, 61-62, III, 7-8).

    For puns we find the clown in *The Winter's Tale* making a play on *sea* and *say*:

> I have seen two such sights, by sea and by land! But I am not to say it is a sea. (III, iii, 84-85)

At least in some dialects with which Shakespeare was familiar, both *sea* and *say* were pronounced with [e:]. Shakespeare makes several puns on *grace, grass,* and *grease,* one of which is found in *The Comedy of Errors*:

> Marry sir, she's the kitchen wench, and all grease. (III, ii, 97)

The pronunciation of *grease* with [e:] was evidently known, as were pronunciations of *grace* both with [e:] and the earlier [æ:].

[†]All examples are from Wyld, *A History of Modern Colloquial English*.

[††]The orthoepic evidence for the Great Vowel Shift is examined in detail in Dobson, *English Pronunciation 1500-1700* and in chapter six of Chomsky and Halle, *The Sound Pattern of English*.

Evidence for comparative study can be found in cognates in other Germanic languages and their English counterparts:

Unchanged vowel		Modern English vowel	
[a:]	German *Staat*	[ey]	state
[o:]	German *Mohr*	[uw]	Moor
[e:]	German *sehen*	[iy]	see

The high tense vowels in German have undergone a change similar to that in English so that earlier [i:] and [u:] have become [ay] and [aw] in such words as *mein* ("mine") and *Haus* ("house"). We may also compare the modern forms of loanwords borrowed from French during the Middle English period.

Modern French		Modern English	
[u]	tour	[aw]	tower
[ɛ]	plaider	[iy]	plead
[a]	grâce	[ey]	grace
[i]	vice	[ay]	vice

The French vowels have not changed to any marked degree, but those in English have.

From all of this evidence we can give a set of correspondences between Middle English and Modern English tense vowels:

Middle English		Modern English	
[i:]		[ay]	mine
[e:]		[iy]	see
[æ:]	[ey] ⟶	[iy]	sea
[u:]		[aw]	house
[o:]		[uw]	moon
[ɔ:]		[ow]	road
[a:]	[æy] ⟶	[ey]	name

The presence of the glides [y] and [w] in the Modern English forms is accounted for by a diphthongization rule which adds [y] after front tense vowels and [w] after those which are back and tense. The apparent exception, [ay], will presently be shown to be regular when we discuss underlying forms.

The other difference between the Middle and Modern English tense vowels is one affecting the features high and low. Except for the changes of [i:] to [ay] and [a:] to [ey], the feature back is not altered. The direction of the change was in a rising pattern; the two vowels that were already high became low. By moving in the direction of the arrows in the following chart, we can see the effect of the change:

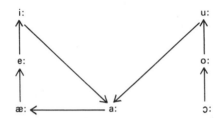

The vowels [a:] and [æ:] each moved two spaces, the others only one.

Vowel Shift and Laxing Rules

Some rules that are added remain in the grammar for only a limited period of time, which may be for only one generation or for many. If the members of a succeeding generation do not have sufficient data to warrant the inclusion of the rules, their grammars will not have them; instead, they will have different underlying forms from those of their predecessors. Umlaut is an example of a rule that remained in English for several generations and then was discontinued after the /i/ and /y/ which had caused it were lost and the front rounded [ü] and [ö] were unrounded to [i] and [e]. After these changes there were not enough data for inclusion of an umlaut rule. Earlier grammars of Old English had the following derivation:

Underlying form:	/fullyan/
Umlaut:	füllyan
/y/ deletion:	füllan
Unrounding:	fillan
Surface form:	[fillan]

Members of later generations would develop the underlying form /fillan/ and not have the umlaut, /y/ deletion, or unrounding rules.

Other rules are added and remain in the grammars of succeeding generations. Since no one can foresee future developments in any language, it would be foolish to speak of any rule as being a permanent addition. Nevertheless some rules, such as spirantization and palatalization, have been in grammars of English for several centuries and are still definitely present. It is useful to distinguish between the rules which once existed in English but which are no longer in existence from those which are still present today.

As we have seen, the reason for the continuation of a rule from the grammars of one generation of speakers to those of a later one is the presence of data which warrant the rule. Such data for continuation of the vowel shift rule are found in alternations between tense and lax vowels seen in words such as the following:

[ay]	derive	[i]	derivative
[iy]	keep	[e]	kept
[ey]	grateful	[æ]	gratitude
[aw]	pronounce	[ʌ]	pronunciation
[uw]	lose	[ɔ]	lost
[ow]	verbose	[a]	verbosity

These words, of course, are only illustrative; for each pair there are many more which exhibit the same alternation. Both spelling and meaning indicate a relationship between these pairs. The glides in the tense forms can be accounted for by the diphthongization rule, but the linking of the [a] in [ay] with [i] or of the [i] in [iy] with [e] appears whimsical. We could stop with a listing of tense-lax counterparts as in the above chart, but such a listing shows no pattern and gives the impression that the correspondence of [ay] and [i] and that of [iy] and [e] are both idiosyncratic and have no relation to each other.

On the other hand, the presence of a vowel shift rule and one which affects the low diphthongs reveals one of the most remarkable systems in English phonology. Confronted with alternations such as those in the preceding paragraph, a person will develop these underlying tense vowels:

$$i: \quad e: \quad æ: \quad u: \quad o: \quad ɔ:$$

To these underlying representations we apply the diphthongization rule:

$$iy \quad ey \quad æy \quad uw \quad ow \quad ɔw$$

The vowels remain tense, but the presence of the glide tells us this, making continued use of the colon unnecessary. The vowel shift rules next apply, effecting changes indicated by the direction of the arrows:

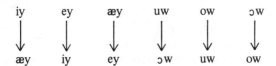

We can state these rules in two parts:

> Rule 8.1   Nonlow vowels reverse their feature value for high. (i.e.,
>   Vowels that are [-low] become [+high] if they are [-high]
>   and [-high] if they are [+high] .)

This part of the rule will have the following effect on the underlying forms:

iy	ey	æy	uw	ow	ɔw
↓	↓		↓	↓	
ey	iy		ow	uw	

The low vowels are not affected.

> Rule 8.2   Nonhigh vowels reverse their feature value for low. This rule
>   applies to the output of 8.1.

Taking the two parts together, we get the following derivations:

	iy	ey	æy	uw	ow	ɔw
Rule 8.1	ey	iy		ow	uw	
Rule 8.2	æy		ey	ɔw		ow

These two parts comprise the vowel shift rule for Modern English.
   We are now ready for a rule which converts [æy] to [ay] and [ɔw] to [aw]:

> Rule 8.3   Rewrite the first element of a low diphthong as [a] .

We call this the **diphthong adjustment rule**. A complete grammar would have to
alter the rule somewhat, as would a grammar for those dialects that do not have
phonetic [ay] and [aw] in *mice* and *house*. The effects of this rule can be seen
in the following derivations:

Underlying:	/miːs/	/beːt/	/gæːt/	/muːs/	/foːd/	/rɔːp/
Diphthongization:	miys	beyt	gæyt	muws	fowd	rɔwp
Vowel shift 8.1:	meys	biyt		mows	fuwd	
8.2:	mæys		geyt	mɔws		rowp
Adjustment 8.3:	mays			maws		
Surface:	[mays]	[biyt]	[geyt]	[maws]	[fuwd]	[rowp]
	mice	beet	gate	mouse	food	rope

By using underlying instead of surface representations, we are much closer to showing the pattern that exists between *derive* and *derivative* and the other pairs we considered earlier:

	Underlying vowel		Surface vowel
/i:/	derive	[i]	derivative
/e:/	keep	[e]	kept
/æ:/	grateful	[æ]	gratitude
/u:/	pronounce	[ʌ]	pronunciation
/o:/	lose	[ɔ]	lost
/ɔ:/	verbose	[a]	verbosity

The correspondences are clear for the front vowels. The lax vowels show no change in going from underlying to surface forms: /i, e, æ/——➤ [i, e, æ]. The back vowels are more complex. For the purpose of this presentation we give the following ad hoc rules, called collectively **backness adjustment**:

$$/u/ \longrightarrow [ʌ] \quad \text{under certain circumstances}$$
$$/o/ \longrightarrow [ɔ] \quad \text{under certain circumstances}$$
$$/ɔ/ \longrightarrow [a] \quad \text{under certain circumstances}$$

Many of the details of these changes are far from clear, and there is variation among dialects in the phonetic forms. Since these changes are of only peripheral interest to our present investigation, we will say nothing further about them.

We have now accounted for the surface differences between the vowels in *keep* and *kept*, *pronounce* and *pronunciation*, as well as a great many other words. What we have not accounted for is the reason that one of the words has a tense vowel but the other word has a lax one. There are two rules which change a vowel from [+tense] to [-tense]. These laxing rules have been in existence since late Old English times with only slight modifications in form.

Rule 8.4   A vowel becomes lax if it is followed by two or more unstressed syllables.

Rule 8.5   A vowel becomes lax if it is followed by a cluster of three or more consonants or by a two-consonant cluster other than /nd/ or /ld/.

The first rule changes /dəri:v + æt iv/ to [dəriv + æt iv], since [i:] is followed by the two unstressed syllables [æt] and [iv]. This rule accounts for the lax vowel in *divinity* (cf. *divine*), *pronunciation* (cf. *pronounce*), *gratitude* (cf. *grateful*), and many more words. The second rule, 8.5, accounts for the lax vowels in *Christmas* (cf. *Christ*) and *children* (cf. *child*), each of which has a three-consonant cluster. It also accounts for laxing before most two-consonant clusters, as in *kept* and *slept* (cf. *keep* and *sleep*). A complete grammar would include additional laxing rules and tensing rules as well, but the two we have given are among the most important.

Let us now examine the derivation of two pairs of words which illustrate the rules we have been discussing. We will not start with the ultimate underlying forms, but rather at the stage at which the rules under consideration become applicable.

	/prəfæ:n/	/prəfæ:n + əti/	/ke:p/	past /ke:p/
Stress:	prəfǽ:n	prəfǽ:nəti	kě:p	past kě:p
Past tense:				kě:pt
Laxing:		prəfǽnəti		képt
Diphthongization:	prəfǽyn		kéyp	
Vowel shift:	prəféyn		kíyp	
Surface form:	[prəféyn]	[prəfǽnətiy]	[kíyp]	[képt]

The final /i/ in *profanity* is tensed by a rule which we have not discussed; it is, therefore, not included in the derivation. Except for a few miscellaneous rules to take care of dialect variation, we are able to account for a large number of alternations in Modern English by means of a few rules. These rules were all added at an earlier period of English, but they survive in the grammars of present-day speakers of the language.

Reasons for Change in Language

We have examined several ways in which a language changes: alteration of a lexical entry and addition, deletion, and generalization of rules. So far we have not asked *why* the changes occur. Additions to and losses from the lexicon are often brought about because of technological and cultural changes. The introduction of Christianity into England during the seventh century brought with it an addition to the English vocabulary of such words as *angel, apostle, disciple, bishop,* and *monk.* The introduction of the automobile during the twentieth century prompted the introduction of such words as *windshield, tail pipe,* and *direction signal.* The space age has witnessed the introduction of such words as *astronaut, moon walk,* and *space age.*

Many changes occur as the result of borrowing. For most people this is the most fruitful source of change in their lexicons. Most of the new words a person learns come from other people either orally or through writing. Large numbers of people can change a lexical entry because of contact with radio, television, or newspapers. A great many people have changed their pronunciation of *greasy* from [griyziy] to [griysiy] and *blouse* from [blawz] to [blaws] within recent years; television commercials have no doubt had a great influence. Also, cherries that are advertised as *pitted* have been influential in causing people to stop speaking of a *seed* or *stone* in a cherry and to start calling it a *pit*. Borrowing has a definite influence on individual lexicons.

As important as borrowing is, it does not tell us anything about the ultimate origins of a change in pronunciation or in a rule of the grammar. Once a change has been initiated, we can often trace its spread among other speakers of the language, but why did palatalization or the vowel shift begin in the first place? In the past there has been a great deal of speculation, and we will briefly consider some of the theories that have been advanced. We will not distinguish among changes which spread uniformly to all speakers of the language and those that do not; that is, changes which result in dialect differentiation will be treated the same way as those which affect all speakers.

Climate is one of the most frequently advanced theories for language change. It is perhaps natural to wonder whether the breathing habits of people living at a high altitude, the sinus problems of people in a humid area, or the lassitude of people in a hot climate has affected their language. It is hard to see how climatic features such as these could influence most of the changes that have occurred in the languages of the world: metathesis, assimilation, epenthesis, changes in syntactic rules. Furthermore, if a particular change is supposedly caused by high altitude or humidity, how are we to account for an identical change occurring in another language spoken at sea level or in a desert region? It has been suggested that the differences in speech in the northern and southern parts of the United States result from the fact that it is cold in the North and hot in the South. To hold this belief, a person has to forget that there are different seasons of the year. New York and Chicago have hot summers just as Atlanta and Birmingham have cold winters. If temperature influences rules in a language, the winter language in Detroit, St. Louis, or Baton Rouge should be different from the summer language in these cities. Apart from vocabulary there has not been a single linguistic change which has been shown to result from climatic conditions.

Nor have the physical or psychological characteristics of the speakers of a language been shown to have any influence. Statements about the high level of intelligence, the desire for liberty, or the industriousness of the people of a nation are fine at patriotic occasions for bringing tears to the eyes and making the heart beat faster, but as proposed causes for change in language they are worthless. People of the world range in skin coloring from fair in Scandinavia to black in Africa, with many shades in between. They range in height as adults from well over six feet to under four. But skin coloring, height, and other physical features used to distinguish groups of people have no influence on whether a language will have equi-NP deletion or how it will treat vowels in unstressed syllables. It is true that adults who learn a new language speak it with a foreign accent, making the English spoken by immigrant Chinese, Germans, Swedes, or Mexicans distinctive. The features that stand out are not the result of physical or mental characteristics of the speakers, but rather of the language they spoke before learning English. If their children have adequate contact with native speakers of English, they will learn to speak the language without a foreign accent.

Another type of situation exists when a group of people have learned a foreign language as a result of military conquest or some other reason which makes them subjects of a ruling class who speak another language. If the subject people are more numerous than their rulers or if language contact between the two groups is limited, it has been suggested that the foreign features in the language of the first generation will be perpetuated in succeeding generations and result in a permanent change in the language. As an example, during the first century B. C., Roman legions conquered Gaul, and in time the native inhabitants gave up speaking Gaulish and adopted Latin, which later evolved into French. It has been suggested that the first generation of Gauls to learn Latin carried features of Gaulish into the Latin they spoke. Members of later generations did not have enough contact with native speakers of Latin to weed out their foreign features, and they were, therefore, incorporated into the grammars of Latin for everyone in Gaul and were perpetuated even after Gaulish was no longer spoken. A language such as Gaulish which a group of people speak before learning another one such as Latin and which has an influence on the new or superimposed language is called a **substratum language**. At one time attributing early changes in such languages as French, Spanish, and German to the interference of substrata was quite common, whether anything was known about the substrata or not. Such influences seem plausible, but many linguists today insist upon evidence beyond fanciful speculation. They want to know whether the substratum actually contained the features involved and whether the change actually occurred at the time of contact or later. Recent studies of creole languages and of languages of bilingual speakers have made an impressive beginning in investigating interference from one language as the cause for change in another, but scholarship in this area is so recent that it is not yet possible to assess its importance as a cause of change in a language.

Some changes such as assimilation seem to result from physical causes. To pronounce *lousy* with [s] requires more effort than to pronounce it with [z]. Since this consonant has a voiced segment both before and after it, it is easier to allow the vocal cords to keep vibrating through [aw], [z], and [iy] than it is to have them vibrate for [aw], stop them for [s], and then have them vibrate again for [iy]. Similarly, [pʌŋ kin] requires less movement of the vocal apparatus than [pʌ mkin]. Epenthesis can also be shown to be a means of adding ease to speech. As attractive as physical causes for phonetic changes may be, they account for only a few of the changes which occur. For example, they tell us nothing about the cause of the English vowel shift. Nor do they tell us why two languages or two dialects of the same language may have the same kind of phonetic structure, but assimilation or epenthesis occurs in one and not in the other. If voicing of [t] to [d] between vowels as in *better, bitter,* and *pity* is a natural change, why has it not occurred in British English as well as in American?

During the last 30 years there have been additional explanations offered for change in language. Since each one requires fuller explanation than our space permits, none of them will be presented here. The works by Martinet, Hockett, King, and Postal cited at the end of this chapter give a good account of these proposals. All of these suggested causes need much more investigation before their validity can be accurately assessed.

Possibly linguists will eventually be able to tell us why changes in language occur. Other questions to which answers would be welcome are why does a change such as the vowel shift occur at one time rather than another, such as a century earlier or later? How are we to account for a similar change occurring at about the same time in two different languages? Why does a change occur in one language or dialect but not in another with the same characteristics? Is change predictable? Research in change in language will no doubt tell us a great deal about language in general as well as about historical linguistics.

Exercises

A. Why is a change in a lexical entry of less importance than a change in a grammatical rule?

B. Apply palatalization and glide deletion wherever the rules are applicable:

1.	/sensyuwəl/	6.	/pliyz/
2.	/sens/	7.	/moystyur/
3.	/edyuwkeyt/	8.	/pantiæk/
4.	/miydiəm/	9.	/kənfyuwzyən/
5.	/plezyər/	10.	/kənfyuwz/

C. What evidence is there that palatalization and glide deletion are still in the grammar?

D. During the 1940s many speakers changed their pronunciation of *route* from [rawt] to [ruwt]. Was this change reflected in the phonological rules or just in the lexicon? Consider such words as *sound, about,* and *house* in arriving at your answer.

E. Under Rule Generalization we discussed the rule of glide deletion. In each of the listings given in that section, add one more word for each preceding segment. Try to determine the degree to which the rule has been generalized in your grammar. Are there some words which you pronounce both with and without the glide, such as [nuwz] and [nyuwz]?

F. In the pairs of pronunciations given below, the first indicates an earlier pro-
    nunciation, the second a later one. Name the process that has occurred.
    Some of the changes have been accepted as standard English, but others
    have not.

    1. [pæmflit]   [pæmplit]   6. [tyuwn]   [tuwn]
    2. [tways]   [twayst]   7. [sʌmθiŋ]   [sʌmpθiŋ]
    3. [pridiy]   [pərdiy]   8. [lætər]   [lædər]
    4. [inpiyəs] [impiyəs]   9. [len]   [lend]
    5. [madərn]   [madrən]   10. [difrənt] [difərnt]

G. What do the following spellings suggest about phonological changes?

    1a. hardily, "heartily"
     b. quarder, "quarter"
     c. postmardom, "postmortem"
     d. Atom and Eve, "Adam and Eve"
     e. parating, "parading"
    2a. ed, "head"
     b. ard, "hard"
     c. eaven, "heaven"
     d. heven, "even"

H. The following pairs of words are cognates, deriving from the same source
    in Indo-European. We know from other sources that the consonants in the
    Latin words preserve the Indo-European system, whereas those in English
    show a change. By comparing the pairs of words, show which consonants
    were changed. Do they constitute a natural class? Which feature was
    changed?

Latin	English	Latin	English
duo	two	pedis	foot
decem	ten	piscis	fish
augere	eke	tres	three
labium	lip	cornu	horn
iugum	yoke	cordis	heart

    Latin c is pronounced [k]; g is [g].

I. Use underlying forms and phonological rules to show how the vowels in the
    following pairs of words are related:

    1. divine, divinity   4. five, fifth
    2. serene, serenity   5. profound, profundity
    3. profane, profanity

Suggested Reading

Bloomfield, Leonard. *Language*. New York: Holt, Rinehart and Winston, 1933.
    Chapters 20–21.

Chomsky, Noam, and Halle, Morris. *The Sound Pattern of English*. New York: Harper & Row, 1968. Chapter 6.

Dobson, E. J. *English Pronunciation 1500–1700*. Oxford: Clarendon Press, 1957, 1968.

Hockett, Charles F. "Sound Change." *Language* 41 (1965): 185–204.

Hoenigswald, Henry. *Language Change and Linguistic Reconstruction*. Chicago: University of Chicago Press, 1960.

King, Robert D. "Functional Load and Sound Change." *Language* 43 (1967): 831–52.

____. *Historical Linguistics and Generative Grammar*. Englewood Cliffs, N.J.: Prentice-Hall, 1969.

Kiparsky, Paul. "Linguistic Universals and Linguistic Change" in Bach and Harms, 1968. Reprinted in Hungerford, Robinson, and Sledd, 1970.

Kökeritz, Helge. *Shakespeare's Pronunciation*. New Haven: Yale University Press, 1953.

Lehmann, Winfred P. *Historical Linguistics, An Introduction*. New York: Holt, Rinehart and Winston, 1962.

Luick, Karl. *Historische Grammatik der Englischen Sprache*. Cambridge, Mass.: Harvard University Press, 1964.

Martinet, André. *Économie des changements phonétiques*. Berne: A. Francke, 1955, 1970.

Paul, Hermann. *Prinzipien der Sprachgeschichte*. Tübingen: Max Niemeyer Verlag, 1920.

Penzl, Herbert. "The Evidence for Phonemic Changes." In *Studies Presented to Joshua Whatmough on His Sixtieth Birthday*, edited by Ernst Pulgram. The Hague: Mouton, 1957. Reprinted in Scott and Erickson, 1968.

Postal, Paul M. *Aspects of Phonological Theory*. New York: Harper & Row, 1968. Chapters 10–15.

Sturtevant, E. H. *Linguistic Change*. Chicago: University of Chicago Press, 1917.

Weinreich, Uriel; Labov, William; and Herzog, Marvin I. "Empirical Foundations for a Theory of Language Change" in Lehmann and Malkiel, 1968.

Wyld, H. C. *A History of Modern Colloquial English*. Oxford: Basil Blackwell, 1956.

Zachrisson, R. E. *Pronunciation of English Vowels 1400–1700*. Göteborg: Wald. Zachrissons Boktryckeri, 1913.

CHAPTER NINE

English Spelling

Even if there had never been a writing system developed for English, the language would have been essentially the way we have described it in the preceding chapters. Speakers of English would have organized morphemes into larger structures identifiable as sentences, which would have been governed by syntactic rules. Units of sound would have been subjected to sequential constraints, and such features as stress placement and palatalization would have been predictable by rule. As time passed the language would have changed. Since any language is the sum of the internalized grammars of its speakers, its existence is in no way dependent on its having a written form.

In the second half of the twentieth century, it is hard for most speakers of English to imagine any language without a writing system. Yet there are a great many even today which are not written, and they are still *languages*, just as English, Italian, and Chinese are. Man has been speaking for many thousands of years, yet the earliest known writing systems, from Egypt and the valleys of the Tigris and Euphrates, are at best five thousand years old. For most of the languages of Europe, including English, there was no writing system until several centuries after the beginning of the Christian era, yet there is no reason to believe that these languages were any less systematic or complex during the preliterate centuries than later.

The fact that a language is not dependent upon a writing system for its existence in no way detracts from the importance of writing. Indeed, it is the most essential tool for the development and continuation of our culture because with writing we can learn from people who are distant in space or in time. The advantages of writing are probably obvious to everyone, and we do not need to dwell on them here. What we do need to investigate is the way in which writing relates to and represents language.

There are three principal writing systems: logographic, syllabic, and alphabetic. The **logographic** system requires more characters than the other two. According to this system, each morpheme of the language is represented by its own unique symbol, and several thousand symbols are needed. There is no attempt to relate the symbol to the pronunciation of the morpheme. Both Egyptian hieroglyphics and Chinese writing are essentially logographic. In both systems it seems certain that the symbols developed ultimately from pictures of the objects or actions named. A **syllabic** system requires fewer symbols than the logographic; in this system each symbol stands for a syllable. If a language has a very restricted number of syllables, say no more than fifty, a syllabic writing system can be learned with relative ease. But for a language such as English with several hundred possible syllables, a syllabic system would be extremely cumbersome. The third type is **alphabetic**. According to this system, each symbol represents one phoneme. Languages vary in the degree to which they carry out the alphabetic principle. In English /e:/ (surface [iy]) is represented differently in *see* and *sea*, yet the principle remains essentially alphabetic. There are a few logographic symbols in the English writing system—&, %, $, 7, 8, 9—but normally the system represents phonemes.

In addition to being alphabetic, the English writing system is essentially based on the underlying forms of words rather than the phonetic forms which result from the application of phonological rules. For example, [g] is pronounced with the lips spread in *geese* but with them rounded in *goose*. Since lip rounding for consonants is determined by the vowel that follows, it is not part of the underlying representation. The writing system ignores lip rounding for consonants, since this feature is found only on the surface. Instead of representing surface manifestations, it restricts itself to underlying representations. As another example, [p, t, k] are aspirated in *pat, tat,* and *cat* but not in *spat, static,* and *skat.* Since aspiration is predictable, it is not given as a feature of underlying forms. The writing system usually represents these sounds as *p, t,* and *k* (or *c*) whether they are aspirated or not. A phonetic writing system would indicate all perceptible features, writing the first consonant in *goose* differently from that in *geese* and the [p] in *pat* differently from the [p] in *spat.* The English writing system is phonemic and represents only underlying forms of words, giving those features not predictable by rule.

The Spelling of Old English

The English writing system is based on the system for writing Latin, which was introduced into England from two sources: in the north during the sixth century from Irish missionaries and in the south from Roman missionaries, who first came in 597 A.D. They equated the English phonemes as closely as they could with those in Latin and assigned the Latin letters accordingly. Following are a few phoneme and spelling correspondences with examples from Latin and Old English:

Phoneme	Letter	Latin	Old English
/p/	p	*p*orta ("gate")	*p*æð ("path")
/b/	b	*b*asis ("base")	*b*æc ("back")
/t/	t	*t*abula ("board")	*t*ien ("ten")
/d/	d	*d*ebitor ("debtor")	*d*æl ("deal")
/k/	c	*c*onsul ("consul")	*c*amb ("comb")

The following letters were adopted to represent approximately the same phonemes they did in Latin: *a, b, c, d, e, f, g, h, i, l, m, n, o, p, r, s, t, u, x*. The scribes wrote some of these letters differently from the way we do today, in particular *f, g, r,* and *s*, but most modern editors of Old English texts print these letters with their modern forms.

In addition to the phonemes which were similar in the two languages, for which spelling presented no problem, there were a few that Old English had but which Latin lacked: /w, θ, æ, ü/. Classical Latin had /w/, spelled *v*, in such words as *via, videre,* and *vesper,* but by the sixth century these words all had /v/. To represent /w/, English scribes borrowed a symbol called *wynn* from the runic alphabet, a writing system which was probably derived from the Greek or Latin alphabet. It was used by the Germanic tribes after the beginning of the Christian era for carving epitaphs and other inscriptions on stone, bone, or other hard surfaces. For /θ/ Irish scribes introduced a crossed variant of *d*: ð, called *eth*. Another symbol was also used for this phoneme: the *thorn, þ*, borrowed from the runic alphabet. For /æ/ the digraph (pair of letters) *ae* was used; this was more often joined as *æ* and called *æsc*, [æš]. The digraph *oe* also occurs in a few early manuscripts as a symbol for /ö/. Both *oe* and *ae* are found in Latin manuscripts. There were other vowels which may or may not have been diphthongs which were represented by digraphs: *ea, eo,* and *ie*. Finally, /ü/ was represented by *y*, a letter which Latin had used earlier to transliterate [ü] in borrowed words from Greek, and which in French is still called "i grec," i.e., "Greek *i*."

The scribes who adapted the Latin alphabet to Old English needs produced a writing system that was workable and logical. The same characteristics that we noticed in the Modern English system were already present in that of Old English: It was alphabetic and phonemic, and not logographic or phonetic.

The phonemic principle can be seen in the representations of nasals. Both [m] and [n] could occur before or after a vowel:

miht "might"	lim "lime"
niht "night"	lin "flax, linen"
miðan "to hide"	ban "bone"
niðan "to hate"	bam "both"

Since there was no way to predict whether the nasal in these positions would be

[m] or [n] , the underlying forms had /m/ or /n/, and different letters were used: *m* for underlying /m/ and *n* for /n/. For nasals occurring before obstruents there was an assimilation rule which insured that the features anterior and coronal of the nasal agreed with those of the obstruent. Hence, [mb, mp, nd, nt] are found but not [nb, np, md, mt] :

[mp]	[mb]	[nt]	[nd]
limpan "to happen"	timber "timber"	winter "winter"	candel "candle"
camp "combat"	camb "comb"	munt "mountain"	standan "to stand"

Although the features anterior and coronal were predictable for nasals preceding obstruents, they were not for those in other positions (*miht, niht*), and different letters were used even before obstruents. There was a third nasal, [ŋ] , but it was more restricted than it is in Modern English. It never occurred at the beginning or at the end of a morpheme, but only before the velar obstruents [k] and [g] . Its presence on the surface was, therefore, predictable, and it did not exist as a separate phoneme in underlying forms. The following derivations illustrate the pattern:

Underlying:	/bindan/	/bringan/	/sand/	/sang/
Assimilation:		briŋgan		saŋg
Surface:	[bindan]	[briŋgan]	[sand]	[saŋg]
Spelling:	bindan	bringan	sand	sang
	"to bind"	"to bring"	"sand"	"song"

Since surface [ŋ] was predictable, there was no separate symbol to represent it. Both [n] and [ŋ] had the same underlying form, and there was one letter, *n*, to represent /n/, whether it was phonetic [n] or [ŋ].

There was also a voicing assimilation rule which affected the underlying continuant obstruents /s, θ, f/, voicing them to [z, ð, v] if they occurred between voiced segments. This was the only position in which [z, ð, v] occurred in Old English. Whether the phonetic result of underlying /s, θ, f/ was the voiced [z, ð, v] or the voiceless [s, θ, f] was, therefore, just as predictable as lip rounding and aspiration are in Modern English consonants. Since both sounds [s] and [z] were derived from underlying /s/, only one symbol was needed: the letter *s*. The following spellings accurately indicate all unpredictable features:

Underlying:	/sumor/	/mu:s/	/fæst/	/nosu/	/la:ser/	/fæsl/
Voicing:				nozu	la:zer	fæzl
Surface:	[sumor]	[mu:s]	[fæst]	[nozu]	[la:zer]	[fæzl]
Spelling:	sumor	mus	fæst	nosu	laser	fæsl
	"summer"	"mouse"	"fast"	"nose"	"weed"	"seed"

Occasionally the letter z did occur, but this was almost exclusively in foreign
names: *Zabulon, Zeb.*

For the sounds [f] and [v] the symbol *f* was used, since both sounds had the
underlying phoneme /f/:

Underlying:	/fæst/	/li:f/	/lufu/	/fi:fel/
Voicing:			luvu	fi:vel
Surface:	[fæst]	[li:f]	[luvu]	[fi:vel]
Spelling:	fæst	lif	lufu	fifel
	"fast"	"life"	"love"	"sea monster"

Similarly, [θ] and [ð] were represented by *þ* or *ð*. Some manuscripts tended
to use *þ* initially and *ð* in other positions (*þæt, pæð, fæðm*), but most of them
followed no discernible pattern: *ðeod* or *þeod, ðusend* or *þusend, maðmas* or
maþmas, ðæt or *þæt*. For purposes of clarity, we are using only *þ* as the spelling
in the examples below:

Underlying:	/wiθ/	/wiθer/	/θank/	/oθer/
Voicing:		wiðer		oðer
Surface:	[wiθ]	[wiðer]	[θaŋk]	[oðer]
Spelling:	wiþ	wiþer	þanc	oþer
	"with"	"against"	"thought"	"other"

The voicing assimilation rule did not alter the underlying forms and, therefore,
was not reflected in the spelling.

Another rule added early in the Old English period was one which palatalized
/k/ to [č] if a front vowel preceded or followed. The rule also affected /g/, but
we will restrict our observations to /k/. Before the palatalization rule was added,
the following surface forms were found:

Underlying:	/kild/	/ri:ke/	/ko:k/	/klæ:ne/
Surface:	[kild]	[ri:ke]	[ko:k]	[klæ:ne]
Spelling:	cild	rice	coc	clæne
	"child"	"strong"	"cook"	"clean"

After the addition of the rule, the following derivations resulted:

Underlying:	/kild/	/ri:ke/	/ko:k/	/klæ:ne/
Palatalization:	čild	ri:če		
Surface:	[čild]	[ri:če]	[ko:k]	[klæ:ne]
Spelling:	cild	rice	coc	clæne

Hence, the spelling remained unchanged since it was based on underlying forms, not those on the surface.

Although this tendency toward phonemic spelling is unquestionable, there was never a time in which the correspondence between underlying forms and letters was perfect. The use of both þ and ð for /θ/ was less than ideal. Also, in Old English, as in Latin, vocalic length was not predictable by rule:

/god/	god	"god"	/goːd/	god	"good"
/lim/	lim	"limb"	/liːm/	lim	"lime"
/ful/	ful	"full"	/fuːl/	ful	"foul"
/dæl/	dæl	"dale"	/dæːl/	dæl	"deal"

No indication was made in spelling to indicate this difference in underlying forms, and *y, i, e, æ, a, o, u* were used for both long and short vowels. Most modern editors mark long vowels with a macron (*gōd, līm, fūl, dǣl*), but these symbols are not in the manuscripts. A few early manuscripts, such as the *Corpus Glossary*, indicated vowel length in some words by doubling the vowel. Others, such as *Beowulf*, marked some long vowels with acute accents, but this practice was rare.

Another factor which prevented the correspondence between underlying forms and spelling from being perfect was conservative spelling practices. Although standardized spelling as we know it today did not exist before the eighteenth century, certain conventions did become traditional and were retained even though the units they represented may have been changed. Early scribes spelled the consonant sequence /sk/ as *sc*, as would be expected. The following spellings resulted:

Underlying:	/skip/	/fisk/	/skamu/
Surface:	[skip]	[fisk]	[skamu]
Spelling:	scip	fisc	scamu
	"ship"	"fish"	"shame"

Sometime after the introduction of the Latin alphabet, a rule was added which changed this cluster to [š]. At first the rule may have been restricted to /sk/ before front vowels, but by 900 it was extended to most other positions. For the generation of speakers who added the rule, the following derivations resulted:

Underlying:	/skip/	/fisk/	/skamu/
/sk/ rule:	šip	fiš	šamu
Surface:	[šip]	[fiš]	[šamu]
Spelling:	scip	fisc	scamu

Although their surface forms were different from those of their predecessors, they had the same underlying forms and had no reason to change the spelling. Later generations would have no reason to set up underlying /sk/ or to have the /sk/ rule; rather, they would have underlying forms with /š/ and the following derivations:

Underlying:	/šip/	/fiš/	/šamu/
Surface:	[šip]	[fiš]	[šamu]
Spelling:	scip	fisc	scamu

The spellings no longer represented the underlying forms. Because of the absence of a symbol for [š] in the Latin alphabet and because of conservative spelling practices, *sc* was retained as the spelling until the end of the Old English period.

Another example of conservatism can be seen late in the Old English period in words with [č] from underlying /k/. As we saw earlier in this section, several generations of speakers had underlying /k/ and a palatalization rule which changed it to [č] if a front vowel preceded or followed. During the latter part of the Old English period, various phonological changes occurred which resulted in surface [k], not [č], before some front vowels. The umlaut and unrounding rules were the ones primarily responsible. As a result, the pattern of surface [č] before or after front vowels, [k] elsewhere, was disrupted, and children developing grammars would not see the pattern. The palatalization rule was, therefore, lost and underlying forms were changed. Whereas earlier generations had underlying /kild/ and /ri:ke/ for surface [čild] and [ri:če], later ones had the following:

Underlying:	/čild/	/ri:če/	/ko:k/	/klæ:ne/
Surface:	[čild]	[ri:če]	[ko:k]	[klæ:ne]
Spelling:	cild	rice	coc	clæne
	"child"	"strong"	"cook"	"clean"

The spellings *coc* and *clæne* for "cook" and "clean" were still representative of their underlying forms; the spellings *cild* and *rice* for "child" and "strong," however, no longer represented the underlying forms, but rather those of an earlier time. The use of *c* for both underlying /č/ and /k/ can be seen even more clearly in the following examples:

Underlying:	/kin/	/čin/	/kičene/	/čiken/
Surface:	[kin]	[čin]	[kičene]	[čiken]
Spelling:	cynn	cinn	cycene	cicen
	cinn	cynn	cicene	cycen
	"kin"	"chin"	"kitchen"	"chicken"

At an earlier time, the umlaut and unrounding rules would have accounted systematically for the differences between *kin* and *chin, kitchen* and *chicken*; by the end of the Old English period, the spelling was no longer representative.

The conservative spelling conventions of the West Saxon kingdom from the time of King Alfred (871–899) until the Norman Conquest (1066) prevented these changes in underlying forms from being reflected in the spelling system. The spelling *c* for underlying /č/ was archaic. Some Old English scribes attempted to remedy the problem by writing *ce* for /č/ in some words:

/tæčan/	/streččan/	/se:čan/
tacean	streccean	secean

But this practice was by no means regular.

This conservative tendency should not be mistaken for a standardized spelling system. If we look at all Old English manuscripts collectively, we find much variation in spelling. There was, however, an unmistakable tradition in spelling, especially in the works written after 900, the period during which most of the extant manuscripts were written. Some works, such as the *Exeter Book* and the *Vercelli Book*, were remarkably consistent in spelling.

The Old English spelling system was one in which letters stood for phonemes, rather than surface phonetic forms. There was an imperfect correspondence between underlying segments and letters because of the use of both ð and þ for /θ/ and because of the failure to distinguish long and short vowels. Conservative trends sometimes resulted in spellings that reflected underlying forms from an earlier time rather than those current at the time an individual manuscript was written.

The Spelling of Middle English

The Norman conquest of England in 1066 brought with it a new upper class who considered the native Anglo-Saxon cultural traditions inferior to the French. This attitude extended to the scribes, who had small regard for English spelling practices. During the period from around 1100 to about 1300, there was neither a prestige dialect of English nor generally accepted spelling conventions. Twelfth-century manuscripts show much variation even in the spelling of simple words, not only from work to work but also within a manuscript written by only one scribe.

One particularly notorious example of inconsistent spelling is the *Canterbury Psalter*, an interlinear gloss to the book of Psalms that was copied near the middle of the twelfth century from an earlier gloss. The glossator's whimsical inconsistency can be illustrated with five different spellings he gave to *arleas*, "dishonorable": *arleasre* (1.1), *arlesan* (1.5), *ærleæsæn* (10.6), *eærleæsæ* (16.13), *arleæsæ* (50.15). It is not unusual to find a half dozen or more spellings of the base of a word in this psalter.

Along with the breakdown in earlier spelling practices, we see a number of innovations from French and Latin spelling conventions. Most of these innovations are merely new spellings for words whose pronunciations did not change. The spelling for /u:/ in Old English was *u*:

/hu:s/	/mu:θ/	/nu:/
hus	muð	nu
"house"	"mouth"	"now"

However, in Old French the long /u:/ was represented by *ou*, the letter *u* being used for /ü/, as it still is in Modern French: *sucre, pur, plus*. The French spelling *ou* gradually won favor during the Middle English period; but because of the absence of standardized spelling practices, both *u* and *ou* existed, often on the same page of a manuscript. Hence, both the earlier spellings *muþ, muth* are found alongside the later ones: *mouth, mouþ, mouthe*. By the fourteenth century, *ou* or *ow* was the usual spelling for /u:/. We can illustrate the spelling change as follows:

Underlying:	/hu:s/	/mu:θ/	/nu:/
Old English spelling:	hus	muð	nu
Late Middle English spelling:	house	mouth	now

The underlying and surface forms for these words remained the same; the only difference was in spelling.

We saw earlier that the Old English change from underlying /sk/ to /š/ did not produce a corresponding change in spelling. The letters *sc* continued to be used in such words as *scip, fisc*, and *scamu*. During the Middle English period several spellings replaced *sc*, as reflected in attested spellings for the word that became *shall*: *schall, sall, ssall, sshall, shall*. Eventually *sh* won out, and *sc* and *sk* were restricted to /sk/ in such borrowed words as *sky, skirt*, and *skill*. The change in spelling from *sc* to *sh* did reflect a change in underlying forms, but the spelling change occurred several centuries after the alteration in the underlying representations.

Another conservative Old English spelling practice which the Norman scribes discontinued was that of using *c* for underlying /č/ and /k/. During the twelfth century they introduced *ch* for underlying /č/ in keeping with French spelling practices. As a result, *cild, cese, rice, bece* were respelled *child, cheese, rich, beech*. Again, a change in underlying forms that had taken place several centuries earlier was not reflected in spelling until the Middle English period.

The usual spelling for /k/ in Old English was *c*, but *k* was found sporadically. During the Middle English period, the practice evolved of spelling this sound as *k* before *n* and front vowels and as *c* before back vowels, *r*, and *l*:

Old English	Middle English
cyning	kyng, king
cyssan	kissen, kiss
cniht	knight
cu	cou, cow
camb	comb
claþ	cloth
cradol	cradel, cradle

The underlying forms for these words remained the same; the only difference was one in spelling.

The Old English spelling for the consonant sequence /kw/ was *cw*; the Norman scribes introduced the Latin and French spelling *qu*:

Old English	Middle English
cwen	quen, queen
cwic	quik, quick
cwacian	quake

The change was in spelling alone and not in underlying form. Nor was there a phonological change in /hw/. This sequence was spelled *hw* in Old English, but in Middle English it was changed to *wh*:

Old English	Middle English
hwæt	what
hwit	whit, white
hwæte	whete, wheat

This change may have been influenced by other sequences of letters with *h* as the second member: *ch, sh, th.*

The changes in spelling discussed so far do not reflect changes in underlying forms except in those cases in which a change had occurred during the Old English period but was not reflected in spelling. After the eleventh century there were additional changes in underlying forms. Until the end of the Old English period, there was probably no underlying /v/, since surface [f] and [v] were predictable by the rule which voiced continuants coming between voiced sounds. In the Southern dialect of early Middle English, a phonological rule was added which voiced all initial /f/ segments:

Underlying:	/foks/	/fiksen/	/fiːnd/	/for/	/fat/
Voicing:	voks	viksen	viːnd	vor	vat
Surface:	[voks]	[viksen]	[viːnd]	[vor]	[vat]
	"fox"	"vixen"	"find"	"for"	"vat"

In addition, during the Middle English period a number of French loanwords with initial /v/ were incorporated into the vocabulary: *voice, vice, venison, very,* and others. As a result of these loanwords and the Southern initial voicing rule, the underlying forms of many words were changed, surface [f] and [v] no longer being predictable by rule. The Norman scribes, therefore, retained *f* as the spelling for underlying /f/ but used *u* and its angled variant *v* for /v/: *find, for, fox, over, love, voice.* In the absence of standardized spelling, all of these words appear with various spellings in the manuscripts.

For Old English /θ/ the earliest documents used *th*, but this was soon replaced by ð and þ. Early in the Middle English period ð died out and *th* was reintroduced. During the fourteenth century, þ became rare and *th* eventually replaced it altogether. At no time in the history of English has there been any consistent effort to provide distinct spellings for [θ] and [ð̌]. During the Old English period these were both surface forms of underlying /θ/, and no distinction in spelling was warranted. For some time linguists have assumed that underlying /θ/ split into /θ/ and /ð̌/ at about the same time as earlier /f/ split into /f/ and /v/. If this is so, then *th* for both /θ/ and /ð̌/ is a weakness in the spelling system. Recent research has suggested that surface [θ] and [ð̌] may still be predictable by rules which take into account whether the word containing the segment is stressed or not in the sentence and whether the word is native to English or a borrowed word. If this system can be proved satisfactorily, then only underlying /θ/ will be required for surface [θ] and [ð̌], and the single spelling *th* will accurately reflect the underlying system.

During the twelfth century (or possibly earlier) underlying /aː/ rounded to [ɔː] in all dialects of English except those in the north. Since the change occurred at a time when conservative conventions were being abandoned, the change was reflected in spelling:

OE underlying form:	/gaːt/	/staːn/	/baːn/
OE spelling:	gat	stan	ban
ME underlying form:	/gɔːt/	/stɔːn/	/bɔːn/
ME spelling:	got	ston	bon
	"goat"	"stone"	"bone"

Another change in underlying forms which was soon reflected in the spelling system was the loss of the /h/ in initial consonant clusters: /hr/, /hl/, /hn/.

OE underlying form:	/hring/	/hlid/	/hnekka/
OE spelling:	hring	hlid	hnecca
ME underlying form:	/ring/	/lid/	/nekkə/
ME spelling:	ring	lid	nekke
	"ring"	"lid"	"neck"

We can summarize these changes by listing representative Old English spellings beside those for Middle English:

Old English	Middle English
1. hus	hous, house
2. scip	ship
3. cild	child
4. cniht	knight
5. cwen	quen, queen
6. hwæt	what
7. heofon	heven, heaven
8. þæt, ðæt	that
9. ban	bon, bone
10. hring	ring

The obvious result of these changes was to make the English spelling system look very much like that which we have today. In fact, almost all of our present conventions were in existence by the time of Chaucer, even if they were not used consistently.

Just as the late Old English period witnessed the first tendency in English toward standardized or frozen spellings that ceased to reflect changes in underlying forms, so the Middle English period witnessed the first spelling reform in English, unofficial and undirected as it may have been. The Old English alphabetic system that attempted to represent underlying rather than surface forms was still definitely in existence during the Middle English period.

The Spelling of Modern English

During the second half of the fourteenth century, the dialect of London attained considerable prestige because of the importance of the city as a governmental, legal, financial, and commercial center. By the end of the fifteenth century, when the first printing presses were introduced, writers in most areas of England were beginning to imitate the London dialect. The spelling of Modern English is, therefore, based primarily upon spelling practices from the London area during the late Middle English period.

The widespread variation in spelling that is so noticeable in medieval English manuscripts gradually developed in the direction of consistency during the sixteenth and seventeenth centuries. By the middle of the sixteenth century the beginning of systematic spelling is clearly discernible. Most educated people in Shakespeare's day (1564–1616) were fairly consistent in their spelling, although this consistency was usually individual, and different practices existed from one person to another. By the middle of the seventeenth century, a system for spelling of printed matter was fairly well established. The dictionaries of the eighteenth century placed the final touches on a standardized spelling system.[†]

Printing was one of the most influential forces in developing the notion of consistent spelling practices. For the first time, hundreds of copies of a book could be produced rapidly, all of them identical. The printers were responsible for a number of our modern conventions.

During the Middle English period, *u* and *v* were looked upon as variants of the same letter, just as they are sometimes today in inscriptions on buildings: MVNICIPAL, VNIVERSITY. MVSEVM. Such variations as the following were common: *use, vse; very, uery; usury, vsvry, usvry, vsury; love, loue*. During the time of late Middle and early Modern English, the system of using *v* initially and *u* elsewhere developed: *vse, very, vsury, loue*. Around the middle of the seventeenth century, the system of using *u* as a vowel and *v* as a consonant became accepted: *use, very, usury, love*. But like a great many other traditions, the treatment of *u* and *v* as the same letter continued long after printing conventions had separated them. Hence, some alphabetical listings as late as the nineteenth century grouped them together as one letter.

Similarly, *i* and *j* were originally variants of the same letter, the principal use of *j* being to prevent the sequence of *ii* in final positions of words. It was also used in Roman numbers: *ij, iij, vij, viij*. The present distinction of *i* for a vowel and *j* for a consonant was made during the seventeenth century, but like *u* and *v* many dictionaries and indexes as late as the nineteenth century alphabetized *i* and *j* as the same letter.

The practice of not ending a word with *i* developed during the early Modern English period. Such optional spellings as *mani, veri, beauti, marri* were abandoned for *many, very, beauty, marry*. This practice is responsible for our present variations between *y* and *i* in such words as *try, tried; baby, babies; marry, marries.*

[†]Albert C. Baugh, *A History of the English Language* (New York: Appleton-Century-Crofts, 1935, 1957), p. 251.

The use of double letters to indicate long vowels was found occasionally in Old English and was continued into the Middle English period; but except for a few exceptions this was not a consistent practice, although it became much more frequent during the late Middle English period. During the sixteenth and seventeenth centuries this system became standard practice. At first almost all vowels were doubled:

miin, mijn	"mine"	boot	"boot"
beet	"beet"	boot	"boat"
beet	"beat"	naam	"name

The spelling *ou* was normally continued for /u:/. During the early Modern English period the practice of doubling the letter was retained only for ME /e:/ and /o:/ as in *beet, feet, boot, moon*. For ME /i:/ and /a:/ the pattern *vowel + single consonant + e* became standard: *mine, mice, name, gate*. Also *ie* for ME /e:/ was used: *field, piece*. For ME /æ:/ and /ɔ :/ the spellings *ea* and *oa* or *o + consonant + e* were established: *beat, read, boat, stone*.

The practice of basing spelling on underlying rather than surface forms has continued during the Modern English period. The rule of palatalization did not affect underlying forms, but rather remained as one of the phonological rules that converted underlying forms into those on the surface. The spelling system, therefore, was normally not affected:

Underlying:	/moystyər/	/prəsiydyər/	/presyər/	/eyzyæ/
Palatalization:	moysčyər	prəsiyǰyər	prešyər	eyžyæ
/y/ deletion:	moysčər	prəsiyǰər	prešər	eyžæ
Surface:	[moysčər]	[prəsiyǰər]	[prešər]	[eyžə]
Spelling:	moisture	procedure	pressure	Asia

We have simplified the underlying forms and omitted rules such as vowel shift and reduction which are not relevant to our immediate concern. That palatalization is still an active rule in Modern English can be seen in such combinations as *can't you, would you, bless you* as they are normally pronounced in regular speech. The rule is needed, of course, to account for the consonant variation in *act* and *actual, press* and *pressure, grade* and *gradual*. It is normally the underlying, not the surface, consonants that are represented by the spelling.

Another rule that affected surface but not underlying forms after it was added to the grammar was the vowel shift. This rule and its lack of influence on the spelling system can be illustrated as follows:

Underlying:	/mi:s/	/be:t/	/næ:m/	/hu:s/	/bo:t/	/bɔ:t/
Diphthongization:	miys	beyt	næym	huws	bowt	bɔwt

Vowel shift:	mæys	biyt	neym	hɔws	buwt	bowt
Adjustment:	mays			haws		
Surface:	[mays]	[biyt]	[neym]	[haws]	[buwt]	[bowt]
Spelling:	mice	beet	name	house	boot	boat

The spellings fairly accurately represent the underlying but not the surface forms.

A spelling system based upon an alphabetic representation of underlying forms will normally not reflect rules that affect only surface pronunciations whether there is a standardized spelling system or not. Usually if there is no standardized system, changes in underlying forms will be reflected in the spelling, as was the case with underlying /a:/ changing to /ɔ:/ in such words as *boat, stone, goat*. On the other hand, if the spellings of words have become frozen, changes in underlying forms may not be reflected in the spelling, as was the case with late Old English /č/.

Early in the Modern English period, the consonant clusters /kn/ and /gn/ at the beginning of a word were reduced to underlying /n/; also the final cluster /mb/ reduced to /m/. Yet the spellings of such words as *knight, gnat,* and *dumb* were not revised to reflect this change since they were already standardized. Because of this conservative tendency, we still have today a number of words whose spellings do not represent their underlying forms: *know, knack, knot, gnaw, lamb, thumb, comb,* etc. These spellings, of course, quite accurately reflected earlier forms.

Words borrowed from other languages, especially Greek, which contain consonant clusters not permitted in English are another group for which the spelling does not represent the English underlying form. For most of these words the underlying forms were restructured to conform with English rules, but the original spellings were retained: *bdellium, ctenoid, pneumonia, psychology, ptomaine.* Spelling conventions from other languages were sometimes introduced even though the English conventions could easily handle the spellings. The French spelling *c* for /s/ was introduced during the Middle Ages for such words as *city* and *cell,* giving both the native *s* and the borrowed *c* as spellings for /s/. The spelling *que* at the end of a word for /k/ is also from French: *clique, sacque.* From Greek we get *ch* as a spelling for /k/ in *choir, chiropractor, Christ, architect* and *ph* as a spelling for /f/ in *philosopher, phenomenon, telephone.*

As in earlier stages of English, the spelling system today is essentially alphabetic and phonemic, but the phonemic principle of representation is not carried out consistently.

Critics and Reformers of English Spelling

Periodically since the Middle Ages there have been those who have found discontent with English spelling, in some periods because it was too flexible and lacked standardization, in others because it was too inflexible and retained archaic spellings which no longer represented the phonological system. Although there have been a great many treatises written on the deficiencies of English spelling, accompanied by suggestions for reform, no single person has ever been able to change the spellings of more than a few words, regardless of how influential he may have been in his other endeavors or how well presented his arguments were.

The earliest would-be reformer of English spelling, Orme, lived during the twelfth century. In his *Ormulum* he followed several spelling conventions with reasonable consistency, the most interesting of which was doubling consonants which followed short vowels:

broþerr	"brother"	off	"of"
Wallterr	"Walter"	itt	"it"
Affterr	"after"	iss	"is"
Annd	"and"	wass	"was"
enngell	"angel"	all	"all"
inn	"in"	whatt	"what"
till	"till"	upp	"up"
wiþþ	"with"	wille	"will"

Some of these words—*till, all, will*—are spelled with double consonants today. Long vowels were generally written singly:

nu	"now"	me	"me"
min	"mine"	to	"to"
lif	"life"	time	"time"
hus	"house"	he	"he"

There is no evidence that Orme exerted any influence upon the spelling of his contemporaries or upon that of anyone who followed him.

The Norman spelling reform and the tendency toward standardization during the fourteenth century were apparently developments that were not effected by any one man. But starting around 1550, there was a rash of critics and would-be reformers of English spelling: John Cheke, Thomas Smith, John Hart, William Bullokar, Richard Mulcaster, Richard Stanyhurst, and Alexander Gil, to name a few. John Cheke wanted to do away with all "unsounded" letters, such as the *l* in *fault*, the *b* in *doubt*, and all silent *e*'s. To indicate vowel length, he doubled the vowel. In a letter he wrote to Thomas Hoby on July 16, 1557, he used the following spellings:

wriit	"write"	mijn	"mine"
saam	"same"	goodnes	"goodness"
debaat	"debate"	tijm	"time"
seek	"seek"	keep	"keep"

Occasionally, like Orme, he doubled a consonant to indicate a preceding short vowel. His contemporary, Thomas Smith, agreed that all "unsounded" letters should be dropped, but he extended this to doubled consonants and vowels. To indicate vocalic length, he proposed the use of diacritics: the circumflex, the macron, and the diaeresis.

A complete discussion of the proposals made during the sixteenth century would go beyond the goals of this chapter, and E. J. Dobson has already done this well in his *English Pronunciation 1500–1700*, Vol. I (Oxford: Clarendon Press, 1968). On the other hand, some of the faults found with English spelling as well as some of the reasons advanced for not changing it are of interest to us here since we find them repeated during the twentieth century.

Many of the sixteenth-century reformers felt that in an ideal spelling system there should be an exact one to one correspondence between sounds and letters. The alphabet did not contain enough letters to handle all the English sounds. As a result, some letters represented more than one sound each (such as *c* represented [k] and [s]). Some sounds could be represented by more than one letter, such as [s] being represented by *s* or *c*. Some letters were superfluous; all spellings with *c*, for example, could be replaced by *s* or *k*. Some sounds were represented by two letters: [θ] by *th*, [č] by *ch*, [š] by *sh*. Some letters, such as silent *e*, did not represent any sound at all. Several of the proposed reforms included dropping superfluous letters such as *c* and *q* and adding new symbols so as to achieve a perfect correspondence between sounds and letters.

Those in favor of retaining the current spellings or at least of making only limited changes also offered their arguments. There were some who opposed any change because of custom, but there were others who gave more cogent arguments. Some said that basing spelling totally upon sound would obscure the derivation of many words and that homonyms would no longer be distinguished. They felt that silent *e*'s and doubled consonants served a worthwhile purpose in marking vocalic length. Some argued that a revised spelling system based exclusively on sound would make the books already in print inaccessible to anyone who learned to read after the reform was instituted. Richard Mulcaster came close to recognizing that spelling is based on underlying rather than surface forms of words when he argued the inadequacy of basing spelling solely on sound. He said that sounds are constantly changing and that there is much individual variation in the way people talk. Today we would say that spelling is not based on the surface forms of words or on performance features.

Most of the sixteenth–century critics of English spelling had little lasting

influence; our standardized spelling conventions would have developed without
any one of them. There were other efforts afoot during the Renaissance, however, that did have a lasting influence on spelling, not all of them beneficial. The
interest in the classical languages was accompanied by an interest in the etymologies of English words. Some scholars were interested in revising the spellings of
individual words to reveal better their real or supposed etymologies. Often these
scholars had more zeal and imagination than real knowledge. In adding a *b* to
det and *dout* to give *debt* and *doubt*, they were correct in associating these words
with Latin *debitum* and *dubitare*. They were being extreme in their restoration,
however, since these words had lost the *b* in spelling and in sound in Old French,
from which English borrowed them. Other respellings were not merely extreme,
but totally wrong. English *iland* had developed normally from Old English
iegland, "water land," and was in no way related to Latin *insula* or French *isle*
(Modern French *île*). But because of the accidental similarity to the French
word, the *s* was added to give the unjustified spelling *island*, and people who followed were gullible enough to accept the respelling. Similar learned errors account for a number of other spellings which later became established: the *a* in
aisle, the *l* in *could*, and the *h* in *rhyme*, to name only a few.

By about 1650, English spelling was fairly well standardized. This trend was
firmly established by the dictionaries of English, which appeared regularly after
Robert Cawdrey's *A Table Alphabetical of Hard Words* in 1604 and included
dictionaries by such lexicographers as Edward Phillips (1658), Nathaniel Bailey
(1721), Samuel Johnson (1755), Noah Webster (1828), and Joseph Worcester
(1820).

Of these lexicographers, Noah Webster exerted the most influence on English
spelling in the United States. Some of his changes affected only individual words,
but others affected larger groups:

Earlier Spelling	Webster's Change
musick, physick	music, physic
honour, colour, labour	honor, color, labor
centre, metre	center, meter
agonise, analyse	agonize, analyze
draught	draft
plough	plow
travelled, waggoner	traveled, wagoner
encyclopaedia	encyclopedia

The entire English speaking world accepted *music* and *physic*, but the others are
the chief words for which British and American spellings differ today. Webster's

changes were accepted in the new world but not in England. Not all of his proposed changes were accepted:

Earlier Spelling	Webster's Change
choral	koral
nephew	nefew
imagine	imagin
crumb	crum
feather	fether
screen	skreen
woe	wo
soup	soop
give	giv

It is probably nothing more than chance that caused some of his revised spellings to be accepted while others were not.

Since the time of Webster there have been a number of influential people interested in spelling reform, among them, Isaac Pitman, A. J. Ellis, William D. Whitney, George Bernard Shaw, Theodore Roosevelt, and Andrew Carnegie. Arguments for a revised spelling system have included the increased speed with which speakers of other languages could learn to read English; the increased speed and efficiency with which English speaking children could be taught to read and to spell; and the reduced expense in typing and printing that would result from the removal of unnecessary letters in many words. In spite of the support of many scholars and such organizations as the Simplified Spelling Board, the results of would-be reformers have been negligible. In the United States, in particular, the masses seem to feel that any change in the spelling system would be in some way immoral and that anyone advocating them would be shaking the very roots of the American way of life and probably perverting something that is God given. So many people have mistaken the printed word for the actual language and speech as a mere symbol of that printed form that they feel any changes in spelling would actually affect the language itself. Such conservatism is not restricted to the semiliterate. Very few scholars feel free to use such spellings as *nite, thru,* and *tho* anywhere except in the most informal of circumstances such as notes or personal letters. Significant revisions of spelling systems are rare in the world, and barring such disasters as a revolution and a resulting dictatorship it is most doubtful that English spelling will change much if at all during the next century.

System in Modern English Spelling

Since it is so unlikely that there will be any major changes in English spelling in the near future, we should examine it to see if there is perhaps some system in the spelling conventions. This is something we would have to do anyway if we were going to reform it. Also, we should see how recent advances in our knowledge of phonology affect the arguments that have been given in the past.

Some of the earlier reformers advocated a system wherein there was a perfect fit between sound and spelling; for each sound a person produces there would be one unambiguous symbol to represent it. By *sound*, some of these people apparently meant the surface form, or perhaps something that is concrete and can be recorded and measured. Such a system if carried out according to the principle of one sound, one symbol would necessitate greatly augmenting the alphabet. The aspirated [t] in *top* is a different sound from the one in *stop* without aspiration. Both are different from the [t] that is unreleased as in *what*, nasally released as in *button*, laterally released as in *battle*, or rounded as in *too*. We would need at least six different symbols for sounds which we now collectively write as *t*. As for vowels, the one in *beet, bead, bees, beam* is different in length in all four words, depending upon the consonant that follows. We currently do not indicate this predictable variation in vocalic length, but we would have to do so if we strictly adhered to one symbol for each surface form. The matter is actually more complicated than this, however. If a person means by *sound* something that can be recorded mechanically and measured, then we probably never have a sound that is repeated. No two people talk exactly alike, or we would be unable to identify a person by merely hearing his voice. In addition, such performance factors as haste, anger, indifference, distraction, and the imprecision of the vocal apparatus further make no two repetitions of a word really alike even when spoken by the same person. A system that not only spelled *cat* differently for each speaker but also altered it according to how he said it at a given time would be totally unusable. No alphabet, not even the International Phonetic Alphabet, has ever gone this far.

We know now that an alphabetic writing system does not represent the *sounds* a person makes, but rather his underlying *conception* of these sounds. Earlier, many linguists felt that this level which was being represented was one intermediate between what we call the underlying and the surface levels. According to this kind of system, the following spellings would be advocated: *telǝgræf, tǝlegrǝfǝr, ækt, ækčuǝl, kænču*. In recent years the relevance of this intermediate level has been questioned, and we are more concerned with the systematic phonemic, or underlying, level of representation.†

We can show the phonemic nature of English spelling by examining several groups of words. Plurals and past-tense forms are spelled according to their underlying forms:

†See especially Morris Halle, *The Sound Pattern of Russian* (The Hague: Mouton, 1959), and Paul M. Postal, *Aspects of Phonological Theory* (New York: Harper & Row, 1968).

Underlying Form	Surface Form	Spelling
/kæt/ + Pl	[kæts]	cats
/mæp/ + Pl	[mæps]	maps
/tæb/ + Pl	[tæbz]	tabs
/bid/ + Pl	[bidz]	bids
Past + /lɔ:f/	[lowft]	loafed
Past + /sip/	[sipt]	sipped
Past + /sæ:v/	[seyvd]	saved
Past + /rab/	[rabd]	robbed

For plurals the surface [s] or [z] is predictable by rule, as is the [t] or [d] for past-tense forms. The spellings *s* for plural and *ed* for past tense represent the underlying, not surface, forms, nor do they represent some level in between.

Modern spellings give no indication of palatalization: *presidential, educate, erasure, measure*. It is the underlying sequence /ty, dy, sy, zy/ not the surface [č, ǰ, š, ž] that is reflected in the spellings *ti, d, s, s*.

Furthermore, the reduced vowel [ə] does not have a symbol to represent it, since it may occur as any vowel in underlying forms. It is not the surface forms which are represented by the following spellings: *grammar, resident, installation, parent*.

Underlying /i:/ and /u:/ have a great many surface manifestations, depending upon the dialect and idiolect, as well as performance factors, especially for underlying /i:/. Yet all of these surface forms are predictable by rule, according to the grammar of each dialect, and all speakers seemingly have underlying /i:/ and /u:/. The spellings *time, kite, ripe, house, pout,* and *loud* reflect these underlying forms, and the words are spelled the same way for all speakers of English, regardless of surface differences among various dialects and among idiolects within a dialect.

Some people have argued that English spelling practices have deviated so radically from the original system that it is now chaotic. They cite the presence of more phonemes than letters to represent them. There are only five vowel letters but fourteen different underlying forms, as illustrated by the following words:

beet	but	boot
bit	bottle	foot
bait	bite	boat
bet	bout	bought
bad	boy	

They point out that one letter or combination of letters is used to represent

different sounds, such as *ch* for *chair, choir,* and *champagne.* Conversely, one
sound may be represented by a large number of spellings, as can be shown for
[iy]:

meet	receive	Caesar
meat	believe	people
mete	key	amoeba
me	quay	machine

The old standby for illustrating inconsistent spellings is *ough* in such words as
tough, through, trough, and *dough.* George Bernard Shaw even coined the spelling *ghoti* for [fiš̌], using *gh* as the spelling for [f] as found in *enough, o* as the
spelling for [i] as in *women,* and *ti* for [š̌] as in *admiration.*

   Some of these examples while amusing are not accurate descriptions of English spelling conventions. The spellings for [iy] in *quay, Casear, people, amoeba,*
and *machine* are rare, existing only in these words and perhaps a half dozen
others. These words do not show that there is no system to English spelling, but
merely that there are exceptional spellings. Furthermore, it is doubtful that any
native speaker of English who has not heard of *ghoti* would pronounce the word
as [fiš̌]. The spelling is a novelty, and it is fun to use it in lectures before unin-
itiated audiences. But it is hardly a possible spelling for [fiš̌]. *Gh* spells [f] only
at the end of a few words, and the sequence is always preceded by *ou: tough,
enough.* Initially and not preceded by *ou,* the sequence usually spells [g]. The
letter *o* is used to spell [i] in the word *women,* but probably in no others. Finally, *ti* spells [š̌] only in the suffix *ion.* But such words as *admiration, perspira-
tion,* and *saturation* have underlying /ty/, whereas *fish* has underlying /fiš̌/. *Ti*
is a perfectly logical spelling for underlying /ty/, but not for /š̌/.

   In spite of such exceptions as *amoeba, women,* and *quay,* there is a regular
system that accounts for the spelling of most English words. As Robert A. Hall,
Jr., has shown in his *Sound and Spelling in English* (Philadelphia: Chilton Books,
1961), most people pronounce the following new words the same way: *meeb,
bez, cack, fidge, stug.* They pronounce them [miyb], [bez], [kæk], [fiǰ], and
[stʌg]. When given new pronunciations—[meyb], [læǰ], [lʌd]—they are
fairly consistent in spelling—*mabe, ladge, lud.* For some words, such as [stiyz],
either *steese* or *stease* may occur unless [z] is interpreted as an inflectional suffix, in which case *stees* or *steas* is given.

   Several of the spelling conventions that had become fairly widespread by the
time of Chaucer are now the regular means for distinguishing between tense and
lax vowels, corresponding to Chaucer's long and short vowels. Tense vowels are
usually spelled with two vowel letters (VV) or with a single vowel that is followed
by a single consonant, which is followed by a vowel (VCV). For the two-vowel
pattern, the letters may or may not be the same: *meet, beet* or *meat, beat.* For

the VCV pattern, the second vowel may represent a sound, as in *major* and *total*, or it may be merely a spelling device to indicate the tenseness of the preceding vowel, as the "silent *e*" in *rope* and *date*. Lax vowels are normally represented by a spelling of a single vowel followed by two or more consonants (VCC) or by a single vowel followed by a single consonant at the end of the word (VC#). The VCC pattern for stressed vowels can be illustrated by such words as *vessel*, *adverb*, and *lasting*, the VC# by *hit*, *sap*, and *but*.

VOWEL SPELLING PATTERNS IN ENGLISH

	VV	VCV		VC #	VCC
/i:/		site	/i/	sit	sitting
		bide		bid	bidding
		biding		clip	clipped
		biting		bit	bitten
/e:/	meet	mete	/e/	met	nest
	meat	Pete		leg	reckless
	beet			bet	betting
	seat			set	settee
/æ:/	break	shame	/æ/	sham	shammed
	breaking	shamed		as	ask
		fame		than	batting
		famous		mad	madder
/u:/	gown		/u/	cut	cutting
	out			mut	rudder
	pronounce				pronunciation
/o:/	moon		/o/		lost
	fool				cost
	poodle				
/ɔ:/	goal	hope	/ɔ/	hop	hopping
		hoping		was	
		code		cod	

Table 9.1

Table 9.1 gives examples of underlying vowels and the regular spellings for each. Phonological rules, such as laxing and tensing, produce different surface forms in some words. The word *bite* shows the regular spelling for underlying tense /i:/: iCV. It is followed by a single consonant; since the consonant is the last sound in the word, a final *e* has been added to obtain the VCV pattern. This *e* is merely a device for indicating the tenseness of the preceding vowel. For the present participle *biting*, the suffix begins with the vowel /i/, which is spelled *i*. The VCV pattern is maintained without the "silent *e*." The word *bit*, on the other hand, illustrates the VC# pattern. If the past participial /en/, spelled *en*, were added without other modifications, the result would be *biten*. This pattern is VCV, the one for a tense vowel; we, therefore, double the *t* to produce the VCC pattern: *bitten*. The same patterns are seen in *hope, hoping; hop, hopping*. It is this spelling convention which has been recognized in two spelling rules which are found in almost every spelling text and English handbook: the rules for dropping final *e* and for doubling a final consonant.

The regular spellings for vowels are given in Table 9.1. In Table 9.2 are found the regular spellings for consonants. The table does not take into consideration doubled consonants, since these are conventions for representing preceding lax vowels, not features of consonants.

Along with this readily observable regularity in English spelling, there are also words in which the correspondence between phonemic representation and spelling is imperfect. As was the case in late Old English times, standardized spellings of words often remain even though phonological rules have changed their underlying forms. The words *gnat, gnaw, know, knack* all have underlying /n/ as their first consonant, yet the spellings are representative of an earlier time when these words had underlying /gn-/ and /kn-/. Similarly, Middle English had two tense vowels /e:/ and /æ:/ whose modern reflexes are usually spelled *ee* and *ea* respectively, as in *tee* and *tea, see* and *sea, beet* and *beat*. Since there was only one corresponding lax vowel for both of these, /e/, there is no longer any way for a person who depends exclusively on Modern English evidence to include both underlying /e:/ and /æ:/ in his grammar. (He does have an underlying /æ:/, but it corresponds to ME /a:/, not to ME /æ:/.) Hence, today both *see* and *sea* have underlying /se:/, yet the spelling preserves an earlier state in which *see* had underlying /se:/ but *sea* had /sæ:/.

Another problem with Modern English spelling is that we preserve conventions from more than one source: the French *c* (*cite*) beside the English *s* (*site*), the French *q* (*sacque*) beside the English *k* (*sack*), the Greek *ch* (*chord*) beside the English *k* or *c* (*cord*), the Greek *ph* (*phase*) beside the English *f* (*faze*). This situation is not so haphazard as it seems on the surface. The spelling *c* for /s/ is almost always found before *e* (*center, cedar, ceiling, face*), *i* (*citizen, citrus, civil*), or *y* (*mercy, lacy, Percy*). In these environments both *c* and *s* are frequent spellings for /s/; in all others only *s* is normally found (*save, slave, sack, sue, soap,*

CONSONANT SPELLING PATTERNS IN ENGLISH

Phoneme	Initial	Final
/p/	pit	up
/b/	big	hub
/t/	toy	at
/d/	do	fad
/k/	cat, kit	back
/g/	get	peg
/č/	chore	which, witch
/ǰ/	just, gem	wedge
/f/	foot, phone	leaf
/v/	vat	leave, of
/θ/	thought	with
/ð/	those	seethe
/s/	see	lass
/z/	zoo	his, fizz
/š/	she	wish
/ž/		rouge
/m/	moon	slam
/n/	now	win
/ŋ/		sing
/r/	red	pear
/l/	live	pal
/w/	wet	
/y/	yet, use	
/h/	how	

Table 9.2

supper, spot, stop, scare, snip). The *q* is found only before *u* and at the beginning of a word represents /kw/ (*queen, quick, quest*). This is the normal spelling for /kw/, rather than *cw* or *kw*. Other uses of *q* in Modern English are exceptional. Most of the words with *ch* for /k/ are of Greek origin (*chloroform, cholera, choir, architect*) and either are or once were technical terms. Neither *ch* for /k/ nor *ph* for /f/ occurs at the end of a word in very many instances.

   With the exception of a few words which have different spellings in England (*kerb, colour, checque*) and in the United States (*curb, color, check*) and a handful that have alternate spellings throughout the English speaking world (*catalog, catalogue*; *judgment, judgement*; *buses, busses*), English spelling is rigidly standardized. Almost all variations in print, even in the trashiest of publications, are the result of oversight by the typesetters and proofreaders. Variations from this standard can have adverse effects if found in letters of application or other persuasive letters. The various dictionaries on the market often differ in usage labels for words, but except for the treatment of compounds they are in agreement on following standardized spellings, even when they do not accurately represent the underlying forms of words. Although there are a great many words in English whose spellings are exceptional, there is a clearly discernible phonemic system which determines the spellings of the majority of words in the language.

Exercises

A. Some of the words below are regular in their spellings; others are irregular. If the word is regular, tell which vocalic pattern it follows. If it is irregular, suggest a revised spelling for it.

1. cave	6. steak	11. chubby	16. city
2. calf	7. win	12. whining	17. patter
3. china	8. heat	13. love	18. cubed
4. berry	9. albino	14. beer	19. spinning
5. head	10. judge	15. mood	20. led

B. Why is the *p* doubled in *dropping* but not in *drooping*?

C. With your knowledge of spelling patterns for English vowels, you should have no trouble in forming the derived words indicated below and spelling them correctly:

1. hum + ing	11. scoop + ed
2. home + ing	12. compel + ed
3. plan + ing	13. appear + ed
4. sole + ly	14. confine + ing
5. occur + ence	15. like + ing
6. care + ful	16. compel + ing
7. stale + mate	17. occur + ed
8. bride + al	18. remit + ed
9. admit + ed	19. refer + ed
10. regret + ed	20. precede + ence

D. In the following pairs of words, one follows the regular spelling conventions, but the other does not. Decide which are regular.

1. maid, said   5. closet, close
2. read (past), read (present)   6. shoulder, bolder
3. could, mouse   7. both, moth
4. blood, mood   8. lead (v.), lead (n.)

E. If you were writing a reader for first-grade students and were emphasizing the relationship between sound and spelling and regular spelling patterns, which of the following words would you omit until the patterns had been learned? Do elementary readers normally omit them?

1. stop	7. help	13. come	19. you
2. good	8. and	14. go	20. laugh
3. look	9. with	15. to	21. work
4. at	10. thank	16. mother	22. busy
5. here	11. Spot	17. me	23. ball
6. run	12. fun	18. see	24. live (v.)

F. The following misspelled words come from student papers. Decide which errors are caused by ignorance of English spelling patterns and which ones result from flaws in the system.

1. grammer	5. buy ("by")	9. instillation	13. collasped
2. describ	6. fourty	10. roomate	14. deviashion
3. seperate	7. requirred	11. acquainte	15. were ("where")
4. especialy	8. completeing	12. poka-dot	

Suggested Reading

Baugh, Albert C. *A History of the English Language*. New York: Appleton-Century-Crofts, 1935, 1957. Chapter 8.

Campbell, A. *Old English Grammar*. Oxford: Clarendon Press, 1959. Chapter 1.

Conlin, David A. *Grammar for Written English*. Boston: Houghton Mifflin Co., 1961. Chapter 17.

Dobson, E. J. *English Pronunciation 1500–1700*. Vol. I. Oxford: Clarendon Press, 1957, 1968.

Francis, W. Nelson. *The English Language: An Introduction*. New York: W. W. Norton & Co., 1965. Chapter 5.

_____. *The Structure of American English*. New York: Ronald Press, 1958. Chapter 8.

Fries, Charles C. *Linguistics and Reading*. New York: Holt, Rinehart and Winston, 1963. Chapter 6.

Hall, Robert A., Jr. *Sound and Spelling in English*. Philadelphia: Chilton Books, 1961.

Jones, Richard Foster. *The Triumph of the English Language*. Stanford: Stanford University Press, 1953. Chapter 5.

Kurath, Hans. *A Phonology and Prosody of Modern English*. Ann Arbor: University of Michigan Press, 1964.

Lefevre, Carl A. *Linguistics and the Teaching of Reading*. New York: McGraw-Hill, 1964. Chapter 8.

Mossé, Fernand. *A Handbook of Middle English*. James A. Walker, trans. Baltimore: Johns Hopkins Press, 1952. Chapter 1.

Pyles, Thomas. *The Origins and Development of the English Language*. New York: Harcourt Brace Jovanovich, 1964. Chapter 2.

Robertson, Stuart. *The Development of Modern English*. 2d ed., revised by Frederic G. Cassidy. Englewood Cliffs, N. J.: Prentice-Hall, 1954. Chapter 11.

Stevick, Robert D. *English and Its History*. Boston: Allyn & Bacon, 1968. Chapter 23.

CHAPTER TEN

Variation in Language

When a person is speaking, the sounds he makes are not the only ones heard. Noises from other sources such as passing cars, coughing, footsteps, and other conversations are usually present. If a person is speaking over the telephone, public address system, radio, or television, electrical noises may coexist with his sounds. We are so accustomed to most of these other noises that we learn to ignore them. Because a certain amount of redundancy is always present in language, these other noises can even drown out part of the speech signal and not seriously interfere with our understanding of the speaker's message. If the speaker becomes aware that competing noises are becoming a hindrance, he may speak more loudly, repeat a sentence, or pause until the disturbance has ceased.

In addition to noise, other environmental features may affect the speech signal. If the speaker is in a large auditorium or at a distance, he will not sound the same as when he is in a smaller room or near by. Atmospheric conditions such as heat, cold, and humidity affect the air waves and the individual's speech apparatus. The person speaking usually adjusts to these conditions without conscious effort, speaking more loudly, more softly, or more deliberately. Studies of the effects of competing noises and of atmospheric conditions on speech are of great interest to some people, such as those who design telephone and other communications systems. Most linguists do not consider them part of the domain of descriptive or historical linguistics since they do not help us to understand how a given aspect of the grammar functions or how rules change. To the listener they are important only if they block communication or make it difficult.

Another influence on speech can be the emotional and physical condition of the speaker. We have learned to associate certain features of speaking with fear, anger, boredom, depression, nervousness, excitement, happiness, condescension, or sickness. Among these features are the rate and loudness with which a person is speaking as well as his range of pitch levels. The signals which indicate that the speaker is bored or sick often have no relation to the communicative content of his utterance, although they may be of great interest to the listener. Other signals, such as those indicating sarcasm or facetiousness, are an essential part of the communicative content. The study of these features, called **paralanguage**, and the study of body motions which accompany speech, **kinesics**, have been very limited so far. Those features which are necessary for proper interpretation of the utterance should no doubt be part of the description of a language, but it is not yet clear how they should be treated.

Although the speakers of a language have much in common linguistically which enables them to understand one another, it is also obvious that no two people talk exactly alike. We recognize certain people's voices even when we do not see them. There are machines which can analyze voices and produce a visual record of their distinguishing characteristics, showing that a person's voice is as distinctive as his fingerprints. Part of this distinctiveness results from the physical characteristics of the person's speech apparatus, part of it from his speaking habits. Although these features are as much a part of the speech signal as are those which distinguish nasals from oral sounds or consonants from vowels, they are normally not included in discussions of phonological features since they do not affect the communicative content of an utterance. For a singer or an actor, of course, they can be of great importance.

There is another way in which each person's speech is distinctive that is of interest to the linguist. Although each child has great resources for learning a language, the exact form of this language is dependent upon his linguistic exposure. Hence, regardless of his ancestry, a child learns the language to which he is exposed, whether it is Japanese, Persian, English, Norwegian, Kikuyu, or any of the other languages of the world. In addition to the choice of language, a person's experience determines which exact form of that language he will develop. Since no two children hear exactly the same sentences or necessarily draw the same linguistic conclusions about the ones they hear, there will be individual differences in vocabulary and in the rules of the grammar. We refer to the total features of a person's grammar as his **idiolect**. Each rule and vocabulary item he possesses will be shared by other speakers of the language, but no one else will have his exact combination. It is the combination of rules and vocabulary items a person has which makes his idiolect unique, not the individuality of any part of it.

All idiolects of a language must have many aspects that are similar, or mutual understanding would be impossible. It is also true that children who live near one another will share much of their linguistic environments and will develop grammars which are quite similar. Hence, the idiolects of Englishmen will contain features which distinguish them from those of Australians or Americans. Within the United States, the idiolects of New Englanders, Midwesterners, and Southerners are noticeably different from one another, yet similar within each group. A collection of similar idiolects constitutes a **dialect**. Often the term *dialect* is used to indicate the nonstandard or the provincial form of a language; this is not in agreement with the technical use of the term. According to our meaning, everyone speaks a dialect unless his form of the language is so unusual that it bears no similarity to that of anyone else. In addition to regional dialects, there are those drawn by social boundaries. Two children may live within a mile of each other as they are developing their grammars, yet encounter vastly different forms of the language because they belong to different social classes. There are, then, two kinds of dialects: regional and social. In this chapter we will examine some features of various English dialects. In addition, we will look at the ways in which an individual's language varies according to the formality of the situation in which he is speaking.

Dialects of English

As we have seen in earlier chapters, every language changes with time. Most changes such as the vowel shift, palatalization, and *do* insertion affect the grammars of all speakers of the language. The rules governing these changes account for some of the differences between earlier English and the language spoken today, but they do not account for those among speakers living now. There are other changes which do not spread uniformly to all speakers of the language. Whether the change involves a lexical item or a rule in some component of the grammar, if it is not adopted by everyone, it will set off the speech of some speakers of the language from that of others. When there are enough incompletely disseminated changes, the language of a person will identify him as to the group to which he belongs.

To illustrate these differences, let us imagine three groups of people who speak the same language, groups A, B, and C. Since no one knows how many rules are in a grammar, let us select one hundred as an arbitrary number. We have, then, three groups of people who have rules one through one hundred in common:

A	B	C
Rules 1–100	Rules 1–100	Rules 1–100

Although change can mean the addition, deletion, rearrangement, or revision of a rule or alteration of a lexical item, let us restrict ourselves to rule addition for our illustration. In the course of time some rules will be added to the grammars of all three groups, but others will not be added uniformly:

A	B	C
Rules 1–100	Rules 1–100	Rules 1–100
101	101	101
102	102	102
103	103	

104		
	105	105
		106
107		107
	108	
109	109	109

In the example all groups have changed; none of them has remained pure and uncorrupted or *stagnant* (depending upon one's perspective). When enough differences exist that it is possible to determine a person's group affiliation from his language, groups A, B, and C are said to constitute three separate dialects. There is only one cause for dialect differentiation: changes which do not spread uniformly.

Restricted communication is the most common reason why change fails to spread to all speakers of the language. So long as all of the people interact freely with one another, any changes in the language will be adopted by everyone. But there are features which may separate people. A physical barrier such as an ocean, a wide river, a mountain range, or a dense forest will often limit communication or even block it altogether. A national or other political boundary can divide people and limit communication. Or social attitudes can restrict relations among people of different social classes, religions, or races. Whatever the reason for separation, if a group of people do not have sufficient exposure to a linguistic change, they will not adopt it.

Sometimes people are exposed to a change but consciously resist incorporating it into their grammars because of their attitudes toward the speakers who originated the change. Teenage slang is added to the lexicon in the same manner as other vocabulary items are acquired, yet a person who does not want to sound like a teenager will not adopt slang from this source, regardless of how frequently he hears it. Or a person may not want to sound like a blue-collar worker, a society matron, a preacher, a jazz musician, a city dweller, a farmer, a fisherman, a bank president, a prostitute, a New Englander, or a Midwesterner. He will not adopt any linguistic features which he thinks are distinctive to the group he finds unfavorable.

On the other hand, a person may find the members of one of these groups attractive and wish to emulate them. He will try to adopt their styles of dress, eating habits, cultural interests, and language. This group may be the social elite in a city such as London, Paris, Boston, or New Orleans; it may be the people of a geographical region much larger than a city; or it may be the people of a particular social class. Whatever kind of group it is whose traits are being emulated, we speak of it as a **prestige group** and the form of language used by its members as a **prestige dialect**.

There have been distinct dialects of English since the earliest times, but information about them in the early years is scant. Although a few written documents in Old English from as early as 700 A.D. have survived, most of them which we now possess were written during the tenth and eleventh centuries. In addition, all but a handful of the extant manuscripts were written in the West Saxon dialect. Any study of Old English dialects, therefore, is severely hampered by a scarcity of information about features of the language from the early part of the period and about features of dialects other than West Saxon. Yet there is enough information to make the existence of at least four dialects quite certain: West Saxon, Kentish, Mercian, and Northumbrian.

The exact boundaries of the dialects of Old English cannot be determined precisely, but it seems that **Northumbrian** extended from the Humber River northward into what is now southern Scotland. **Mercian** was spoken in the Midland area between the Humber and the Thames, extending as far west as, but not including, Wales. **Kentish** was spoken in the southeastern part of the island, in the region that was to become the modern counties of Kent and Surrey. The rest of the south of England with the exception of Cornwall comprised the **West Saxon** dialect area. Bede (673-735), writing almost 300 years after the Anglo-Saxon invasion began, seemingly attributed the origin of these dialects to the settlement history of the Germanic tribes. According to him, the original settlers of Northumbria and Mercia were Angles; Saxons settled in Wessex, Sussex, and Essex; Jutes settled in Kent. If there were already differences in dialect among the Germanic tribes at the time of their invasion of Britain, these differences which they brought over with them from the continent would provide a plausible base for the Old English dialects which were documented several centuries later. Regardless of whether there were already differences at the time of settlement or not, at each dialect boundary was a large river or a forest. Also, the four different dialect regions were in different kingdoms for the most part of the Old English period. Hence, there were physical and political boundaries to hamper communication among the people in the various kingdoms during this period.[†]

There is a possibility that West Saxon attained the status of a prestige dialect during the last part of the period. From the time of Alfred (871-899) until the Norman Conquest (1066), the West Saxon kingdom was the most important region on the island. Although all parts of England were hard hit by the Viking invasions which began during the eighth century and continued intermittently until the eleventh, Wessex was affected less drastically than the other kingdoms. The stability provided by the West Saxon kings permitted economic growth, and the interest shown by Alfred and his successors in education, literature, law, and other areas helped make the West Saxon kingdom the dominant cultural center

---

[†]For a suggestion of how various dialectal differences may have originated in Old English times, see David DeCamp, "The Genesis of the Old English Dialects: A New Hypothesis." *Language* 34 (1958): 232-44.

on the island. Most of the manuscripts which have survived from Old English times were written in this kingdom. Many of them were copies of manuscripts from other regions which were transformed into the West Saxon dialect in the process of copying. There also seem to have been scribes whose native dialect was Northumbrian or Mercian but who wrote in West Saxon. We derive our information about the original dialect of a manuscript or a scribe from non-West Saxon features which remain in the manuscripts. Because manuscripts were converted from other dialects in the process of copying and because scribes from other regions wrote in a dialect other than their own, it has been suggested that West Saxon was a prestige dialect during the last 150 years of the Old English period. This may be so, but there is not enough evidence available to make it more than a possibility. The scribes could just as easily have been using West Saxon because that was the dialect of the audience for whom the manuscript was being written or copied.

It is impossible to say whether the West Saxon dialect attained prestige outside of its own area or not. We do know that within the West Saxon kingdom certain writing conventions became established. As a result, there appears to be a period of linguistic stability during the 150 years from around 900 to 1050 and a period of abrupt change during the next 150 years, from 1050 to 1200. A close inspection of all the manuscripts from 900 to 1050 suggests that the stability of the period is illusory, that conservative writing conventions were not reflecting the changes occurring in the spoken language.

The Norman Conquest of 1066 brought with it a French-speaking aristocracy, relegating native Englishmen to lower social ranks. As a result, no dialect of English retained prestige. Until the end of the thirteenth century, French was the language of the royal court, of law, of medicine, and of education except for the places in which Latin was used. Nevertheless, there was a great deal of writing in Middle English, enough of it having survived for us to speak of the dialect boundaries with more certainty than we can of those from the Old English period. Because of this increased information, it is customary to give different names to the Middle English dialects. The **Northern** dialect had approximately the same limits as did the Old English Northumbrian, from the Humber River northward into southern Scotland. The **Midland** dialect occupied the region between the Humber and the Thames with the exception of Wales. It is clear in Middle English times that this dialect should be subdivided at least once into **West Midland** and **East Midland**. The **Southern** dialect was found south of the Thames essentially in the same area as the earlier West Saxon. Only **Kentish** remained unchanged in name. Some scholars group Kentish with Southern. Still others refer to the dialects south of the Thames as *Southeastern* and *Southwestern*.

Although we know a great deal more about the geographical limits of the Middle English dialects than we do about those of Old English, there are still

Northern

West
Midland

East
Midland

Southern

Kentish

Middle English Dialects

many varieties of the language which remain unknown to us. We derive our knowledge of Middle English from written documents which have survived; hence, we have recorded the written language of the literate minority. At this time the majority of Englishmen could neither read nor write, and their dialects are irrevocably lost. Since the typical member of the lower classes never went more than a few miles from his birthplace, each person came in contact with only a very limited number of people. There were no doubt noticeable linguistic differences among communities only twenty or thirty miles apart.

By the fourteenth century London had become the most important city in England. With a population of around forty thousand, it was the largest city in the kingdom as well as the most important trading and commercial center. No other city in England approached it socially and culturally. Equally important, the center of government had been moved from Winchester to Westminster, near London, late in the Old English period. For all of these cultural, economic, and political reasons, the city of London was looked upon favorably. When the people of a region gain favor, all aspects of their culture rise in the esteem of others; and their variety of the language becomes a prestige dialect. When Caxton established the first English printing press in London in 1476, the East Midland dialect was well on its way to being the prestige written variety of English; the centering of the printing trade in London assured the continuation of this trend. Just as the variety of English written in London became the standard for writing throughout the kingdom, the dialect spoken by upper-class Londoners became the prestige form for the rest of England. The other dialects were not replaced, but many people in other parts of the country found it advantageous to learn this prestige dialect.

During the Modern English period the regional dialects of England have survived, seemingly with the approximate boundaries of those in Middle English times. Research in English dialects is active at the universities of Leeds and Edinburgh, and perhaps more exact information will be available before long. Among Englishmen, the prestige of the upper-class London dialect has remained, but during the Modern English period it has broadened its regional limits and is no longer identifiable with any particular part of England; rather, it has become a class dialect for the entire country.

Starting with the seventeenth century, Englishmen have transplanted their language to such places as New Zealand, Australia, South Africa, Canada, and the United States. At first the language of the colonists was probably indistinguishable from that of Englishmen who remained at home, but as time passed separation inhibited the spread of many of the changes originating in England. Similarly, changes originating in the colonies would normally not spread to other parts of the English–speaking world. Early settlers in the American colonies were often isolated not only from people in England but also from one another. One remark made by English travelers in the American colonies during the eighteenth century was that the language sounded more like that of the members of their grandparents' generation than of their own. Similar statements have been made during the twentieth century by French visitors in Quebec and by German visitors in Texas. There are reasons that the language in a colony would be more conservative than that in the mother country. Limited communication caused by separation would block the spread of some changes. Also, whereas people in the mother country would feel linguistically secure and adopt changes regularly, the colonists would resist anything which would make them sound provincial. Hence, they would try to avoid linguistic changes, even though they might be occurring in the mother country, unknown to them.

Today it is often possible to identify a person's nationality by the variety of English he uses. For this reason some people have felt that it would be better to restrict the term *English* to the dialects spoken in England and to refer to the others as *Australian, Canadian, American,* etc. At the time of the American Revolution and for a period afterward, there were people such as Thomas Jefferson and Noah Webster who aspired to develop an American language which in a few years would be radically different from English. Starting in 1919 with the first edition of his monumental *American Language*, H. L. Mencken set out to prove that such a separate language had evolved. To achieve his goal, he often compared rustic and nonstandard American usage with urban standard British usage. If mutual intelligibility is the test of whether two varieties constitute different languages, then there is no reason to refer to the language spoken in the United States, Canada, Australia, and elsewhere as anything but English. Books, newspapers, and magazines are not translated when they are shipped from one English speaking country to another, nor are movies dubbed in or given subtitles. Furthermore, the spoken standard in San Francisco, Toronto, or Cape Town is closer to the British standard than are many dialects spoken in the north and west of England.

Just as there are differences among the varieties of English spoken in various parts of the English–speaking world, there are regional differences within each of the countries. Starting in 1931, various projects have been under way to give a survey of English in Canada and the United States. Although many areas are still to be surveyed, and much of the information already collected has not yet been edited, a fairly reliable picture of the dialect situation in the United States has emerged. Hans Kurath's division of the estern seabord into **Northern, Midland,** and **Southern** dialect areas[†] has been generally accepted, along with a subdivision of Midland into **North Midland** and **South Midland**. Surveys from the states bordering Canada and others as far south as Kentucky, Iowa, and Nebraska have shown that the boundaries for the East run more or less

---

[†]Hans Kurath, *A Word Geography of the Eastern United States* (Ann Arbor: University of Michigan Press, 1949).

Dialects of American English

Solid lines indicate approximate dialect boundaries as determined
by various linguistic surveys. Dashed lines are based on incomplete
evidence. The divisions farther west are still not determined.

horizontally across the nation. This is in keeping with the routes followed by
the English speaking settlers of the interior of the country. The earlier belief in
a dialect called *General American* was shown to be a myth.

For American English there has never been a single spoken standard; each
dialect or subdivision within that dialect has its own standard. This point can be
illustrated by the speech of a succession of American presidents, all using the
standard of a region different from the others: Franklin D. Roosevelt, Harry S.
Truman, Dwight D. Eisenhower, John F. Kennedy, Lyndon B. Johnson, and
Richard M. Nixon.

These differences should not be exaggerated, either within one country or
from one country to another. The various standards are in close agreement regarding verb forms, comparison of adjectives and adverbs, pronoun cases, agreement of subject and verb and of pronoun and antecedent. Epenthetic vowels in
athlete, film, and *elm* are universally nonstandard. In spoken English the differences between one social class and another within a given region are usually much
greater than those among the various regional standards throughout the English
speaking world. As far as written English is concerned, there is close agreement
as to what is standard. It is usually impossible to determine an author's origin
within a given country, whether he is writing an editorial for a newspaper, an

article for a learned journal, a popular novel, or a lurid report for a more sensational publication. Even national differences in written standards are few, as a person can readily see by rewriting a paragraph of standard British English into the American standard or vice versa.

Attitudes of people toward dialects other than their own are rarely neutral. As early as the twelfth century there are accounts of Englishmen complaining about the weird sounds made by people in other parts of England. References to the speech of certain regions as sounding *clipped, nasal, harsh,* or *soft* have been as common in the past as are those of today about *drawls, burrs, brogues,* and *twangs.* The term normally applied to a form of speech different from one's own is *accent.* To the person with limited exposure to different forms of language, everyone outside his region speaks with an accent, whereas neither he nor his friends have an accent. Since most people hear the variety of English used on television and in the movies as the same as their own, they are given support in their belief that theirs is the only unaccented form of English, whether they live in the Northeast, the Southeast, the Midwest, the Southwest, or the West. In his *Essay on Criticism*, Alexander Pope made a statement which is appropriate:

> 'Tis with our judgments as our watches, none
> Go just alike, yet each believes his own. (lines 9–10)

He was speaking of judgment in literary criticism, but his comparison is equally applicable to judgments about dialects.

From an unbiased viewpoint there is no reason to set one regional or social dialect higher or lower than another. Research has failed to show that one is any more logical or systematic than another. They have all changed from earlier forms of English, and in many cases they have made the same changes. They differ from one another in those areas of the grammar or vocabulary for which they have not adopted the same changes. A change usually fails to spread to all speakers of the language as the result of chance, not aesthetics or logic. However, few people are without prejudices.

Variation in Vocabulary

Vocabulary is that aspect of dialect variation which has received the most attention in the past. No doubt this is because information about vocabulary can be collected with relative ease. Excellent discussions of vocabulary have appeared in such works as H. L. Mencken's *The American Language*, Albert H. Marckwardt's *American English*, Thomas Pyles' *Words and Ways of American*

English, E. Bagby Atwood's *The Regional Vocabulary of Texas*, and Hans Kurath's *A Word Geography of the Eastern United States*. Special dictionaries have been prepared: *The English Dialect Dictionary* by Joseph Wright, *A Dictionary of Modern American Usage* by H. W. Horwill, *American Dialect Dictionary* by Harold Wentworth, *A Dictionary of American English on Historical Principles* by William Craigie *et al.*, and *A Dictionary of Americanisms on Historical Principles* by Mitford M. Mathews. More limited lists appear regularly in the *Publications of the American Dialect Society* and in the journal *American Speech*. Compilations have been made of slang and of special words used by cowboys, jazz musicians, tramps, gamblers, drug addicts, and others.

Vocabulary differences between American and British English began developing during the seventeenth and eighteenth centuries as the colonists encountered new plants, animals, and topographical features for which they had no names. Frequently they coined new words by the use of compounding: *egg plant, water oak, live oak, copperhead, catfish, blue jay, underbrush, backwoods*. Or they used existing words and gave them new meanings. *Bluff, creek, robin, blackbird, corn,* and *polecat* refer to different objects in England and America. Often the unfamiliar objects had already been named by people speaking other languages, and the English-speaking settlers adopted the names from these languages, usually with phonological and semantic alterations. From the various American Indian languages they borrowed such words as *moose, skunk, raccoon, squash, hickory,* and *sequoia*. They borrowed *bayou, prairie, gopher, pumpkin,* and other words from French. From Spanish they borrowed such words as *mustang, pinto, mesquite,* and *canyon*.

Other differences in vocabulary between British and American English result from institutions which are not the same in both countries. Differences in government, law, religion, and educational systems are responsible for such terms as *barrister* and *solicitor* in British English and *lawyer* in American English. An American *prep school* is roughly equivalent to an English *public school*, whereas an American *public school* corresponds to the English *council school*. In England a *college* is usually a division of a *university*, and in the United States this distinction survives in most larger universities with their *colleges* or *schools* of business, agriculture, arts and sciences, medicine, and others. At the same time, *university* can be part of the title of any institution of higher learning in the United States even if it offers no graduate programs and has very limited undergraduate offerings. In many cases the governing bodies of schools have found a change of name from *college* to *university* to be the easiest and least expensive means of acquiring prestige.

Any new idea or invention which has been developed since the American colonies were settled often results in different terms in the United States and in England. If an American visiting in London asks how to get to the nearest *subway*, he will be directed to a walkway which crosses under a main street; if he wants a train which moves under the ground, he must ask for the *underground*. An Englishman visiting in New York would probably not be understood if he asked for directions to the *underground*; in Atlanta or Houston he might be directed to an underground shopping center. The most common use of *underground* in the United States is in a figurative sense, as relating to railroads, movies, or newspapers.

The railroad industry is relatively recent, and since it developed independently in both countries, different terms were coined. The American *engineer, fireman,* and *conductor* are equivalent to the English *engine driver, stoker,* and *guard,* respectively. The American *baggage car, caboose,* and *crossties* are the English *luggage van, brake van,* and *sleepers.* Many terms, of course, are the same: *express train, railway, line,* and the like.

In most cases there is nothing particularly American or British about the terms. In fact, it is probably nothing more than chance that most of them were coined in one of the countries rather than in the other. With automobile terms, for example, one can think of a part as muffling or as silencing noise and call it a *muffler* (American) or a *silencer* (British). One can name the covering for the engine for an article of headwear and call it a *hood* (American) or a *bonnet* (British). One can think of an enclosed car with a nonmovable top as being like a covered chair which is carried on poles and call it a *sedan* or like an elegant public hall and call it a *saloon.* One can think of the glass in front of the driver as shielding him from the wind or as screening him from it: *windshield* or *wind screen.* It seems as logical to *dip* the *headlamps* as to *dim* the *headlights* or to drive with the lights on *main beam* as on *bright.*

Although one could prepare an impressive list of words which differ between British and American English, they should not be exaggerated. If a person wishing to compile such a list begins looking in current publications, for example, he soon learns that he must limit himself to articles or advertisements on certain subjects. Nor can an American hope to find many Briticisms in popular novels such as those by Agatha Christie or Daphne du Maurier. An Englishman in the United States or an American in England may have some difficulties filling out a laundry list or discussing automobile repairs, but for most topics there are few vocabulary differences.

In addition to the words which are found primarily in one of the English speaking countries but not in others, there are those which are found only in certain sections of a given country. The term *roller shades* or *shades* is found in all parts of the United States; but *blinds* is also found in the Midland area and *curtains* in New England, both terms synonymous with *roller shades.* A certain piece of playground equipment is known as a *seesaw* in all American dialects. Competing with this term in the Northern area are such terms as *teeter board* and *teeter totter.* Hans Kurath in *A Word Geography of the Eastern United*

States gives other terms with more limited distribution: *tilting board, tiddle board, tippity bounce, ridy horse, cock horse,* and *hicky horse,* as well as variants of each of these. Depending upon the region, a person may refer to a small stream of water as a *creek,* a *brook,* a *run,* a *branch,* or a *kill.* The part of a chicken which is referred to as a *wishbone* in the North and North Midland is often called a *pullybone* in the South Midland and in the South. To call cows, one may use *co-Boss* or *come Bossie* in the North, *sook* or *sook cow* in the Midland, and *co-wench* in the South. In many regions *bull* is an obscene word which a gentleman does not use in conversation with a member of the fair sex. Rather, he uses such terms as *sire, gentleman cow,* or *masculine,* depending upon where he lives.

Since vocabulary is the most rapidly changing aspect of language, it is not surprising to see that many words which were once regionally limited are now found in all dialects and that others are becoming obsolete. Originally *pail* was a Northern term which corresponded to Midland and Southern *bucket.* In recent years both terms have spread to all dialect areas. Although *bucket* is still the more usual general term in the Midland and the South, *sand pail, lunch pail,* and *milk pail* are fairly common. The urban term *frying pan* is replacing the Midland and rural *skillet* as well as the New England *spider.* *Kerosene* in many areas has replaced *coal oil* and *lamp oil.* Many words which once were widely used in certain areas are now becoming obsolete as large numbers of people are moving away from rural areas. If the closest a person comes to a farm animal is his television set or the dining table, he does not use (and probably does not know) any of the regional terms for calling cows, horses, sheep, pigs, and chickens or those for the various sounds the animals make. He probably has no occasion to refer to a corn crib, hay stack, barn yard, privy, or wagon tongue by any of the terms normally applied to these objects. Contact with advertising has caused some words to gain wider use. Cherries advertised as *pitted* have been influential in replacing *stone* and *seed* of the cherry with *pit.* Restaurants known as *pancake houses* have reduced the use of *hot cakes, griddle cakes,* and *flapjacks* and increased that of *pancakes.*

The addition of a word to a person's language affects only his lexicon, not the rules of the grammar. Many words that the individual adds are accepted by most other speakers of the language, but others have only restricted acceptance. To the person adding the word, all new words seem the same. It is only when he comes in contact with people from outside his environment that he learns how widely they have been adopted. Most people have little difficulty in making alterations in their vocabularies. They can drop a word such as *bag, bucket,* or *couch* and begin using *sack, pail,* or *sofa* fairly easily. As with other aspects of linguistic change, regional vocabulary items are far less stable than rules in syntax, morphology, or phonology.

Variation in Syntax and Morphology

Since all aspects of language change with time, an alteration in any part of the lexicon or grammar can fail to spread to all speakers of the language and become one of the features which distinguish dialects. We have seen several regional differences in vocabulary; let us next look at differences in syntax and morphology.

As with vocabulary, a change in a syntactic rule may be extended to all speakers of the language who have adequate exposure to the change. If there are barriers which isolate the people who originated the change from other speakers of the language, the change probably will not spread beyond the original group. Physical features such as mountains, oceans, and deserts may isolate people. People may also be isolated because of economics, religion, or race, all of which we collectively call social reasons. Not only in cities, but even in small towns, social barriers often separate people and limit communication. In such a situation it would be unusual if linguistic differences did not arise. Language is constantly changing for all speakers, but if their contact with one another is restricted, the same changes will not be made in all dialects.

One group of people who have often been socially separated from speakers of the prestige dialect of English are black Americans of lower economic status. Since they usually have only limited contact with black or white speakers of the prestige dialect, it is natural that distinctive features have developed in their language. Following the practice of Ralph W. Fasold, we will refer to this dialect as **Black English.**† Although it is probably no longer possible to find a term which is totally neutral for any group of people, this one has been selected because it is closer to being neutral than the others which have been suggested. At the same time it has one disadvantage in that all black people do not speak this dialect. Since the addition of any qualifier such as *nonstandard* has a pejorative connotation which is not warranted by the linguistic facts and since the black Americans who speak the prestige dialect need no special term for their form of the language, the disadvantage is not insurmountable. Probably research will eventually show that Black English is in reality several dialects. It is contrary to what we know about language in general to expect uniformity in all geographical regions.

For most of the rules of the grammar there are no differences among dialects. It is probable that all dialects of a language share the same deep structures and that they differ only in a few rules. One frequently observed difference between the surface structures of Black English and those of the prestige dialect involves forms of *be*. Differences exist in practically every structure in which *be* is used, and it seems likely that a few rules will be able to account for them. Since the

---

†Ralph W. Fasold, "Tense and the Form *be* in Black English," *Language* 45 (1969): 763–76.

overall pattern is not yet clear, we will restrict our discussion to one structure in which *be* occurs.[†]

    10.1   The barber shop *be* full every time I get a haircut.
    10.2   She *be* out of town sometimes.
    10.3   Every Saturday they *be* getting up early.

These sentences differ from those in the prestige dialect in their use of *be* instead of *is, are, was,* or *were*; that is, tense is missing. Our first reaction might be to say that tense does not exist in the deep structures of sentences in this dialect, but the following examples show that this is not true:

    10.4   Didn't you see him?
    10.5   He ate and left.

The structure we are examining is restricted to sentences with *be* and actions or occurrences which are repeated. It does not exist with continuing action or with a situation or action found at a single time in the past or at the present. Often an adverbial such as *every time, sometimes,* or *usually* indicates the repetition.
    Since tense is needed for other kinds of structures, the least complicated means of accounting for sentences such as 10.1–10.3 is to assign tense to their deep structures and give a rule which deletes it before *be* in case of repeated occurrence. Hence, the derivation of 10.2 is something like the following:

Intermediate: she present be out of town sometimes
Tense deletion: she   be out of town sometimes
Surface: She be out of town sometimes.

Dialects which do not have this deletion rule will obtain *She is out of town sometimes* from the same underlying structure.
    It is interesting that we find similarities in different syntactic rules. Notice the expression of the subjunctive in the following sentences:

    10.6   We recommend that she *be* prompt.
    10.7   I insist that you *be* here on time.
    10.8   If this *be* treason, make the most of it.
    10.9   I suggest that he *answer* all questions.
    10.10   I move that the treasurer *deposit* the money.

In each of these sentences, tense has been deleted. The difference between the

[†]See, Fasold, "*Be* in Black English" for a fuller discussion of this topic and for justification of the analysis given.

rule accounting for these structures and the one for 10.1-10.3 is the condition under which it applies. In 10.1-10.3 tense is deleted for repeated occurrences; in 10.6-10.10 it is deleted for subjunctives.

We know even less about most social dialects of English than we do about Black English. In the past the general consensus was that any form of language other than the prestige dialect was unsystematic, illogical, and very much the same for all speakers. These beliefs have been shown to be false. No doubt there are as many social dialects as there are levels of society in any English-speaking community, all of them equally systematic and logical. There is no reason to believe that any of these dialects will be identical to those of corresponding social levels in other regions. Let us examine several morphological changes which have occurred in two of these dialects since the seventeenth century. In the absence of satisfactory terms, we will refer to them merely as dialects A and B.

In Chapter Five we saw that the regular development of nouns after numbers was without suffix: *two mile, four foot, three gallon.* In Old English, nouns following numbers were in the genitive plural: *feower fota,* "four of feet." With the later loss of final unstressed vowels, *four foot* developed. Dialect A has retained this system for nouns of measurement, regardless of how they are used:

10.11a   He is six *foot* tall.
10.12a   He reached it with a six-*foot* pole.

Dialect B has made a change for structures like 10.11, but it has retained the original form for modifiers such as 10.12:

10.11b   He is six *feet* tall.
10.12b   He reached it with a six-*foot* pole.

For structures such as 10.11, Dialect A has retained the original system, but Dialect B has not.

The reflexive pronoun is another structure which has undergone change in some dialects but not in all. Normally the reflexive is formed by adding *self* to the possessive:

my	+ self	myself
your	+ self	yourself
her	+ self	herself
its	+ self	itself
our	+ selves	ourselves
your	+ selves	yourselves

For two pronouns there is a different formation. With *himself* and *themselves* the objective pronoun is used instead of the possessive. Dialect A has altered this inconsistency and made these reflexives conform to the pattern: *hisself* and *theirselves*. Dialect B has retained the older formation. So far we have seen one change which has affected Dialect B but not A (*six feet* vs. *six foot*) and one that has affected A but not B (*hisself, theirselves* vs. *himself, themselves*). In each case the change caused an exception in the language to follow the regular pattern.

Another change in pronouns involved the possessive. By the end of the Middle English period, phonological changes had caused the first and second person singular pronouns to have two possessives: *my* and *thy* for unstressed and *mine* and *thine* for stressed positions. Since the change which produced this differentiation affected just final [n], the other pronouns were left with only one form each: *his, her, our, your, their.* Eventually the system developed which used only *my* and *thy* before nouns

10.13   This is *my* book.

and *mine* and *thine* elsewhere

10.14   This book is *mine.*

There was an inconsistency in that two of the pronouns had different forms depending upon whether or not a noun followed, whereas the others did not make this distinction. Two possibilities existed for regularizing the system: (1) eliminate the distinction in the first and second persons singular or (2) extend it to the other pronouns. Both dialects took the second choice, but they did not execute it in the same way. Dialect A extended the *mine* and *thine* pattern:

10.13	This is *my* book.	10.14	This book is *mine.*
10.15	This is *thy* book.	10.16	This book is *thine.*
10.17	This is *his* book.	10.18a	This book is *hisn.*
10.19	This is *her* book.	10.20a	This book is *hern.*
10.21	This is *our* book.	10.22a	This book is *ourn.*
10.23	This is *your* book.	10.24a	This book is *yourn.*
10.25	This is *their* book.	10.26a	This book is *theirn.*

Dialect B selected a different course, apparently using *his* as the model:

10.13	This is *my* book.	10.14	This book is *mine.*
10.15	This is *thy* book.	10.16	This book is *thine.*
10.17	This is *his* book.	10.18b	This book is *his.*

10.19   This is *her* book.   10.20b This book is *hers*.
10.21. This is *our* book.   10.22b This book is *ours*.
10.23   This is *your* book.   10.24b This book is *yours*.
10.25   This is *their* book.   10.26b This book is *theirs*.

Both dialects have changed the form of certain possessives, but in different directions.

In Chapter Four we saw that in Old and Middle English there was no restriction on the number of negatives which might occur in a sentence. Dialect A has maintained this lack of restriction:

10.27a He did*n't* want *nothing*.
10.28   You ca*n't* just sit still and do *nothing*.
10.29   She is*n't un*happy.

Dialect B has added a condition which restricts structures such as 10.27 to one negative:

10.27b He didn't want anything.

In special cases such as 10.28, however, the restriction does not hold, nor is there any restriction on negative prefixes co-occurring with *not*, as in 10.29.

Turning next to verbs, we saw in Chapter Five that many verbs which were formerly strong are now weak. The earlier past tense of *melt* was *molt*, but both Dialects A and B have reclassified it as weak, giving *melted* as the past form. With many verbs they have made the same change from strong to weak; for others they have not:

	Earlier English	Dialect A	Dialect B
10.30	The ice molt.	The ice *melted*.	The ice *melted*.
10.31	He clumb the tree.	He clumb the tree.	He *climbed* the tree.
10.32	He holp me.	He holp me.	He *helped* me.
10.33	He knew it.	He *knowed* it.	He knew it.
10.34	It grew fast.	It *growed* fast.	It grew fast.

Dialect A has retained *climb* and *help* as strong verbs but has converted *know* and *grow* to the weak category. Dialect B has made the opposite choice.

For one final example, many strong verbs no longer have different forms for past tense and past participle. In the case of *cling* and *sting*, the original past-tense forms *clang* and *stang* are now archaic, *clung* and *stung* serving both for past tense and for past participle. During the seventeenth century this trend was apparently extended to all strong verbs, but it was arrested. Today, Dialect A has made more changes in this direction than Dialect B has:

	Dialect A	Dialect B
10.35	She *clung* to me.	She *clung* to me.
10.36	She has clung to me.	She has clung to me.
10.37	It *stung* me.	It *stung* me.
10.38	It has stung me.	It has stung me.
10.39	He *taken* it.	He took it.
10.40	He has taken it.	He has taken it.
10.41	He *seen* it.	He saw it.
10.42	He has seen it.	He has seen it.

Dialect B is the prestige dialect, or standard English. Dialect A is one of the other dialects of the language. To classify all dialects other than B under one heading may be useful for some purposes, but there is no more reason to expect agreement in their rules than there is to expect it in the non-English languages of Europe. There are a great many dialects of English, and A is only one of those usually labeled *nonstandard*.

Several points should be observed from our examples. First, neither A nor B has remained "pure and uncorrupted"; both have changed. Furthermore, both have made about the same number of changes. Second, A is not a corruption of B. Both dialects evolved from the same source, not one from the other. Third, there is nothing about the changes in either dialect which makes them more logical or tasteful than those in the other dialect. In many instances they have made identical changes. In others, the changes are remarkably similar. Finally, the dialects are equally systematic, and there is no linguistic reason to prefer one over the other.

Although these points are true, anyone who is unable to use the prestige dialect is severely limited professionally and socially, not because of any features of the language per se but because of popular attitudes. Since there is no indication that these attitudes will be altered in the near future, anyone who does not already speak the prestige dialect is advised to learn it. While he is doing this, he should realize that he is not changing from a state of sin to a state of grace or from wrong to right, but rather that he is merely learning a new dialect, an activity similar to learning a new language.

Variation in Phonology

All parts of the grammar change. If we look at a language over a period of several centuries, we find many more changes in phonology than in the other components of the grammar and more in morphology than in syntax. The same proportions exist for dialect differences. The fewest are in syntax, and the most are in phonology. This situation explains why even the linguistically untrained person recognizes that a person is from a different region or social class more by his pronunciation than by the way he forms sentences. We have examined differences in vocabulary, syntax, and morphology. Let us now turn to phonology.

During the Early Modern English period, [u] in most words changed to [ʌ] in the dialects spoken in the East Midland area and in the South of England. This affected such words as *cut, hut, but, dull, rug,* and *love.* A few words such as *pull, push,* and *full* retained [u]. As a result of this change, various surface correspondences between tense and lax vowels appear to be unusual:

Surface [aw] Underlying /u:/	Surface [ʌ] Underlying /u/
abound	abundance
profound	profundity
pronounce	pronunciation
denounce	denunciation
announce	annunciation

Because of these correspondences, we give /u/ as the underlying vowel for surface [ʌ], at least for these words and others which follow the same pattern. At present it is not clear whether /u/ should underlie all instances of [ʌ] or just those which alternate with surface [aw] and [uw], such as *resume, resumption* and *consume, consumption.* This rule changing /u/ to [ʌ] did not spread to all parts of the English-speaking world. For most of the dialects spoken in the northern part of England, [u] has remained. Hence, these dialects have surface [u] corresponding to [ʌ] elsewhere in such words as *come, love, luck, must, much, month, money, number, up, cup, sun, husband, some, us, stuff, done, enough,* and *clumsy.* If all instances of [ʌ] have underlying /u/, all dialects of English have the same underlying vowel; they differ only on the surface, depending upon whether or not they have the rule changing /u/ to [ʌ].

During the Late Modern English period, a phonological rule which voiced underlying /t/ to [d] in certain positions was added to most of the dialects of American English. The position for which voicing occurred was between two vowels, the first stressed and the second unstressed: *bitter, latter, pity, Patty,* and the like. Only surface forms were affected, since the rule can be bypassed for emphasis or clarity, for example to distinguish *bitter* from *bidder* or *latter* from *ladder.* Further evidence for underlying /t/ rather than /d/ can be seen in the following derived words:

[t]	[d]
sit	baby sitter
cut	paper cutter
late	latest
pat	patting

The same pattern is found even if the following unstressed vowel is in a different word:

[t]	[d]
What have you bought?	I bought a hat.
He got the raise.	He got up.
Sam went to bed.	Sam went abroad.
Shut the door.	Shut up.

All of the words in these examples have underlying /t/. The voicing rule determines whether the surface form will be the voiceless [t] or the voiced [d]. The dialects of British English have the same underlying forms as American English, but they have only surface [t] in these words since the voicing rule was not added in these dialects.

During the second half of the eighteenth century, some dialects of British English added a rule which deleted /r/ after a vowel if a consonant or word boundary followed: *barn, lurk, beard, far, here, care.* This position is often referred to as "postvocalic /r/." Also, the preceding vowel was lengthened [ba:n], or [ə] was added [biəd]. These rules did not affect initial /r/ (*red, rave, round, right*) or intervocalic /r/ (*worry, parrot, parade*). A base ending in /r/ might or might not have surface [r], depending upon which suffixes were added, if any:

Without [r]	With [r]
poured	pouring
poor	poorest
pore	porous
clear	clearance
bear	unbearable

The rules became part of the grammar of standard British English, but they were not accepted by all of the other dialects. In American English the rules were added in the Southern dialect and in eastern New England. The Northern dialect area west of the Connecticut River and the Midland areas did not adopt them. No doubt the rules failed to spread farther because many speakers of the language were isolated and the colonists at the time of the American Revolution had a negative attitude toward anything British.

In England as in eastern New England, the rule was generalized to disregard word boundaries. Underlying /r/ was not deleted before a vowel, whether it was in the same word or not:

Without [r]	With [r]
poured	pouring
Pour the tea.	Pour us some tea.
Rubber was expensive.	Rubber is expensive.
The offer sounded good.	The offer appeared good.

In the Southern dialect of American English, this alteration was not made. Underlying postvocalic /r/ was retained only if a vowel followed in the same word (*worry, porous, pouring*). If it occurred at the end of a word (*pour, rubber, offer*), it was deleted regardless of whether the next word began with a vowel or a consonant.

For many people in England and in eastern New England, various changes occurred. Not only did their surface forms of such structures as *rubber is* and *the offer appeared* have [r], but they added [r] to any word ending in [ə] if the next word began with a vowel. The following pattern emerged:

Without [r]	With [r]
Pou(r) the tea.	Pour us some tea.
Rubbe(r) was expensive.	Rubber is expensive.
The offe(r) sounded good.	The offer appeared good.
The banana was ripe.	The bananar is ripe.
The sofa by the wall. . .	The sofar in that room. . .
law for everyone	lawr and order
Cuba was	Cubar is

The [r] in constructions such as *Pour us some tea* is often called "linking /r/," and that in *The banana is ripe* is called "intrusive /r/."

Most of the changes which occurred in English before the settlement of the American colonies in the seventeenth century are preserved in dialects on both sides of the Atlantic Ocean. After the seventeenth century, changes which originated in England did not necessarily spread to the colonies and vice versa. Voicing of intervocalic /t/ is an addition to the grammars of the dialects of American English; deletion of postvocalic /r/ originated in British English. For other changes in British dialects since the seventeenth century, we can cite the change of [æ] to [a] in about 150 words such as *path, fast, half,* and *aunt*; for many words such as *sand* and *gas* the change did not occur. Except for eastern New England, the earlier pronunciation has been preserved in American English. The change to [-ayl] for the last syllable of such words as *missile, fertile, projectile,* and *hostile* has been limited to British English, as has the change from [sk] to [š] in *schedule.*[†] The change from earlier [a] to a back rounded vowel in such words as *hot, stop, God,* and *rob* is a British development, as is the loss of stress and vowel in the third syllable of such words as *military* and *secretary.* It has sometimes been said that the existence of a standard dialect provides a stabilizing influence which inhibits change. If we consider the changes we have just mentioned and add to them others that have occurred during the same period, we arrive at a sizable number. Although spelling does not reflect it, standard British English has changed considerably during the last three centuries, and no scholar has shown more changes for any of the other dialects of the language, standard or nonstandard. The statement that the presence of a standard dialect inhibits change may be a myth influenced by spelling conventions.

As a final group of phonological changes which did not spread to all speakers of English, we will consider several examples of vowels which have become neutralized in various dialects of American English. Our knowledge of the distribution of features in American dialects is far from complete. In many cases changes have altered the patterns described in the literature. There may have developed differences between older and younger speakers or between different social groups which the surveys conducted twenty or thirty years ago do not indicate. Also, a feature which is described as Northern or South Midland, for example, may be restricted to only a subdivision of that area.

For both Midland dialects, /æ/ and /e/ neutralize to [e] before /r/. As a result of this rule, the following derivations result:

	Underlying	Surface
marry	/mæri/	[meriy]
merry	/meri/	[meriy]
fairy	/færi/	[feriy]
ferry	/feri/	[feriy]
Harold	/hærəld/	[herəld]
herald	/heræld/	[herəld]

Whereas the Northern and Southern dialects distinguish these words on the surface by [æ] or [e], in the Midland dialects they are homonyms, as are other pairs such as *air, heir; Barry, berry; vary, very.*

[†]Both *projectile* and *hostile*, of course, are not pronounced the same way by all speakers of American English, many of whom use the so-called British pronunciation.

In Western Pennsylvania and perhaps in much of the Northern area, / ɔ / and /a/ become neutralized except before /r/. Hence, surface *caught, cot*; *taught, tot*; *caller, collar* all have the same vowel. These pairs of words are homonyms in these areas, whereas they are kept distinct elsewhere.[†]

For a final example, in the South and South Midland, /e/ and /i/ are neutralized to [i] before nasals. For these dialects the following words all have [i]: *pen, pin*; *ten, tin*; *gem, Jim*; *sense, since*; *many, mini*; *Ben, bin.*

The same reasons which cause differences in other components of the grammar produce phonological differences among dialects. A change fails to be adopted by all speakers of the language. This failure may result from isolation and restricted communication, or it may be caused by unfavorable attitudes toward the people among whom the change originated. From a linguistic viewpoint the changes which do not spread to all speakers of the language look very much like those which are adopted uniformly, and there is nothing which distinguishes the changes originating in any one dialect from those in the others.

Contextual Styles

In this chapter we have been examining several kinds of variation in language which exist among people from different regional or social backgrounds. We have not been examining variations within the idiolect, yet the language of an individual is not the same at all times. Each year a person makes a number of lexical alterations, adding words, dropping words, and revising the entries for others. Within a person's lifetime he also makes changes in the rules of his grammar. An idiolect does not remain constant, but changes with time. In addition, performance features are influenced by nervousness, boredom, curiosity, and other emotions so that there may be noticeable differences in a person's speech within a short period of time such as an hour or an afternoon. Finally, the individual adjusts certain aspects of his language according to the content of his message and according to the person with whom he is speaking. These adjustments produce various **contextual styles** (or **levels of usage** or **registers**). We are concerned now with this last kind of variation.

There are noticeable differences in syntax, morphology, phonology, and word choice in the language which a person uses for various occasions: making a speech to a large group, participating in a panel for the discussion of some current problem, consulting with a professional person for advice on some matter, talking with a new neighbor, or chatting with a close friend or member of the

[†]For a fuller treatment of this topic and of phonological variation in general see Rudolph C. Troike, "Overall Pattern and Generative Phonology" in Harold B. Allen and Gary N. Underwood, eds., *Readings in American Dialectology* (New York: Appleton-Century-Crofts, 1971).

family. It is not easy to mark divisions among contextual styles since they are part of a continuum with any number of possible dividing points. The first extensive treatment of the subject was made by Martin Joos in *The Five Clocks*. H. A. Gleason, Jr. in *Linguistics and English Grammar* followed the divisions made by Joos but renamed some of the styles:

1. *Oratorical*: for formal speeches to large groups
2. *Deliberative*: primarily for less formal speeches to groups of any size
3. *Consultative*: for conversations with someone other than a close friend
4. *Casual*: for conversations with close friends
5. *Intimate*: for use with members of the family and friends with whom one is especially close

Although this classification is not perfect, as Joos and Gleason readily admit, it is much better than one which recognizes just formal and informal styles.

Usually we are not aware of variations in contextual styles but adjust to them without conscious effort. We begin noticing them when a person uses a style inappropriate for the occasion and sounds too *bookish* and *stiff* or too *chatty*. At times a person may intentionally shift styles for some specific purpose. A sudden change from deliberative or consultative to casual can indicate flippancy or actual contempt: "Are you in agreement with our proposal for the new project?" "It sounds like a hell of a good idea to me." Even less respect can be shown by the use of slang, especially if it is used primarily by an unfavored group or if it is outdated: "It sounds just ducky." Or a person can show aloofness by using a style more formal than the one used by the other person: "Wanta come?" "I should like to, but unfortunately I have a prior commitment." If two people meet on the sidewalk and one says, "Hi!" and is greeted by "How do you do," he will probably not feel free to stop and chat. A parent reprimanding a child may employ consultative style to indicate firmness, whereas under normal circumstances he uses intimate or casual.

Most of the rules of the grammar remain unchanged regardless of which contextual style a person is using. His syntactic rules for forming questions and negatives are the same whether he is being oratorical or casual. In morphology, the plural of *cat* is *cats* and the past tense of *drop* is *dropped* regardless of the style. Nor does he alter most of his phonological rules or most of his vocabulary items. Many entire sentences such as *Would you open the door?* do not belong to any single style. Yet there are a few rules in each component of the grammar and a few lexical items which do show variation.

The most obvious syntactic adjustment for contextual styles results from a rule which deletes certain unstressed words. In questions, the auxiliaries *be, have,* and *do* which precede the subject noun phrase are deleted for casual and intimate styles but not for consultative, deliberative, or oratorical:

	Consultative	Casual
10.43	Has he been here long?	He been here long?
10.44	Is Bill going with us?	Bill going with us?
10.45	Does she ever stop complaining?	She ever stop complaining?

If the subject noun phrase is *you*, it is also deleted:

10.46	Have you already eaten?	Already eaten?
10.47	Are you expecting someone?	Expecting someone?
10.48	Do you need some help?	Need some help?

If the verb is *be* and there is no auxiliary except tense, it is deleted in questions. If the subject is *you*, it may also be deleted if an adjective follows:

10.49	Is he your brother?	He your brother?
10.50	Are you the teacher?	You the teacher?
10.51	Are you at home?	You at home?
10.52	Are you hungry?	Hungry?

In statements *it*, whether an expletive or a pronoun, is deleted for casual and intimate styles; the auxiliaries *have* and *be* are deleted after the expletive *it*:

10.53	It sounded fishy.	Sounded fishy.
10.54	It looks like rain.	Looks like rain.
10.55	It's raining again.	Raining again.

The reason for deletion in these cases is probably the same as that for other kinds of deletion in English: to avoid boring the listener with obvious information. Furthermore, the use of casual or intimate style indicates a degree of rapport and shared knowledge between speaker and listener, and thereby permits the omission of much redundancy which would be useful in other situations.

Another syntactic difference found among different contextual styles is the amount of embedding used in each sentence. Although it is found with all styles, intimate has the least amount of embedding, and oratorical has the most. As a result, some transformations such as extraposition are rarely found in some styles:

10.56   It is unfortunate that our bank account must be closed.

This sentence is more in keeping with oratorical or deliberative styles than with the other three.

For most people, noun plurals, verb forms, and other morphological features remain the same regardless of the style used. It is primarily with pronouns that distinctions are made. For many people *whom* is found only with the oratorical and deliberative styles. A few people use it with consultative. *Who* is the usual form for all uses in intimate and casual styles. There may be other variations in case forms, but clear-cut examples are not abundant. Possibly *It's me* is the form used for the less formal styles and *It is I* for the more formal, but it is doubtful that the sentence occurs with any frequency—if at all—with the more formal styles. It would certainly be unusual in a formal address. Similarly, *This is he* and *This is she* are normally restricted to consultative style and are used primarily over the telephone by people who do not know each other well enough to recognize their voices. Whether *him* or *her* would be used under less formal circumstances cannot be answered, since the sentence would probably not occur when one is speaking to a close friend or member of the family.

Pronoun number can show variation within the idiolect as well as case forms. For a sentence such as *Everyone should do his best,* some people use *his* for all styles; others use *their* for less formal situations. For some structures a singular pronoun with an indefinite antecedent is objectionable at any level:

> 10.57   *We encouraged everyone who entered and hope he continues to the end.
> 10.58   *I invited everyone in the room and think he will come.

In other sentences *they* is used to avoid making a commitment about sex:

> 10.59   "Someone was asking for you." "What did they want?"

Apparently sentences such as these are rare on the more formal levels.

Most verb forms are the same for all styles, but there are some differences in auxiliaries. In American English, *shall* occurs only on the most formal levels, if at all. Also, *have to* and *have got to* usually replace *must* in casual and intimate usage: *I must go* (consultative) vs. *I have to go* or *I've got to go* (casual).

Although phonological variations are less easily defined than those in other components of the grammar, vowel reduction and palatalization are applied much more extensively on the informal levels than on those which are more formal. Also, some people who have [ŋ] as the final segment in the past participial *-ing* for the more formal styles have [n] for casual and intimate. As a result of these variations and syntactic deletion, the following surface structures can be found:

Consultative	Casual
[hwat did yə bay]	[hwa̯jə bay]
[hæv yə gat ə daym]	[gadə daym]
[hwat ər yə duwi ŋ]	[hwačə duwin]

Although these surface structures show considerable difference, it is easy to show that they have the same deep structures. Certain features which are needed for clarity when a person is speaking with a stranger or before a group may be dispensed with when he is talking with someone who knows him well.

For a final example of phonological variation, we can consider the treatment of [h] before an unstressed vowel. Even with oratorical style [h] is frequently deleted in this position. For styles less formal than oratorical, it is deleted with more consistency:

10.60   Will *he* go?
10.61   We went with *her*.
10.62   Did *his* plane leave?
10.63   There's something about *him* I don't understand.
10.64   Does *her* mother know it?

Before a stressed vowel [h] is not deleted in most dialects:

10.65   This is a *history* book.

Differences in vocabulary among the various contextual styles are more numerous and obvious than those involving rules of the grammar. Certain words such as *animosity, derive, relegate,* and *perspicacity* are found primarily in the more formal styles, whereas others such as *a lot of, terrific,* and *funny* ("odd") are informal. For many people slang is reserved for casual and intimate usage, although they may use the jargon of a particular profession or group on any level provided that they have an appropriate audience.

The five contextual styles we have been discussing describe spoken English. In writing there are differences as well. The usual division into **formal** (material for publication, business letters, reports) and **informal** (personal letters, notes) is more satisfactory for the written form of English than for the spoken, although there are various degrees of formality. For many reasons written English can be considered a dialect separate from any variety of the spoken language, and the criteria for differentiating spoken styles are only partially applicable. Whereas contractions such as *isn't* and *don't* occur freely even in oratorical speech, they are normally avoided in formal written English. The varying complexity of sentence structures which distinguishes the different styles of spoken English is also noticeable in writing, with considerable embedding found in formal usage. However, it is not unusual for the syntactic complexity of a friendly letter to exceed that of deliberate speech. Many of the structures in even semiformal writing are not found in speech of any level.

The popular belief that the English language is something immutable and fixed is as inaccurate as the one which claims that there is a single norm which some people are too ignorant to attain and from which others sometimes depart because of laziness. The only existence any living language has is in the internalized grammars of its speakers. Each of these grammars is highly systematic, and they all have much in common. Since all living languages change with time, the English language is not static but shows differences among successive generations. At any particular time the regional and social backgrounds of the speakers of the language can be recognized by their dialects. Finally, each person has a unique idiolect which permits him to use the contextual style which the situation demands. It would be a mistake to underestimate the complexity and diversity of a language.

Exercises

A. Examine several British magazines or newspapers for words which are not used or have a different meaning in American English. Try to determine the American equivalent.

B. Use the *Oxford English Dictionary* and several of the dictionaries mentioned in this chapter under Variation in Vocabulary to determine the difference between British and American usage of the following words: *braces, caravan, clerk, chapel, chemist, garage.*

C. Use Kurath's *Word Geography of the Eastern United States* to determine the regions in which *stoop* ("porch"), *pot cheese* ("cottage cheese"), *bellybump* ("face down on a sled"), and *light bread* ("wheat bread") are found. Use the same source to find alternate names for *dragonfly, paper bag, burlap bag,* and *doughnut.*

D. Read the entries in *A Survey of Verb Forms in the Eastern United States* to determine the regional and social distributions of the past-tense (or *preterite*) forms of the following verbs: *blow, burst, drag, dream, drink, eat, lie, shrink, swim, wake.*

E. Most American dictionaries give British as well as American pronunciations for common words. British pronunciations are also found in the *Oxford English Dictionary.* Determine the British pronunciation for the following words: *advertisement, again, been, clerk, either, figure, hover, lieutenant, nephew.*

F. Examine the different pronunciations for one of the following groups of

words and decide whether the differences are of a regional, social, or historical nature. Consult the following sources: (1) *Oxford English Dictionary*,
(2) *Webster's Third New International Dictionary*, (3) Kenyon and Knott,
A Pronouncing Dictionary of American English, and (4) Kurath and
McDavid, *The Pronunciation of English in the Atlantic States*. You may
add other sources if you choose. In addition, survey the pronunciation of
at least ten people for the words you are studying. Give enough information on each informant to establish his approximate age and regional and
social background:

1. can't, aunt, pants
2. Mrs.
3. either, neither
4. Negro
5. tomato, potato
6. coop, Cooper, hoop
7. iodine, quinine
8. Missouri, Miami, Cincinnati
9. Massachusetts
10. wash, Washington

G. Use a standard dictionary, handbook, or other work on usage to determine
the contextual style or social dialect for which the italicized words are appropriate:

1. I felt *absolutely* miserable last week.
2. I was *aggravated* by his answer.
3. I'm on the list, *ain't* I?
4. I'm on the list, *aren't* I?
5. You are *apt* to get lost if you aren't careful.
6. I was *awfully* upset over what she said.
7. Don't feel *badly* about it.
8. *Contact* me if you can't make it.
9. Being *disinterested* in the lecture, I fell asleep.
10. I *expect* you know this better than I do.
11. Some of my *kinfolks* from Kansas are visiting me.
12. I *got* sick and had to go home.
13. I don't *get* your meaning.
14. I was *good and* wet when I arrived.
15. It should arrive *inside of* a week.
16. *Irregardless* of what you say, I'm going!
17. Would you *loan* me your pen?
18. She was so *mad* she couldn't speak.
19. I can't find it *nowheres*.
20. He ran *towards* the window.
21. We'll *try and* get some sleep.
22. He gave a *most unique* solution.
23. He *goofed* when he said that.
24. I could not *shake off* the cold.
25. She did a *real* good job on your dress.

H. Study a conversation in which you are not actively participating and decide which contextual style is being used. Which features do you notice which are characteristic of this style?

I. Compare the results from the preceding question with a study of one or more of the following: an interview or unrehearsed conversation on television, a news report or analysis which the person is probably reading, a lecture or speech which is not being read. You may wish to limit your investigation to one aspect of language (vocabulary, syntax, phonology) or even to some very specific feature (vowel reduction, palatalization, deletion).

Suggested Reading

Allen, Harold B., and Underwood, Gary N., eds. *Readings in American Dialectology*. New York: Appleton-Century-Crofts, 1971.

Atwood, E. Bagby. *A Survey of Verb Forms in the Eastern United States*. Ann Arbor: University of Michigan Press, 1953.

Brook, G. L. *English Dialects*. London: Andre Deutsch, 1963, 1965.

Gleason, H. A., Jr. *Linguistics and English Grammar*. New York: Holt, Rinehart and Winston, 1965. Chapter 15.

Joos, Martin. *The Five Clocks*. Bloomington: Indiana University Research Center in Anthropology, Folklore, and Linguistics, 1961.

Keyser, Samuel Jay. Review of *The Pronunciation of English in the Atlantic States* by Hans Kurath and Raven I. McDavid, Jr. *Language* 39 (1963): 303–16.

Kurath, Hans. *A Word Geography of the Eastern United States*. Ann Arbor: University of Michigan Press, 1949.

_____. and McDavid, Raven I., Jr. *The Pronunciation of English in the Atlantic States*. Ann Arbor: University of Michigan Press, 1961.

Labov, William. "The Social Motivation of a Sound Change." *Word* 19 (1963): 273–309. Reprinted in Scott and Erickson, 1968.

_____. *The Social Stratification of English in New York City*. Washington, D.C.: Center for Applied Linguistics, 1966.

Marckwardt, Albert H. *American English*. New York: Oxford University Press, 1958.

McDavid, Raven I., Jr. "The Dialects of American English." In *The Structure of American English* by W. Nelson Francis. New York: Ronald Press, 1958. Chapter 9.

Mencken, H. L. *The American Language*. Abridged by Raven I. McDavid, Jr. New York: Alfred A. Knopf, 1963.

Pyles, Thomas, *The Origins and Development of the English Language*. New York: Harcourt Brace Jovanovich, 1964. Chapter 9.

_____. *Words and Ways of American English*. New York: Random House, 1952.

Sledd, James. "Breaking, Umlaut, and the Southern Drawl." *Language* 42 (1966): 18-41. Reprinted in Hungerford, Robinson, and Sledd, 1970.

Wolfram, Walter. *A Sociolinguistic Description of Detroit Negro Speech*. Washington, D.C.: Center for Applied Linguistics, 1969.

Bibliography

To avoid needless repetition of works listed in the suggested readings at the end of each chapter, we are restricting this bibliography to collections of readings which have been referred to in the various chapters of this book and to introductory linguistics textbooks which follow a transformational model.

Collections of Readings

Allen, Harold B., and Underwood, Gary N., eds. *Readings in American Dialectology*. New York: Appleton-Century-Crofts, 1971.

Bach, Emmon, and Harms, Robert T., eds. *Universals in Linguistic Theory*. New York: Holt, Rinehart and Winston, 1968.

Dinneen, Francis P., ed. *Report of the Seventeenth Annual Round Table Meeting on Linguistics and Language Studies*. Washington, D.C.: Georgetown University Press, 1966.

Fodor, Jerry A., and Katz, Jerrold J., eds. *The Structure of Language*. Englewood Cliffs, N.J.: Prentice-Hall, 1964.

Hungerford, Harold; Robinson, Jay; and Sledd, James, eds. *English Linguistics*. Glenview, Ill.: Scott, Foresman, and Co., 1970.

Jacobs, Roderick A., and Rosenbaum, Peter S., eds. *Readings in English Transformational Grammar*. Waltham: Ginn and Co., 1970.

Lehmann, Winfred P., and Malkiel, Yakov, eds. *Directions for Historical Linguistics*. Austin: University of Texas Press, 1968.

Reibel, David A., and Schane, Sanford A., eds. *Modern Studies in English*. Englewood Cliffs, N.J.: Prentice-Hall, 1969.

Scott, Charles T., and Erickson, Jon L., eds. *Readings for the History of the English Language*. Boston: Allyn & Bacon, 1968.

Introductory Texts

Bach, Emmon. *An Introduction to Transformational Grammars*. New York: Holt, Rinehart and Winston, 1964.

317

Jacobs, Roderick A., and Rosenbaum, Peter S. *English Transformational Grammar*. Waltham: Blaisdell Publishing Co., 1968.

Koutsoudas, Andreas. *Writing Transformational Grammars*. New York: McGraw-Hill Book Co., 1966.

Langacker, Ronald W. *Language and Its Structure*. New York: Harcourt Brace Jovanovich, 1968.

Langendoen, D. Terence. *Essentials of English Grammar*. New York: Holt, Rinehart and Winston, 1970.

_____. *The Study of Syntax*. New York: Holt, Rinehart and Winston, 1969.

Lester, Mark. *Introductory Transformational Grammar of English*. New York: Holt, Rinehart and Winston, 1971.

Liles, Bruce L. *An Introductory Transformational Grammar*. Englewood Cliffs, N.J.: Prentice-Hall, 1971.

Lyons, John. *Introduction to Theoretical Linguistics*. Cambridge: Cambridge University Press, 1969.

Roberts, Paul. *English Syntax*. New York: Harcourt Brace Jovanovich, 1964.

_____. *Modern Grammar*. New York: Harcourt Brace Jovanovich, 1968.

Thomas, Owen. *Transformational Grammar and the Teacher of English*. New York: Holt, Rinehart and Winston, 1964.

INDEX